THE COMPLETE

parrot

THE COMPLETE

parrot

arthur freud

HOWELL
BOOK
HOUSE

MACMILLAN•USA

Howell Book House
Macmillan General Reference
A Simon & Schuster Macmillan Company
1633 Broadway
New York, NY 10019-6785

MACMILLAN is a registered trademark of Macmillan, Inc.

Designed by George J. McKeon

Library of Congress Cataloging-in-Publication Data

Freud, Arthur
    The complete parrot/Arthur Freud.
      p. cm.
    Includes bibliographical references
    ISBN 0–87605–905–1
    1. Parrots. 2. Parrots—Anecdotes. I. Title.
SF473.P3F734   1995
636.6'865—dc20   95–4031
                CIP

Manufactured in the United States of America
10 9 8 7 6 5 4 3

*The photograph on the title page shows a gold-mantled Rosella
showing the full adult colors of the species.* Bill Whala

DEDICATION

To my wife, Hannah,
who has always been my inspiration,
and to my children and grandchildren,
who always loved the parrots.

CONTENTS

This beautiful Eleonora subspecies is often referred to as a "medium" Greater Sulphur-crested Cockatoo (opposite). Lynne Schoppe-Viola

FOREWORD

I could not say whether it would be more accurate to describe Arthur Freud as an enthusiastic aviculturist or a highly effective avian publicist; in reality, both descriptions apply equally. More than any other single individual, Arthur Freud has dynamically publicized the joys of pet bird ownership, and he has experienced the deep personal fulfillment that will be the reward of all who take up breeding psittacines, particularly the endangered species.

Teaching people about birds comes naturally to him. Arthur Freud is an educator by profession with a strong background in the sciences. He first became known to the followers of aviculture in 1974 through his widely read, regularly appearing articles in *American Cage-Bird Magazine*, and also to professionals in the pet industry in his role as a contributing editor to *Pets/Supplies/Marketing*. Interestingly, both periodicals, while addressed to completely different audiences—one to the potential bird owner and the other to pet shops and their suppliers—contributed equally to the growth in the industry that has occurred since Arthur Freud's influence was first felt over two decades ago. Today, the economic principle of supply and demand is alive and well in the world of birds, and the author of this book had a lot to do with it. In one format, by extolling the virtues of domestically bred birds, he helped to create the demand. In the other format, he educated the pet industry on the wisdom of meeting that demand and on the viability of supplying healthy, well-cared-for, captive-raised stock for this purpose. His has been a distinctly positive contribution to the advancement of the popularity of aviculture.

Anyone who reads Arthur Freud's writing is invariably infected by his delightfully contagious enthusiasm and affection for parrots of all kinds. It was inevitable that his prolific output of magazine articles would someday translate into a full-fledged book. His first, *All About the Parrots*, was published in 1980 by Howell Book House. This popular book struck an excellent balance between clearly explained technical information, revealing considerable research, and a host of delightful

Rows of tiny black feathers produce the delicate cheek markings typical of the Blue and Gold Macaw (opposite).
Sharon and Ray Bailey

anecdotes based on extensive personal experience. Like his subject, Freud's writing style is unique, allowing his readers to remember his words as one would remember a pleasant voice, a kind face, or a special friend.

Now, following a fifteen-year hiatus, Arthur Freud offers the parrot fancier *The Complete Parrot,* an even more comprehensive volume than his first. This is truly an in-depth view both of parrots with which we are familiar and quite a few lesser-known species with which to become better acquainted. For the newcomer to aviculture, this delightfully readable, informative work will surely inspire even greater interest in the many-faceted, intriguing world of aviculture. To those who have faithfully read the writings of Arthur Freud for the past twenty-plus years, *The Complete Parrot* will reaffirm his ongoing status as a friend to aviculture and to all who own and love pet birds.

Tom Marshall
Past President, American Federation of Aviculture

Arthur Freud began his career as a teacher of biology in a Long Island school district, eventually becoming a science department chairperson and then a principal. In the early 1970s he obtained his first parrot, which was to become the nucleus of a fifteen-bird collection that included macaws, Yellow-napes, Double Yellow-heads, cockatoos, African Greys, and others. His consuming interest in parrots led him to write a column on hookbills for *American Cage-Bird Magazine*, which he began in 1974. In 1980 he became editor of the magazine, and in 1984 he retired from the school system and became the publisher while continuing as editor. Also, in 1980, his first book, *All About the Parrots*, was published by Howell Book House. It was also Howell's first bird book and the start of what was to become a quality list of books dealing with birds.

In 1994 Mr. Freud sold *American Cage-Bird Magazine*; he is currently serving as a contributing editor to *Pet Business*, a pet trade magazine.

Arthur Freud with "Tutu," one of his special favorites. Tutu is a domestically bred, hand-raised Greater Sulphur-crested Cockatoo that is as charming as a bird can be.

INTRODUCTION

People throughout the world have loved and been fascinated by parrots since they decided to bring certain animals into their homes and make them a part of their lives.

Parrots have often been considered a sign of prestige as well as an indication of exotic taste. After the imposition of restrictions on their importation in the 1930s, many people told of someone they knew whose father or grandmother had a green or gray parrot screeching in the kitchen. Invariably there were stories about the cleverness and speech abilities of these unusual pets, and usually the bragging was fairly accurate.

"Parrot fever," or psittacosis, is a dangerous and debilitating disease that is now correctly referred to as ornithosis, since it can afflict all birds, not just parrots. Ornithosis is one of the few bird ailments that can be transmitted to humans, in whom it resembles a severe case of pneumonia. If untreated it can result in death. Concern over this threat resulted in a ban on parrot importation by the U.S. Public Health Department in 1930. This ban continued until 1967 when it was lifted, as effective treatments for both birds and humans had been developed. A new total ban on parrot importation began in 1971 as a reaction to a serious outbreak of Newcastle Virus in California, which caused the loss of a large number of chickens and nearly put a portion of the poultry industry out of business. In 1973 federally inspected quarantine stations were set up; parrots and other exotic birds were again permitted to enter the United States legally if they passed through stations where the birds were closely monitored and tested for thirty days. All birds coming in were medicated with chlortetracycline and meticulously examined during this period. Any who showed Newcastle Virus symptoms were shipped back to their country of origin or destroyed. The efficacy of this system put a virtual stop to the ravages of Newcastle Disease, with the exception of cases brought into the United States by smuggled birds that had not passed through quarantine.

From 1973 until the mid-1980s, very large numbers of parrots were legitimately imported into the United States. Prices were within reach of many people, and birds such as the Yellow-naped Amazon, the African Grey, Scarlet and Blue and gold Macaws, and various white cockatoos quickly became favorites. Once again, parrots were a sign of prestige and the "in" pet to own. Models, movie stars, politicians, and royalty appeared in news photos with their parrots, and the average person was determined not to be left out. Many hundreds of thousands of parrots were imported until two types of legislation took hold at the end of the 1980s and in the early years of the 1990s. Parrot exportation from many Central and South American countries was slowed and then halted, and ultimately the importation of exotic birds into the United States was forbidden, with the exception of certain rare exemptions for zoos, licensed breeders, and research.

Domestic breeding of both rare and common parrots is now widespread in the United States, as well as a number of other countries. Enough pairs of mature birds are available that this situation is likely to continue and even to improve. Many clubs and other organizations are attempting to popularize stud books and breeder bird loans so that suitable mates can be located and brought together. An additional advantage of this type of cooperation is that it also enriches the gene pool, which is vital if successful domestic breeding is to continue and species are to survive.

With the virtual cessation of the importation of exotic birds into the United States and the tragic devastation of the habitat of so many species taking place in many parts of the world, advances in breeding techniques are a welcome development. Now we have a chance to preserve species that will eventually disappear from the wild, and scientists can study psittacine birds in a number of ways that enhance our knowledge. If the species are successfully preserved for posterity, we will have the opportunity to observe them in collections of exotic animals provided for public viewing.

Finally, the strides that have been and will be made in domestic breeding of parrot-family birds mean that we can enjoy these unique pets in the comfort of our own homes. Because we can produce parrots without first having to capture them, we can more easily enjoy these large-beaked, querulous-looking birds and learn firsthand what wonderful additions to our families they can make.

Enjoy the parrot family. Discover the depth of affection of which a pet parrot is capable and revel in that affection for the long life span of the parrot that becomes part of your personal circle. Your voyage of discovery begins in the pages of this book.

Happy reading.
Arthur Freud

part I

WHAT ALL PARROT LOVERS SHOULD KNOW

1 GETTING STARTED WITH PARROTS

At the start of the 1990s, many newspapers and magazines indicated that the outstanding pets of the decade would be birds. Recent studies by seed and pet-food manufacturers confirm this. Although vast numbers of dogs and cats are still maintained as household pets, cage birds are rapidly growing in popularity.

The ease with which one can care for a parrot is a factor in the growing interest in these charming birds. As our population ages, not having to walk a pet on a rainy or snowy night becomes a real advantage. In addition, pet owners are learning that parrots can offer a degree of affection for their owners exceeding that of cats and rivaling that of dogs.

From 1973 until 1992 legal imports of large numbers of parrots made them available at prices many could afford. By 1992 this situation had changed dramatically as many countries that had previously exported parrots restricted or ended

The lighter-colored margins on its feathers give the African Grey (opposite) a "scalloped" appearance that is one of the hallmarks of this popular talking bird. Greta Johnson

such practices. In October 1992, the Wild Bird Conservation Act became part or federal law, and this virtually ended the importation of parrots with exceptions made only for zoos and certain research groups. The act did not restrict the keeping, breeding, selling, or exporting of parrots or their offspring that were already in the United States. Thus, a compensatory action is taking place as more and more individuals become involved in the domestic breeding of parrots and other exotics. Although the prices for domestic specimens are higher than for the birds that were formerly imported, these prices will eventually level off as the law of supply and demand takes hold.

The most popular pets in the United States are cats, dogs, and birds. Surveys made in the early 1990s indicated that there were 54.6 million cats kept as pets in the United States, outnumbering the 52.4 million dogs that had been an earlier favorite. During the period studied, the cat population grew by 4.6 percent while the number of dogs kept as pets declined by 4.6 percent. A very recent study by a national bird pellet and seed manufacturer determined that there are 31 million pet birds in this country, of which 1.2 million are parrots,

4.9 million are cockatiels, and 11 million are budgies. The balance includes finches, canaries, and other miscellaneous pet birds.

A number of factors have caused these changes in pet demography. Paramount among these is our changing lifestyle, with more people living in urban areas and in multi-unit dwellings, which makes keeping a dog or cat a problem. Walking a dog down the elevator and out into a city street on a cold, wet night can take the edge off anybody's enthusiasm. Can a parrot replace a dog in terms of sharing warmth and affection? Absolutely! These clever creatures inspire love with their willingness to accept physical contact, their whimsical, mischievous behavior, and their ability to mimic speech while appearing to understand some of what they are saying. (I have a cockatoo who scolds "No bite!" every time she nips.) Many parrot owners compare their birds to dogs when it comes to love, friendliness, roughhousing, and the ability to respond to the mood of the owner after he or she has had a difficult day.

Increasingly, we see the term "companion animal" used. Perhaps this is better than "pet" as it suggests a more mutual relationship between humans and domestic animals. The bond can be very healthy for people, as is clearly recognized by those enlightened retirement facilities and nursing homes that encourage the presence of animals among individuals or groups. Several recent studies indicate that stroking a pet can actually lower blood pressure as it calms, an excellent therapy for young as well as old. A good friend of mine resides in a Florida retirement facility that permitted her to bring her African Grey with her. What a boon for her and for her neighbors who share the pleasure and love of this noncritical being that doesn't care if people are in wheelchairs or if ill health has slurred their speech. Treated kindly, animals will love those around them unconditionally.

Parrots are ideal pets for older persons living in their own homes. They are clean and easy to care for, and, because they are still relatively unusual, they can help to boost the self-esteem of retired individuals, who no longer share the common link of children or a job with other members of their community. Many a friendly intergenerational conversation has been initiated between an older parrot owner and a young, fascinated admirer.

In the United States, well-known entertainers own parrots, as the ownership of these exotic birds has been an "in thing" for a number of years. Their widespread appeal is reflected in the use of parrots as design elements by well-known stylists on fabrics, pottery, umbrellas, bank checks, and other objects.

One factor that has added greatly to the mystique surrounding the parrot is its claim to exceptional longevity. For young people, this can mean having a pet that will be with them through childhood and that may very well accompany them into adult life. An older person can generally be assured that he or she will be spared the trauma of losing a pet, but is now faced with the new problem of having to make provisions for the time when it is no longer possible to care for the parrot.

Sometimes parrot owners or sellers become overenthusiastic and claim life spans of 100 or more years for the typical parrot. Actually, although their longevity is great, parrots do not live that long, nor are they as long-lived as the ostrich, the raven, or the condor. When a parrot is credited with an unusually long life span, it may be due to misunderstandings that can occur when a bird outlives its original owners. If such an older parrot dies and is replaced, confusion may arise in the future among members of the next generation, who may assume, for example, that the second parrot is actually the same bird that was purchased by their grandfather many years previously. Fortunately, careful studies have been made and accurate records kept on individual parrots, and in some cases it is possible to document extremely long life spans in hookbills.

Amazons can easily reach the age of forty or more, and the life span of cockatoos is similar to that of humans. My personal favorite was Cocky Bennett, a Greater Sulphur-crested Cockatoo of Tom Ugly's Point, near Sydney, Australia. Cocky has been referred to in a number of books, and if the records are correct he died in May 1916 at the age of 119 years. He belonged to Mrs. Sara Bennett, owner of the Sea Breeze Hotel, and a photo of Cocky's stuffed remains suggests that he was indeed a Methuselah among cockatoos. He had been almost featherless for the last twenty years of his life, and his upper beak was so overgrown that he resembled a Long-billed Corella rather than a Sulphur-crested Cockatoo.

My most delightful experience with a long-lived parrot took place when I discovered Leo and Marjorie Esser of Des Moines, Iowa, who owned a seventy-five-year-old Yellow-naped Amazon named

"Oh Boy." They purchased him from a teacher of Iowa State College in 1924, when Oh Boy was a mere stripling of nineteen. His previous owner had two sons named Leroy and Herbert. According to a story about Oh Boy and the Essers in the *Des Moines Tribune*, Mr. and Mrs. Esser had forgotten the name of the original owner of the parrot but had no trouble remembering his sons' names, as each morning Oh Boy would loudly call "LEE-roy! HER-bert!" with the same inflection that the boys' father had used when he would call them for meals or chores. A short time after this story appeared, a visitor arrived just as the Essers were sitting down to dinner. The handsome, gray-haired man introduced himself by saying, "I'm LEE-roy!" Oh Boy failed to recognize his childhood friend, who turned out to be a long-term member of the Des Moines School Board, as well as a successful engineer. He informed the Essers that Herbert ("HER-bert!") was an army colonel stationed at the Aberdeen Proving Grounds in Maryland.

Buying a parrot can be a major investment, and when you own one of these intelligent birds you have also made a significant commitment of time and effort. Before making a decision to bring a parrot into your home, you should do some intensive research to determine the bird that is most suitable for your circumstances and to select a bird that has a pleasing personality and is in good health.

Cockatoos, macaws, Amazons, African Greys, and conures make up the largest groups of full-sized parrots currently available in reasonable quantities for purchase. Unless you buy an older bird, the parrots available today are domestically bred birds that were sold to a pet shop by a breeder or are resales of older birds whose owners no longer wish to keep them. You can also buy directly from a breeder if you are able to make contact with such an individual. Bird breeders often keep a low profile, as they are concerned with theft and vandalism. In most cases I would recommend choosing a young, newly weaned parrot so that you and the bird can bond together as the bird develops parrot skills of speech and acrobatics. Of course, there are exceptions. I never could resist an old, clever, tame, and talking parrot; they seemed to know this, and would seek me out when I visited pet shops.

Young, domestically bred birds are tame and gentle, and if the breeder has done his or her job properly they will be healthy birds. If you can visit the breeder to select your bird, ask whether or not the babies have been hand fed. This is crucial information, as babies that have not been hand fed are usually not much tamer than imported birds, and if a breeder has a large number of pairs producing young, he or she may let the parents do all the feeding. When you examine the parrot you are thinking of buying, ask permission to hold or touch it. If the parrot is tame, it will permit contact either by letting you touch it or by mounting your hand. Qualities such as speech cannot really be checked, as most parrots will not talk on demand, but only when they prefer to do so. If speech is very important to you, think about a Yellow-naped Amazon, Double Yellow-head, or young African Grey, as these are the best candidates for talking. Some of the other Amazons will learn to speak, but not as well as the birds noted above. Although cockatoos and macaws will learn a few loudly articulated phrases, they are generally not great talkers. The cockatoos compensate for this deficiency with their flamboyant behavior, and the macaws, of course, are so beautiful and exotic looking that you may want one in any case.

Keep in mind that, in addition to being able to speak, most parrots are also quite capable of screaming. African Greys are probably the most

A Blue-eyed Cockatoo. Courtesy of the San Diego Zoo

A pair of hand-raised Indian Ringnecks. Courtesy of Ron Goebel

quiet of the full-sized parrots, while the cockatoos and macaws are the loudest. Amazons fall somewhere in between. Many a parrot has lost a good home because it screamed loudly and almost continuously while members of the family were trying to read or watch TV.

Try to bring an experienced individual with you when you choose your parrot. In addition to helping you with identification, this person can also advise you on value. Remember that an extremely tame parrot or one that is already an exceptional talker may command a higher price than those advertised in bird magazines. Mated, proven pairs as well as birds of a particular sex that are hard to come by may also be very expensive. Is it worth it? Only you and your desire to own a particular bird can answer the question.

In some cases, baby birds can be purchased while still unweaned. If you do this, you may be able to negotiate a lower price, as hand feeding chicks takes up many hours of a breeder's time. Be cautious about doing this if you do not feel fully capable of hand feeding a parrot chick, as improper hand feeding can result in the bird's death.

The health of the bird you wish to buy should be determined even before you investigate its tameness and talking ability. You can save yourself many problems by learning to recognize a healthy bird. Take the following information with you when shopping:

Droppings: In a healthy bird, droppings are a combination of fecal solids and urine. In general, solids are excreted first and then followed by the whitish urine. Thus, the bottom of the cage housing a normal bird will show droppings that are a mixture of the fecal matter, which may retain some of the tubular shape of the intestine, mixed with the whitish liquid portion of the wastes. Totally liquid droppings are not normal unless the bird has been drinking excessive amounts of water, and this itself is not normal behavior. Don't reject an otherwise desirable bird because of one example of loose stools. Instead, check it again in thirty or forty minutes and see if the condition persists or was merely the result of something watery it may have eaten.

Vent: Checking the bird's vent is closely related to checking the waste products. If a cage has just been cleaned, you will not be able to judge the quality of the stools. You can, however, examine the vent, or anal opening. A vent over which feathers are pasted together or with droppings adhering to it indicates loose stools; normally, the muscular activity involved in a bird's act of excretion prevents the accumulation of visible waste matter in the area of the vent.

Nostrils: These should be fully open and clear. A powdery residue that may clog a nostril is a sure sign that the bird has a respiratory problem or has had one recently. Liquid oozing from one or both nostrils is, or course, also an indication of respiratory problems. Sneezing, on the other hand, can merely be a sign that the bird is clearing its nostrils, and unless it is chronic it is not significant.

Ears: Most people forget that birds have external openings to take in sound because they have no fleshy "sound-scoops" to aid auditory pickup. The openings are there, however, and are in line with the eyes and to the rear of the skull. Normally you should not see them, as, unless he has just bathed, the feathers of a healthy bird will cover these openings. In a normally feathered bird the ear openings should not be visible.

Eyes: They should be equal in size, have a clear, bright appearance, and be fully open, without visible fluid or other secretions. Eyes that do not meet these conditions may have been injured or may be a sign of other illness.

General appearance: Choose a bird with all his toes. Although a missing claw will probably grow back, a toe that is gone is gone forever. Birds lacking one or more toes are considered imperfect, and this is a disadvantage at shows or if you wish to sell the bird. It may also make the bird unsteady on the perch, which can interfere with copulation. If the seller offers a discount on a bird with a missing claw or toe, it is worth considering. Do not purchase a bird that has plucked his feathers. This habit is extremely difficult to break; and not only is

plucking ugly, it is also a health hazard, as the bird needs constant feather replacement. Molting and plucking are quite different. Birds that are molting do not normally show bare spots.

Consider taking a good reference book with you when you are checking the health of a prospective purchase. Select one with good color photos to help you in identification as well as one that includes information on health and personality.

Before concluding your transaction, ask the seller about the guarantee policy. It should include an opportunity for you to take the bird to an avian veterinarian for a full workup. Do not, however, be surprised if you are limited to only a few days to do this, as livestock is delicate and ignorance on the part of a new owner could cause a healthy bird to become ill. Guarantees may take the form of a refund or a replacement. In a small shop you may have to wait a long time for a replacement, so a refund is to your advantage.

LIVING WITH A PARROT

During the last twenty-five years, I have kept Amazons, cockatoos, macaws, African Greys, and other parrot-family birds. For a few years I also owned a mynah bird, but although Charlie was lovable and clever he was also extremely loud and messy. His efforts to "kill" grapes by vigorously shaking them would cause bits of grape to fly and adhere to the nearest wall. He was subsequently given to my wife's uncle, who tolerates this behavior and considers Charlie incapable of having any faults.

My collection of parrots eventually numbered fifteen full-sized birds, and over the years that I kept this large group I developed various timesaving approaches, along with techniques for keeping the birds safe, happy, and healthy. This was a necessity, as, even if only ten minutes of care were given to each parrot, a group of fifteen would still require more than two hours of daily attention.

TIPS ON BEHAVIOR

With most parrots, putting your fingers through the bars of the cage is a bad idea. Even the tamest parrot may look upon this as an invitation to nip. Of course, there are exceptions. Tutu, my Sulphur-crested Cockatoo, kisses my fingers if I put them through the bars, and Jaco, my African Grey, is so enthusiastic about having her neck scratched that she will permit me to do it through the bars if I am too busy to open her cage as I walk by. Blondi, my Double Yellow-head, would grip my fingers and attempt to perch on them if I put them through the bars. I do not risk fingers with any of the others, however, as I can never be sure what the response will be. In general, it is not a wise move to put your fingers through the bars of any parrot's cage.

Do not leave any feathers lying about your bird's cage. If he drops a feather or pulls one out that is ready to come out, remove it from the cage as soon as you see it. Never play with your parrot with a feather. Interesting a parrot in playing with feathers could lead to the plucking of his own plumage.

Don't give up on a parrot that nips. Be patient, and even if he seems to be waiting with a ready beak for your finger to touch the door of his cage, give him a chance to show his true intentions. You are dealing with an animal whose mind in many respects is similar to that of a bright, but young, child. He may not have any intention of biting, and his swipe at your fingers may well be a little game. If not, try to distract or out-wait him. Getting the bird out on your hand and eventually being allowed to pet and scratch him is well worth a bite or two in the early stages. Also, you will never know what he really intends to do unless you take a chance.

If you have a new and timid parrot and you're not sure if he's moving around the cage, try hanging a little "telltale" from the top of the cage. This could be a bit of wood or a piece of paper. If, when you next come into the room, the wood or paper has been removed, your timid friend is having a grand time when you are not there.

Have you noticed that, if you own several parrots and they are in adjoining cages, your attention to one bird results in a great flurry of activity in nearby cages? I see this quite often. This combination of jealousy and desire for attention and affection is further indication of the great intelligence of our favorite pets.

Have you ever noted the cautious attitude that parrots display toward new objects in the cage or bird room? Most of my parrots will not go near anything new until it has been in the room for several weeks. Once they realize that the new object does not pose a threat they generally accept it and show

no fear of it. Jaco, my African Grey, sneaks up on new objects. Recently I put a stainless steel feeding dish in her cage. She approached it carefully and examined it from every angle. After about five minutes, she said, "Hello" to it in her soft little voice. A little later I caught her saying, "Suppertime?" to the dish. Actually, Jaco talks to all her toys. She often says "come on" to her swing as she waits for it to move back to her so she can grab it. This is truly an indication of high intelligence, as I say exactly the same words to her (in the same voice) while waiting for her to climb on my extended hand.

Some parrots reach plateaus of learning and you may think that they will never again learn anything new. Don't give up on such birds, as after a period of time elapses, they may very well show new spurts of learning. The same phenomenon has been noted in human students. Jaco is a perfect example of this: After failing to learn anything new for almost a year, she has suddenly started picking up a new word or phrase almost every week. Jaco and Tutu, my cockatoo, both love to talk into hollow containers or tubes. Apparently they like hearing the echo of their own voices.

Many parrots that are normally sweet and gentle when alone with their owners or family members become savage when there are strangers in the room. This is, of course, due to their fear of the unfamiliar. If you have such a bird, you should resist taking him out to show to company. If he is already out, wait for the visitors to leave before handling the parrot and you will spare both you and your bird unnecessary unpleasantness.

TOYS AND EQUIPMENT

If you have a swing in your bird's cage (a large handmade swing is highly recommended), do not crimp the sides of the swing so tightly that it cannot be moved from side to side. Tighten it just enough so that the parrot cannot remove the swing from the bar. By leaving it loose, you provide a means for the bird to travel with the swing by sliding it along the bars for at least part of the distance across the cage. This is fun and also good exercise.

Although many people prefer not to, I like to use old newspapers to cover the bottom of the bird cages. The *New York Times* and the *Wall Street Journal* are perfect for large cages and the tabloids for the smaller ones. Just be sure that you avoid using the color sections, which have ink that can be toxic, and that you let the papers age (rotating them with the oldest on top is the best way) for a few weeks so that they do not soil the bird's feathers. Working with old newspapers brings an interesting perspective on fame, which really is a fleeting thing when last week's heroes invariably wind up lining a feathered friend's cage tray. The biggest stories of the previous week or two rapidly fade into insignificance as the newspapers age on the shelf.

HEALTH AND SAFETY

If for some reason you are thinking of placing a cage fairly high in a room, test the temperature of the air at that height. You can do this by standing on a ladder. Since warm air rises, you will be amazed to discover that a room with a temperature of about seventy degrees can be eighty or eighty-five degrees close to the ceiling.

If your favorite big-beaked squawker has figured out how to open the closing device you've put on his cage, try using the stainless steel clips that hikers and mountain climbers use to attach their ropes. These come in many sizes, are inexpensive, and are a real challenge to most parrots. You can find them in any large sporting-goods store. One device I favor can be opened only by pulling out and away from the cage. This one is impossible for a bird to manipulate from inside the cage, although a parrot could free a neighbor if the liberator were outside his own cage.

When you add a new toy or any other object to your parrot's cage, try to anticipate whether the addition poses a possible danger to the parrot. For example, if you add a toy on a chain, the links of the chain should not be so small that the parrot could catch his claw in one of them. Sharp objects should be avoided, and, of course, never put something in the cage that the parrot could form into a loop that might trap his head.

Many cages are built with doors referred to in the trade as guillotine types, which slide up and down instead of folding out. To prevent them from becoming actual guillotines, always lock them in an up position with more than one clamp or clip when your bird is playing on or near the cage.

Raising the temperature for a sick parrot is a standard procedure. In addition to relieving the clinical state of shock that the ill bird suffers from,

the higher temperatures create thirst that forces the bird to drink more. If you have medicated its water, the extra drinking will ensure that more of the medication gets into the parrot. Of course, this must not be carried to extremes, which would lead to dehydration.

New parrot owners are frequently confronted with difficulties such as biting, screeching, fear of the owner, and other undesirable forms of behavior. They would be wise at such times to give some thought to the way they are dealing with the bird. The same intelligence and sense of curiosity that makes a parrot so interesting as a pet can also detract from his relationship with you if he is treated in a thoughtless manner. The following examples may be useful.

If your parrot begins to engage in behavior that appears senseless or mean, try to analyze the situation to see if something has occurred that might have provoked him. A physical change in circumstances or a subtle change in your daily relationship with the parrot may be trivial to you but upsetting to him. A bird that is used to being played with or taken out before the other birds in your collection may bitterly resent a change in that pattern. The important thing to remember is that these intelligent creatures generally have a reason for what they do, and some detective work on your part may help you to determine what has gone wrong and to resolve the problem by changing things back to the way they were, if possible.

Parrots are famous for their curiosity. When you are introduced to a new bird or when you bring a new bird into your home, you will notice that at first he will not get too close to you or permit you to get too close to him. If you have the patience to sit quietly near an open cage, perhaps with your hand or finger in the doorway, the parrot will work or play his way closer and closer to you, usually casting quick, furtive glances to see if you are watching. If you are patient and pretend to be unaware of these small attentions, the parrot may get close enough to allow physical contact. Over a period of time, this can be a stepping-stone to your ultimate goal—getting the parrot to mount your hand.

Many parrots playfully try to nip as food dishes are moved in and out of their cages, and sometimes what may have started as a game becomes a real problem. I remember feeding every parrot in my bird room before taking care of Frodo, a giant

Scarlet Macaw with a whimsical but changeable personality, because I dreaded his occasional attacks on my hands and fingers. You can, however, discourage just about any parrot from such nasty activities by dripping a little water from the dish you're putting in the cage on or near him as he waits with opened beak. The parrot will not be sure that your action was done on purpose, so the problem can be solved without any hard feelings.

Parrots are sometimes referred to as noisy. This is rather like calling river wet. Noise and parrots go together, and if noise would be a problem in your home you probably should not own a parrot. Some people use a cage cover for a particularly noisy bird. Covering the cage will usually quiet down a screamer. I would recommend removing the cover after about twenty minutes and then leaving it off unless the bird starts to scream again. In this way he can learn to realize the cause-and-effect relationship between screaming and having the cage covered. One of my Amazons used to mutter "Cover the cage" right after I had done so. He was either reading my mind or had heard me use this phrase often enough to learn it.

Parrots in the home follow a daily cycle that closely parallels that of their owners. Thus, they awaken at daylight but generally do not go to sleep at dusk, which is what they would normally do in the wild. Instead they tend to stay awake until their owners put out all lights at bedtime. This lengthy day means that most parrots, even if they are in good health, will nap several times a day. When a parrot catnaps, in addition to closing his eyes, he will frequently tuck one foot up under him.

Because parrots see very poorly in darkened or dimly lit rooms, it is important to provide a low-level night light for them so that if they leave their perch they can find their way back without accident. A bird room in total darkness can be dangerous to its occupants and disastrous to eggs and chicks during breeding. Try to place the parrot in a room or area where he need not be disturbed by someone coming in and turning on the light when he is sleeping, a sure way to encourage late-night screaming. On those occasions when I must disturb my sleeping birds, a wave of grumbling goes through the bird room, as if they are saying, "What's he doing in here now?"

Your parrot will be happier and healthier if permitted exercise and playtime outside the cage.

Most cage manufacturers offer playpen tops that are excellent locations for fun and activity. Some parrots enjoy being on the floor of the bird room, and a clean floor makes an excellent playground. If your birds are permitted to walk around the floor of your bird room, you can make an interesting toy for them out of an empty tin can and a lot of small clean stones. Those of my birds who walk on the floor delight in an opportunity to perch on the rim of the can and empty out the stones. The game becomes more interesting as the can gets close to being empty, at which point it generally tips over and the parrot flutters away complaining loudly.

When dealing with new parrots, it is always a good idea to watch the bird closely while handling him. A new and frightened parrot may behave in an unpredictable fashion. Don't become overconfident and get into a conversation with someone while handling your new bird, as he might be getting ready to sample your fingers or fly towards a window; watching him closely can help you anticipate and prevent such actions. If you think a bird is getting ready to bite, move the hand on which he is perched up and down. This will unbalance the bird, who will have to flap his wings and for the moment forget all about biting. Solving a problem this way without hurting or frightening the parrot is crucial to the development of a friendly and lasting relationship.

Many times you will read of toys or devices that sound great but that just do not work with your bird. You must keep in mind that, although parrots have keen minds and relish a challenge, they will reject tasks that seem impossible. For example, parrots love to chew on pieces of wood and are particularly pleased with wood turnings that have different shapes that they can grasp easily. When my cockatoo neglected the lovely pine blocks I cut for her, I started drilling holes through every surface to give her a start. This solved the problem, and she now demolishes several of these blocks each day. This is an excellent method of keeping her entertained and at the same time helps to avoid overgrowth of her beak and nails. You can get clean pine scraps at any lumberyard or wood milling shop; even if you must pay for them, a few will go a long way.

It can be very helpful if you learn to read the body language with which your bird sometimes communicates. When your parrot spreads his wings and tail feathers and stalks about the cage with very deliberate steps, he is not sick or angry but is just feeling especially good and showing it. This is referred to as display behavior and is typical of most Amazons. One of my Yellow-napes would do this regularly, and when he did, he practically doubled in size. Of course, an effort to look larger and more intimidating is another reason for display behavior.

This same Yellow-nape loved to come out but hated to be returned to his cage. I eventually arrived at the technique of carrying him on his back in the palm of my hand, so that he would not be able to grab the bars as I placed him in his cage. He would usually go through his entire vocabulary in a frantic, high-pitched voice when I started to take him back to his cage in the hopes that, if he was particularly entertaining, he would be kept out for a longer period of time. Since he would generally repeat everything in his repertoire in a foghorn-like voice moments after using his favorite falsetto, he usually did get to stay out longer. Sometimes I wonder who was training whom.

Non–bird lovers often ask me why I am so enthusiastic about parrots. I believe that we find them captivating because of their intelligence and ability to show affection. Another charming aspect of their behavior is their exaggerated way of reacting, turning their heads with a great sweeping motion, and if something alarms them, rearing back and moving their wings. Even a sick bird will generally try to put on a bit of a show for the owner he loves. I do not know of any animal that will go as far out of its way to please humans as a parrot will.

If you are going to maintain a good relationship with your parrots, you must find ways to show that you return their affection. Several of my macaws always seemed to enjoy having their tongues scratched or even gently squeezed. This activity reminds me of an old joke about porcupines: How do you scratch the tongue of a macaw? Carefully!

Fiorello, one of my Scarlet Macaws (and a member of the tongue-scratching club), always hated to say good night. Just before I put out the main lighting in the bird room I would say good night to each bird. (This is an ideal time to observe them and to see that all is well with them.) Fiorello would accept my good night and then run to the other side of his long cage so that as I moved to the next cage he could pretend to be another bird and thus be entitled to another good night.

You can avoid many difficult moments with your birds if you give some thought to how your normal human behavior may appear to them. When handling your parrot with one hand, don't make the mistake of a quick move with your other hand just because he is calm and playful. Move that other hand slowly and engage in some maneuvers to reassure him that the hand is attached to and is a safe, non-threatening part of you.

When you work with people, you do not deal with someone who is angry or agitated in the same way that you do a calm individual. It would be equally foolish to treat an excited or agitated parrot the same way you treat him when he is calm. If his eyes are dilating and contracting and his tail feathers are spread out, don't make a point of insisting that he politely step onto your hand or eat a peanut from your lips.

Try to avoid haste in your dealings with your birds. If you are in a hurry on a particular evening, remember that the parrot is totally unaware of your need for urgency and will not like the fact that you push and shove dishes quickly and roughly into his cage. You can actually frighten a bird in this way or set back the training of a new bird. Give yourself more time, slow down, and don't rush the important activities of feeding and playing.

Behavior is the primary reason that hand-fed baby birds command such high prices. Hand-fed baby parrots grow up to be more sensitive to the moods of their owners than do imported birds or birds purchased as adults. Very few birds, or other animals for that matter, will return your love as completely as a parrot you have worked with from an early age. It is very easy for you to love these helpless creatures. Immature baby parrots, with their prickly looking quills, fierce expressions, and wild eyes, hardly look like babies at all. It is not until you start to feed them and see their awkward, hungry, and jerky movements that you realize what truly delightful babies they are.

SOME PARROT TALES

My first parrot was an extremely loud Bee-Bee Parrot whose neck had been rubbed raw in his efforts to put his head through the bars of his cage. Because of this ugly affliction and his piercing squawks, Bee-Bee was offered to me in exchange for some scientific volumes. I jumped at the chance to own a parrot, but it wasn't long before I discovered that there is something about the pitch at which little parrots screech that is particularly grating to the nerves. In addition, I realized that although I expended much time and effort on Bee-Bee, there was no reciprocity. Although I fed and cared for him and even tried to medicate his featherless neck region, his only interest in me was the nightly dish of food and the morning vegetable treats. Bee-Bee eventually was given to a friend who owned a screaming Bee-Bee Parrot of his own, and all I could think of when I dropped him off was that his new owner would now have to bear twice the harsh din that I had been suffering with. Oddly enough, Bee-Bee's new owners were quite pleased with him and he became a permanent member of that household.

I, on the other hand, had learned an important lesson. My next parrot would be selected much more carefully, and it would be a bird I really wanted. This was the late 1960s, when there was no legal importation of parrots and thus the only birds I could choose from were those offered for sale by people who were giving up older pets. Unlike today, there was no newspaper advertising of parrots, as very few were ever offered for sale. Some pet magazines did have a number offered each month in their classified columns, but the pickings were sparse. I began to haunt those local pet shops that had parrots on consignment, another parrot-selling technique in those days. Since there was no importation of parrots, pet shops would accept birds on consignment and the owner of the bird would share the purchase price with the shopkeeper. In short order I purchased a Blue-fronted Amazon. Fogel, as I named him, was a handsome parrot but he had almost no ability to speak. He did, however, dance and perform quite acrobatically. I now learned a second important lesson about buying and owning hookbills: Parrots that can speak are wonderful, but speech is not the only talent of which these clever birds are capable. A bird that is gentle and friendly and will perform for you can be a greater pleasure to keep than a really splendid talker that bites so fiercely you are afraid to take it out of its cage. If I were to choose between two such birds, I would certainly select the tame nontalker.

The next member of my collection was Birl, a hefty Mealy Amazon who had also been placed on consignment in a pet shop. Birl was an excellent example of the largely underrated group of plain Amazons. Although not colorful, he was extremely loving and gentle and liked nothing more than being held and played with. He had a tendency to shriek out his words and phrases, but these were much more pleasant to listen to than the meaningless and annoying sounds Bee-Bee had made. Birl really seemed to want to perform the role of a clown. If placed in a small cardboard box, he would roll on his back and attempt to chew the sides of his cardboard playroom. In later years I was surprised to learn that Birl was actually a hen when he (she) laid an egg for his (her) new owner. This lesson brought home the woeful inadequacy of the books available at that time on parrots and their qualities. Blue-fronts, for example, were rated as top-notch talkers, and little if anything was mentioned about the magnificent pet qualities of the Mealy Amazon. Information from those who collected parrots (and, later, those who actually bred them) was generally much more accurate than derivative books by writers who were largely repeating the opinions of other authors.

By 1974, importation laws had changed and parrots of all types began to enter the United States. On a visit to a well-known shop, I admired a Blue and Gold Macaw who spoke beautifully and permitted me to pet him. A perfect bird, I thought. Unfortunately, his owner felt the same way, and this parrot was very definitely not for sale. He drew so much attention to the shop that he was worth much more than the price of selling him. The owner did urge me to look at the older Double Yellow-head he had in the back of the shop, but this bird did not speak. I later realized that with markings that resembled a yellow rain slicker and extended down the length of his mantle, this parrot was actually a Tres Marias that I could have had for as little as $100. I had ignored my earlier lesson and passed up an excellent parrot whose beauty and rarity more than made up for any lack of speaking ability.

Over the next few years I obtained Tutu, a true Greater Sulphur-crested Cockatoo; Jaco, the African Grey; Frodo, a huge Scarlet Macaw; Bill, the Yellow-nape; Fiorello and Bluebell, a young Scarlet Macaw and Blue and Gold, respectively; Major, a hand-fed Hyacinth; and a number of other delightful parrots. I was no longer making mistakes in my choices, but I was rapidly approaching what might be called the burnout point: With fifteen full-size parrots, I was now spending hours each day in feeding and cleaning chores, with very little time left to actually enjoy the birds. This was probably my biggest mistake. Unless you are a breeder or have a staff to do your bird-room tasks, you should limit the number of parrots you purchase. This will enable you to have quality time to enjoy with them and will also improve their care, as it is almost impossible not to let certain important activities slide when you are cleaning fifteen cages and thirty seed and water cups each evening.

By 1985 I had reduced my collection to one bird, Tutu the cockatoo. I had owned her since she was four months old and would never part with her. I also vowed never again to be tempted by another parrot, no matter how charming it might be. Yet now somehow I find I also own Jaco II (a Grey, of course); Blondi II, a marvelous Double Yellowhead; and Mexico, the friendliest little Redhead I have ever seen. I don't quite know how it happened, but please, don't offer me any more parrots.

Useful Hints for Making Life Better

Since most of us either have to go to work in the morning or tend to our families, a good morning routine can be helpful in getting the bird-room chores completed without having to miss breakfast. A routine I find useful (and that takes care of several birds in about twenty minutes) is as follows:

1. Place greens and fruit in clean cups that have been washed the previous evening.

2. Put clean paper on top of the soiled papers (these can also be separated and prepared the previous night).

3. Allow larger and more active birds out of their cages while these activities are going on.

4. Dump the previous night's water and vitamins and wash cups (if you have not added vitamins to the water, you can get by with a thorough rinse at this time) and replace with fresh water without vitamins.

5. As you leave, say goodbye and turn on the radio. My evening routine is much more involved and takes about an hour. Of course, most of us look upon these activities as pleasure rather than work (most of the time).

I am sure most aviculturists use paper towels in the bird room. I economize by keeping an empty carton in which I throw the paper towels used for drying seed dishes. These crumpled but clean towels can be reused for the endless wipe-ups that are necessary when birds are allowed some degree of freedom. I have learned not to buy bargain brands that may tear if used with wet hands and really don't do as good a job as the more expensive brands.

I've been experimenting with methods of trying to keep my parrots' claws at a reasonable length. As I do not particularly relish the job of clipping, and in some cases this is almost impossible to do, I've purchased small grinding blocks and wheels from my local hardware store. The wheels can be hung and the blocks, ideally one-by-one-by-six inches in size, can be glued to a wood backing and then clipped onto the side of the cage. It's not possible to drill the blocks, as they are much too hard. Make sure you get stones made of carborundum, a form of sand, and not those made of aluminum or other metallic particles.

Another way to keep a parrot's nails worn down is to regularly replace older, smoother tree-branch perches with new ones. Many people hate the job of replacing perches because mounting them is time consuming and getting them just the right length is a real challenge. There are also commercially designed perches that are made of abrasive material such as concrete or carborundum. I don't suggest using these, however, as a parrot that spends a lot of time on one of these perches may injure the skin of his feet.

LONGEVITY
IN PARROTS

The parrot has always been known for having an extraordinarily long life span. Other birds such as the ostrich, the raven, and the condor are also believed to have comparable life spans. Among mammals, the elephant is a contender for long-life honors, while fish such as the halibut and the sturgeon are not far behind. The animal that seems to hold the record for longevity appears to be the box turtle, which has achieved a documented 123 years of life. Naturally, most records are based on captive animals, as accurate record-keeping for those in the wild is virtually impossible.

W. C. Osman Hill, an early and highly respected member of the British Avicultural Society, wrote about the length of life in parrots. In April 1954 he received a parrot for autopsy that weighed about ten ounces. It had been with its last owner for fourteen years, who had saved an article published about the bird in a local newspaper ten years earlier that gave the bird's age as eighty-seven years. It was noted that it had been in the care of its previous owner for forty-two years and in the same family before that for thirty-seven years. The post

mortem revealed the senile degeneration typical of this ancient Blue-fronted Amazon.

Mr. Hill received a second specimen for study in July 1954. The last owner had known the bird personally for twenty-five years, although he had been its owner for only nine and a half years. It had previously been owned by his wife's aunt, who had kept it for nineteen years. She had received it from an elderly lady of eighty who had gotten the parrot as a gift when she was a ten-year-old girl. If the history of this parrot is accurate, it was nipping fingers and perhaps saying clever things before the American Civil War and well after World War II, dying at approximately ninety-nine years of age. The bird was eventually euthanized because of progressive weakness and the fact that it had almost stopped eating.

In 1951, in some earlier notes on parrot longevity, Mr. Hill commented on still another Blue-front that had been in the possession of his owner for forty-nine years and was believed to be eighteen months old when she obtained him. Thus, this parrot had survived for more than half a century. His owner indicated that his diet was highly varied and included animal protein and fat in the form of cheese.

Apparently responding to Mr. Hill's comments, the duke of Bedford noted in April 1951 the story of a Lutino Blue-front that he had obtained in 1929. The duke believed the parrot to be quite old at that time, but, if we are limiting ourselves to specific recorded observations, his mutant can be credited only with being more than twenty years old at the time he wrote about the bird, when the parrot was blind but otherwise quite healthy and vigorous.

The final note in this burst of reports occurred in August 1951 when H. P. Williams of Birmingham, England, told the story of a male Blue-front he had obtained in 1921. This bird suffered through the bombings of the war years and frequently shared an air raid cellar with the writer's mother and her dog and cat. Force of circumstance often compelled the animal trio to share the same food dish, which they apparently did without friction. Mr. Williams advises that it was rather amusing, and probably morale-lifting, to see the little group partaking of the same food under these adverse circumstances. This Blue-fronted Amazon was, thus, thirty-plus years of age when the letter was written and was in such fine shape that it had won a third prize in the Birmingham Open Show two years previously.

In *A Guide to the Names of the Parrots* (1969), A. A. Prestwich mentions, with some skepticism, a macaw living in Venice in 1900 that was reputed to be 136 years of age. It was said that this parrot was originally the property of Charles IV of Spain, who died early in the 1800s. Prestwich also mentions a Scarlet Macaw that was still in the Adelaide Zoo in 1954 and was believed to have been in the possession of the Royal Zoological Society of Australia for at least seventy-five years. He also discusses my own personal favorite, Cocky Bennett, who is described in the previous chapter. A woman in Clearwater, Florida, owns Loro, a Double Yellowhead that may be close to eighty years old. Loro was obtained in Mexico during World War II, when he was fully mature and considered to be between forty and forty-five years of age. He had been owned by a doctor and his wife, but when the doctor's first wife died and the doctor remarried, Loro (the word for parrot in Spanish) took an

immediate dislike to the new wife. On one occasion the sight of her hair in curlers apparently offended him, and he attacked. He was therefore asked to leave this household. The doctor knew of my correspondent's interest in parrots, and after checking on Loro's potential new home he invited them to adopt the bird. To this day Loro has never learned to appreciate women and he continues to make swipes at them even if they merely pass his cage. This is all bluff, however, as even though he is generally permitted to fly free he never attacks anyone. When Loro is in the mood he sings (in both English and Spanish) in a beautiful, high soprano voice.

A friend from Northport, New York, reported on Lovey, a most charming Blue-fronted Amazon who could dance and talk. Lovey was purchased for $10 in 1933, when she was thought to be about twenty years old. At the time the story was related to me, this would put Lovey somewhere in her sixties. Lovey did not like children, as she apparently remembered all the teasing and tricks perpetrated by the children in her original home.

Although the smaller parrots have comparatively short life spans, no story on longevity would be complete without a reference to Bobby, Marie Olssen's cockatiel, who lived until he was almost thirty-eight years old.

In general it would appear that cockatoos in captivity can approach a human life span. Macaws and Amazons appear less long-lived, with most not exceeding half a century. For the smaller parrots, twenty to twenty-five years would be a ripe old age. As with humans, there are notable exceptions to these parameters and a number of the birds described in this chapter probably are such exceptions.

In my book *All About the Parrots* (1980), I wrote about Louis, a Blue and Gold Macaw that resided in an impressive mansion in Victoria, British Columbia. Louis was originally owned by Victoria Wilson, a prominent member of her community. I described how Miss Wilson's will provided for Louis's future by indicating that the Wilson mansion, a sprawling, gabled affair, could not be sold while Louis still lived and that he was to have a home there for his lifetime as well as the care of Miss Wilson's gardener, Wong Wah Yue. At the conclusion of my story, I appealed for more information about Louis and Wong and specifically asked if area residents who knew anything about this intriguing pair would write to me.

Friends in Kitchener, Ontario, sent me a complete history of Louis that originally appeared in the Canadian magazine *Westworld*, and I was delighted to receive additional information on Louis from Ethel Todd of Vancouver, British Columbia.

Louis was without a doubt the richest old bird in Canada, and he was famous for his money and his white, three-story house in Victoria. After his story appeared in *Life* magazine he was called everything from a "brandy-swigging lush" (he received a ration of brandy each day) to a "stumbling block in the path of progress" since while he lived his mansion could not be demolished and the property further developed.

Victoria Wilson received Louis as a present from her father when she was five years old. At that time, Louis was estimated to be about ten years old and had just arrived from South America.

The enigmatic Mr. Wong, Louis's steadfast keeper. Could he have trained understudies? Courtesy of Jim Ryan

Louis, the indestructible Blue and Gold Macaw that started it all. Courtesy of Jim Ryan

The famous house on the bay that was home to Victoria Wilson and Louis for many, many years.

Victoria Wilson never married, and when her father died he left his only daughter enough money to make her a very wealthy woman. A quiet, kindly lady, Miss Wilson lived in her own small world within the boundaries of the big, white house on Courtenay Street. She seldom traveled and seemed content with her garden, with its fish pond, sundial, and an aviary housing about sixty birds. Among this chirping flock was Louis, who became a favorite, perhaps because he had learned to imitate his mistress's tinkling laugh and also because he could talk.

Louis's conversation must have been entertaining enough for Miss Wilson to take him along for an occasional ride in an early gasoline-driven car. He was sufficiently vocal to let her know that he certainly didn't like the noise it made, so in 1913 she bought a Hupp-Yeats electric automobile that was

much quieter. Miss Wilson hoped that the electric car would please Louis, but even this vehicle frayed his short temper. Louis rasped his displeasure and the car was quickly put into storage. It has been confirmed that at the time of Miss Wilson's death, a 1913 Hupp-Yeats with solid tires, a glass roof, a vase for flowers behind the driver's seat, and less than one hundred miles on the odometer was found in her garage.

In another effort to appease Louis, Miss Wilson decided that she would provide him with company in the form of his own parrot, an Amazon named Morrie, who was forty years his junior. Morrie was never considered Miss Wilson's pet, but strictly as company for Louis. The group's companionship lasted for sixty-seven years, until Miss Wilson's death in July 1949. It was then that Louis and the rest of his feathered friends became famous.

In her will, Miss Victoria Wilson left close to $345,000 to be shared between the Royal Jubilee Hospital and the Victoria Branch of the Red Cross. In addition, she left $22,000 to the Queen Alexandra Solarium for Crippled Children and the Protestant Orphanage.

The remainder of her money, $60,000, she bequeathed to "one of the birds and other pets." Nowhere did she mention Louis by name but he was known to be her favorite. The will stipulated that a person was to be chosen by her lawyer who would be a suitable and capable person to care for the birds and other pets.

The immediate problem was where to house such a large bevy of birds. The lawyer wisely decided that the old, white mansion would be best.

The person chosen to care for the birds and other pets was Mr. Wong, who had not only been Miss Wilson's gardener for many years but had also cared for the aviary. For the next seventeen years, until his death in February 1967, Wong Wah Yue tended the birds.

During this period, publication of occasional newspaper articles helped Louis become internationally famous. This was due mainly to the clause in Miss Wilson's will that stipulated that, should there be any money left at the time of the last bird's death, it was to be divided between the Royal Jubilee Hospital and the Victoria Red Cross. Louis just happened to be the last bird and it looked as if he were going to live forever.

To add to the problem, the big white house, along with five choice city lots, became a battleground for contractors. The five lots were finally sold leaving Louis's house standing, although it was divided into apartments and called The White House. The properties on either side of the house became parking lots.

Louis, however, was protected by the will and had not lost his house. Although every one of the other birds had died, the old parrot continued to thrive in a temperature-controlled aviary attached to the mansion. Thus, the ancient parrot ruined the plans of several real estate men, who could hardly build a high-rise with an aviary and a gardener's cottage stuck in the middle. In the meantime Louis teetered on his perch with a satisfied gleam in his yellow eyes while Wong catered to his every whim and provided a diet of white grapes, nuts, boiled eggs, sunflower seeds, and a daily teaspoonful of brandy. One reporter wrote that he had visited Louis's ornate parrot house and peered through the wire mesh window only to see "one bloodshot eye and a bundle of moldering feathers."

In 1965, Louis was quietly removed from his home on Courtenay Street. No one would say why and when asked, Mrs. Wong, the wife of Louis's caretaker, refused to say where the bird was now living.

As Louis continued to enjoy good health and his daily brandy, the members of the Royal Jubilee Hospital board began to worry that there would be no money left at all. They wondered, indignantly, which was more important—parrots or people? It was even suggested that it was about time for Louis to be turned over to the S.P.C.A.

In the year of Canada's 1967 centennial, Louis was believed to be older than Canada! Whenever people asked about him they were told, "Louis is fine, thank you." It was also made clear that other members of his species had been known to live to extraordinary ages.

Later that year, Louis's faithful friend and caretaker, Mr. Wong, died at the age of seventy. Louis, though, despite having been moved to an unnamed location, was assured of an allowance for his continued care.

According to Jim Ryan, well-known Victoria photographer, Louis had not had his photo taken since 1960, at which time the old bird showed considerable distaste for flashbulbs. "Mrs. Wong," Jim said, "would not let anyone near the bird." This helped to encourage a rumor that the ancient bird was dead and a succession of other macaws had posed in his place. Mrs. Wong vigorously denied this. Louis was still alive, she insisted, and he still talked in a late nineteenth-century manner with a perfect imitation of Miss Wilson's tinkly laugh. "Naughty bird!" he would scream, "Oh, naughty bird!"

In recent years Miss Wilson's mansion has been replaced by a building that is aptly named the Chateau Victoria, featuring a restaurant on its top floor that is, of course, known as The Parrot House. A place mat from the restaurant features a drawing of the original house and a photo of a Blue and Gold Macaw who looks a bit like Louis.

3

TAMING AND
TRAINING PARROTS

Some of the questions that are most commonly asked by new parrot owners concern taming and training their birds. The word *taming* is a misnomer, as virtually every parrot starts off with a tractable personality and this is one of the factors that makes them so attractive. It is up to the owner to work with a new bird in a reassuring, non-threatening manner. The owner who starts this way is already halfway to enjoying a well-behaved, responsive parrot.

If you are fortunate enough to be able to purchase a hand-fed baby parrot, he will be pleasant when you bring him home. However, unless he is very young, you will still have to prove to this new companion that you mean him no harm and that you can be a source of food, security, and companionship.

The same is true of older birds, but these will require even more patience on your part, as it is possible that they have already had unsatisfactory experience with breeders, shopkeepers, or former owners.

Taming requires patience and careful consideration to prevent your behavior from frightening the bird. After all, you are dealing with an animal whose instincts tell him not to let a human get too close. Some birds find it difficult to take this step,

It is always easier to teach tricks that are part of a parrot's natural behavior. Russel Gordon

and it is possible to compromise with what is called "stick training." Offer the parrot a short length of perch instead of your hand, but be sure to hold it parallel to his feet rather than pointing it like a weapon. Move the stick perch the way you would your fingers and the bird should climb onto the stick.

A second technique is somewhat slower but is also less confrontational: leave the door of the cage open. Most parrots will ultimately climb up the side of the cage and then sit on the top. You can then offer the bird your hand or the stick perch, either of which should work more effectively now that he is out of the cage.

When I first obtained Blondi, my Double-Yellow-head, her owner warned me that she bit if anyone tried to touch her but had no hesitation about coming out on top of her cage by herself. I soon discovered that the former owner was wrong on one count: Blondi had no intention of biting, although she did pretend that she might. Whenever I reached for her, she tried to intimidate me with swipes of her beak accompanied by a musical snarl. I decided to try something creative, and stood with my back to the cage while Blondi was perched on top of it. After a moment I felt a gentle prodding from her beak as she checked my ear and then slowly climbed onto my shoulder, behavior I reinforced by offering her a peanut. I moved slowly, letting her see the nut before it got to her beak. In such situations it is important to be inventive, but make sure that your creativity will make sense to the parrot.

One behavioral idiosyncrasy can be used to manage even the most timid birds. If the parrot is sitting on the top of his cage, close the door to the cage and move the palm of your hand towards him from the back of the cage. He will probably fly off onto the floor. (Do not use this method with birds that have just had their wings clipped.) Once he is on the floor it is almost guaranteed that he will walk onto your hand if you offer it to him.

Return him to his cage and keep trying to get him out in a normal fashion. This is simply a technique for helping the parrot begin to become tame; you will not have to go through your entire relationship forcing the parrot to the floor to get him onto your hand.

You eventually will want to move your bird from your hand to a T-stand perch, which a newly tame parrot can do without any problems. If you begin future training sessions from the outside perch, things will proceed much more rapidly and you will soon be able to show friends and relatives what a charmer your parrot is.

Although all of this may sound like a lot of work (and it is), the payoff comes when you suddenly realize that you are now able to walk up to your bird's cage, open his door, and have him hop out onto your hand. Having achieved this level of trust, many other activities will be possible.

When your bird first arrives home, he will probably be in either a traveling container, a sky kennel, or some other animal-transporting device. Do not be so anxious to start working with him that you attempt to drag him out of the container. If you put your hand into the container to grab him, he will either bite you (a natural reaction) or move as far to the back of the container as he can and clutch the wires or bars.

A newly acquired parrot generally arrives at the home in some sort of carrier. Such birds are usually somewhat stressed as a result of their experience, so great care should be taken in any handling that is required. Michael DeFreitas

A much better technique is to bring the traveling container level with the new cage, using a chair or table or several cardboard cartons. Place the open door of the traveling cage directly against the open door of his new home. If there are big spaces around the opening, stuff them with newspaper to block them temporarily. Put a small lamp behind the cage and turn it on. Cover the traveling container with a towel to darken its interior and then sit some distance from this arrangement with a good book or a newspaper.

The parrot will be attracted to the light and after a reasonable time will move into his new cage. Moving slowly, as one should with a new bird, remove the traveling container and gently close the door of the new cage. If you can bear to do so, you can now leave the room for a while.

Later that day or evening, visit your new pet and bring him fresh water, food, and some treats. If you purchased the bird from a breeder, he or she will almost always have provided you with some of the pellets or seed mixture that the new arrival had been eating. If you try to use this food during the transition period, there will be one less strange thing for the parrot to get used to. Regarding treats, there are some that very few parrots can resist. You will seldom if ever go wrong with roasted peanuts in the shell or pistachio nuts. Fresh corn-on-the-cob sliced into rounds is another winner; in addition to its nutritional value, most parrots will enjoy tearing the cob apart.

Now is the time to begin your efforts to acclimate the new parrot by placing his cage in the area where he will normally live and letting the life of the household function around him. He may not make it obvious, but he will be observing everything intently. Talk to him as you feed him, change his water, and clean his cage, but wait a day or two before attempting any overt familiarities. If you can sneak in an "accidental" touch of his toe or foot while engaged in the above activities, he will begin to learn that you pose no threat to him, a critical lesson in that his natural fear of a large stranger is the only thing that stands between the parrot and tameness. Depending on his age, his reaction to your touching him will range from passivity to a loud snarl. Don't be concerned if he growls; this is the normal reaction of an alert parrot in a new situation.

Parrots' personalities continue to develop throughout their lifetimes. Ronald N. Wilson

HAND TAMING

During the early stages of training, keep the new bird's cage empty of swings, toys, and other clutter. Provide at least two perches, one giving him access to his seed and water dishes and the other towards the back of the cage to which he can retreat if he is frightened. Without this escape perch, he will cling to the bars of the cage when you first try to pick him up. Attempting to dislodge a parrot from cage bars is a major challenge.

Parrots love having the back of the neck gently scratched. This can be a great help in winning a bird's confidence and in all training efforts. Trish Spencer

Some people begin hand training while using a glove, but this is a great mistake. People in a hurry may have previously handled the parrot while wearing gloves, and thus the sight of a glove may frighten him. In addition, the bird has already noticed that your hand is similar to those of other humans. When you suddenly cover your hand with a large canvas or leather sheath, he may become confused and insecure. If you are afraid that the bird will bite you, a perfectly reasonable fear, you can offer your wrist instead of your fingers. The parrot's beak cannot open very far, and an attempted bite on the wrist may pinch but will not normally draw blood. Incidentally, keep in mind that parrots use their beaks as a climbing and exploring tool and that a squeeze or pinch is not really a bite.

You are now at a point where you can attempt some additional friendly gestures. Place your hand in the cage with your palm down and rest it on the perch near the parrot. Try to make physical contact with the bird's feet or body, but do it slowly, as rapid or abrupt movements will alarm him. Do not be intimidated by threatening noises or gestures; in general, a parrot's reaction to danger is to avoid it, and if he doesn't want to make contact with you at this time he is much more likely to move to the back of the cage than to try biting. He may also fluff up his feathers and raise his wings in an effort to look larger and more dangerous, but this behavior is generally a bluff to convince you to leave. Regardless of whether or not you have been able to touch him, you can now remove your hand and sit down near the cage. Talk to the parrot gently, calling him by the name you have chosen for him. Both you and the parrot will discover that ten or fifteen minutes of this is plenty for a training session.

After several lessons your parrot should realize that your hand does not pose a threat to him. Your next step is to close your fingers (again with the palm down) and extend your index finger while placing it either under his claws or against his belly. If he intends to climb onto your hand, he may very well use his beak to steady himself. This is a moment of truth for you and the bird. Is he going to bite or board? Take the chance and see what happens. It's worth it because when a parrot finally does mount your hand, there is a wonderful feeling of accomplishment. If he stubbornly ignores you, gently push with your fingers against his belly and give him a choice between mounting your hand or falling off the perch; in all likelihood he will choose the former.

Slow, gentle movements are best around any parrot, even more so when working with a new bird. Ronald N. Wilson

Parrots are very bright, and as your parrot learns that you are not a threat he will permit you more contact and greater liberties. Keep in mind that the activities you engage in during these first few days will probably largely determine your whole future relationship.

A photogenic Moluccan with a taste for grand opera.
Robert Pearcy

I cannot claim complete success in the training and taming of all the birds I have owned. Fred, a huge, deep pink Moluccan, came to me as a boarder until his owners could resettle in a new state. They were never able to arrange for Fred to live with them, probably because whenever the urge struck him, he would produce a series of loud shrieks sounding like a train or tugboat warning horn. Unfortunately, Fred was timid in the presence of men, and although he would eventually let me touch his feet and scratch his neck, he never gained enough confidence in me to freely leave and return to his cage. This meant that his outside time was severely limited. Fred ultimately was given to a good friend who loves parrots and who seems to have a special aptitude for dealing with frightened birds. She has provided an excellent home for Fred, who is now out of his cage more often than he is in it.

This same lady purchased an imported African Grey, whom she named Jayjay. This bird is a great talker and quite tame but because he is so active, he injured one of his toes during a typical African Grey swinging game. My friend noticed the injury when Jayjay held his foot up so that it would not make painful contact with the perch. Years have passed since the toe healed, but when Jayjay wants attention he still holds that foot in the air in a pitiful, lame manner.

TEACHING PARROTS TO TALK AND PLAY

People are attracted to parrots for many reasons but usually it is their aptitude for speech and hint of what appears to be the ability to reason that initially spark an individual's interest in these birds. A pet shop with a group of parrots on display will always draw the largest crowd around the baby parrots because of their amusing, puppy-like behavior. The only thing that will tempt visitors away from these delightfully awkward and large-headed babies is an older, experienced talking parrot that appears to be loudly uttering phrases for the express purpose of getting you away from the young upstarts and over to admire him.

Talking parrots are wonderful lures for prospective purchasers. A shop I used to visit fairly regularly kept a loquacious Blue and Gold Macaw to greet all visitors. He was never put up for sale, although many people eagerly offered to purchase him.

Yellow-naped Amazons have long enjoyed a well-earned reputation for vocal talent. They also become relatively tame, but older birds unfortunately tend to bite without apparent reason. This seems to occur when you behave in a way that displeases them, such as putting them back in their cage before they are ready to return or paying attention to another bird or person.

In the early 1970s, Alba Ballard introduced me to Yuba, her opera-singing Yellow-nape. This bird was strongly bonded to a Severe Macaw named Loretto, and the two birds were inseparable. Yuba not only sang operatic arias (albeit in a high-pitched, silly voice), but also spoke quite well. My affection for him developed to the point where I asked Mrs. Ballard to sell him to me but she wisely pointed out that it would be a mistake to separate him from Loretto and I had to agree with her.

Truly tame parrots are able to coexist happily with all members of the family. Ken Orr

It was this disappointment that led to my purchasing Bill, who also developed into a notable talking pet. Bill would always greet arrivals to his area with a hearty hello. His voice, however, could be either gruff and deep or high-pitched and feminine. Bill, a large Yellow-nape, was an imported bird who had become extremely tame, although one quickly learned never to take great liberties with him. My wife admired Bill and was slowly gaining the confidence to hold him and play with him. Bill, however, merely tolerated her as I was the person who fed him and tended to most of his needs. One evening we placed Bill on a small table between our arm chairs. He nibbled at my fingers and then climbed up my arm to kiss me. When my wife and I laughed, Bill proceeded across the table, traveled up her arm, bit her on the cheek, and laughed loudly! (My wife still says that his laughing was the

worst part of the incident.) Bill was a jealous bird and considered her a definite rival for my affection.

Ollie and Duke were a pair of clever Yellownapes who lived with me for several months while waiting to be shipped to their new home. They made the trip to the airport in roomy sky kennels that I covered with a blanket to help keep them warm. They maintained a continuous conversation, punctuated with cries of "help!" and "stop!" that could have been a problem if anyone else had heard.

Jaco, my first African Grey, grew up with my children. Eventually they all left home to begin families of their own, my daughter Carol being the youngest and last to leave. She was an active and popular teenager, and eventually most of the phone calls in our house were for her. Whenever the phone would ring, my wife or I would answer and then invariably call: "Carol!" Eventually Jaco began to mimic us and when the phone rang he would call my daughter's name even before we determined who the call was for.

Tutu, my Greater Sulphur-crested Cockatoo, is a better screamer than talker. Because this is typical of the species, I am quite content with her ability to say "Hello Tutu." She normally adds a little shake of her head to this greeting, which she has heard so many times that she assumes these are the words you say when someone comes to your cage. Tutu's cleverness is usually expressed more with body movements and head gestures than it is with speech. If she wants attention she will swing upside down while looking at her visitor; if she is really anxious to attract someone, she will swing while holding on with only one foot, looking something like a feathered white ape. One of her better phrases is the loud "No biting!" that is often heard in any bird room. Tutu uses it rather indiscriminately in any unusual or noisy event, including the dropping of a seed dish or a can cover. Her cage is next to Jaco's, and while they tolerate each other, they are not openly friendly.

Tutu is now more than twenty years old and recently learned to repeat "cockatoo" over and over again when she wants attention. I can only assume that she heard the term when someone said it in her presence and that the sound appealed to her. I, of

One of the best-known parrots of our time is "Alex," shown opposite with his teacher, Dr. Irene Pepperberg. This bird has shown a phenomenal ability to learn and communicate with humans. Here he is learning that noses are not like beaks. Photo courtesy Rick Padden and the Lafayette, Indiana, *Journal & Courier*

course, reinforced her new achievement by delightedly repeating "cockatoo" each time she said it.

TALKERS VERSUS SQUAWKERS

The parrot's reputation for speech and mimicry is so great that the very word *parrot* is used to describe the act of mimicking or imitating. The ability to mimic speech lends a touch of humanity to these birds, which explains the great value people have placed upon parrots in all the societies to which they have been imported over many centuries.

The casual observer is under the impression that all parrots are capable of great feats of speech, but this unique ability varies widely among the parrots, with some showing virtually no talking skills and others speaking and mimicking so well that legitimate reports of their achievements are looked upon with suspicion. In some species, the skills are so impressive that there is no need to exaggerate.

Parrot speech is actually sound articulated in a meaningful fashion rather than the shrill pipings or garbled noises that often send deluded owners of budgies and cockatiels into a rapturous state. The vocalizations of a parrot are frequently used at what appears to be an appropriate time and in a reasoned manner. This is, in all likelihood, a form of conditioning. On a given occasion the parrot screams "goodbye!" as its owner leaves the room, and is rewarded with such an enthusiastic response that the bird is encouraged to repeat these same sounds the next time its owner leaves.

Of course, there may be exceptional parrots who do exhibit a form of reasoning power. Alex, the African Grey owned and trained by Dr. Irene Pepperberg, not only mimics sounds and speech but will also properly answer questions about the number and category of objects shown to him.

A considerable body of misinformation has risen regarding the speaking ability of various parrot species. Some of this stems from dubious experts who have made broad generalizations after spending time with a particular parrot. When information of this type is published, it may later be repeated periodically and eventually accepted as fact. A great many observations must be made before a sweeping characterization about the speaking powers of a particular species can be made.

The following information is based on such observations. Of course, there will always be exceptions to almost any rule, but these ratings have proven valid for large numbers of parrots over a period of many years.

African Greys

These birds are the best talkers, with one stipulation that may sound like hedging: Not all African Greys learn to speak. Those that do, however, speak with a voice that is close to human (unlike other parrots, which have shrill, "parrot-like" voices). An African Grey that speaks will generally continue to learn new words, sounds, and phrases throughout his lifetime. African Greys obtained as young, dark-eyed birds are the best students; it is the older birds who may never learn to verbalize. The same is true of the Timneh Grey subspecies, which is usually sold for a lower price because it is smaller, somewhat less attractive, and not as well known.

All African Greys have a natural whistle markedly resembling a "wolf whistle." During World War II, U.S. troops stationed in those parts of Africa where the African Greys are found assumed that either they or their comrades had taught this to the birds. Do not bother teaching your parrot how to whistle; it is like teaching fish to swim.

If an African Grey has learned the words, accents, and speech patterns of its original owner, it is quite capable of adding vocabulary and accents in a new home. Ultimately, it may even forget the phrasing practiced in its earlier life. If a talking bird is crucial to your happiness, choose a young African Grey.

Amazon Parrots

The Yellow-naped Amazon is unquestionably the outstanding talking member of this group. Although the speech is typically parrot-sounding, one can safely say that all Yellow-napes learn to speak and that their skills range from eloquent to incredible. As is the case with most parrots, those who do best in this area are birds that were obtained while still quite young. As an added bonus, tame Yellow-napes, as well as the other full-size Amazons, enjoy making physical contact and playing games with their owners, which is not always true of African Greys, who are often easily frightened.

Yellow-napes do not suffer bovine liberties gladly. Frank Simon

The Panama Amazon is second in speaking ability among the Amazons only to the celebrated Yellow-nape. David A. Wurzbach

As a talker, the Panama Amazon, a close relative, is equal to or runs a close second to the Yellow-nape. Panama Amazons are not commonly available, but those who own them praise their speaking skills highly. Unfortunately, this type is often confused with the Yellow-fronted Amazon, which is something of a look-alike but lacks a high level of speaking proficiency.

Double Yellow-heads are another group of Amazons that speak and mimic to a noteworthy degree. Although their vocabulary is smaller than that of the Yellow-nape, they show a marked propensity for mimicry, including the silly laughter that to me is often more amusing than speech. The Double Yellow-heads I have owned or visited had wonderfully amiable personalities. In this respect I prefer them to Yellow-napes, which seem, as noted above, to develop a jealous streak that can result in severe bites.

The Yellow-lored, Blue-fronted, and Mealy Amazons are capable of learning to speak but do not rank high in this category. Mexican Redheads are lovable and friendly but lack a great potential for speech, and the small Amazons, such as the Orange-winged, Spectacled, and White-fronted, generally do not learn to speak more than a word or two.

Macaws

As a general rule, the full-size macaws, such as the Blue and Gold, Scarlet, Military, Greenwing, and Hyacinth, have a limited vocabulary consisting of a few words or short, sometimes distorted phrases that are generally spoken in a loud, attention-getting voice. The Blue and Gold often utters a natural, guttural sound that sounds like the name "Robert" (if the bird were a frog it would probably be "Ribert"); if such a macaw happens to belong to a person with that name, his cleverness will be widely celebrated.

The miniature macaws, with the exception of the Yellow-collared, are usually not capable of learning to speak, but the Yellow-collared Macaw can achieve a limited vocabulary.

Macaws are in demand more for their appearance and personality than for their usually limited speaking ability. Shown here is a young Scarlet (left) and a Blue and Gold.

Parrot Training Tips

You will find it easiest to teach your parrot endearing actions and responses by working with activities that bear a close relationship to characteristic behavior. Many parrot owners demonstrate the tameness and cleverness of their parrots by having the bird hang from the owner's finger by one claw. Although this may look very impressive, in reality it's just an everyday activity for a parrot, comparable to the way his forebears behaved in the wild. Conversely, attempting to force a parrot to learn an activity involving a prop that may be unusual or alarming to him is a big mistake.

Think about your body movements when working with your birds. Parrots consider movements from above a threat (as they are in nature from hawks and similar predators) and react automatically. Always move your hands slowly and when reaching toward your parrot always move from below.

Parrots enjoy being scratched in the nape of the neck; many people refer to this as "head scratching," but it is actually scratching in the nape and cheek regions that is most pleasurable for parrots. The first scratch is the most difficult, as this is a pleasure that has to be learned. Start your movements from below, beginning with the bird's foot or side and working your way up.

Avoid contact with the parrot's back, as he will not be able to see what you're doing and generally even a tame bird will not react well to this type of touch.

Many parrots show a natural response to music. Try beginning your training session with some pleasant music playing softly in the background.

Training results will come faster if you reinforce each success with praise and rewards. In many cases your laughter and enthusiasm will be sufficient encouragement for the parrot, but you can also provide small treats, such as a pistachio or other type of nut, that the parrot does not get regularly.

Cockatoos

The Bare-eyed Cockatoo and its close relative the Goffin's lead the group in the speech category. These parrots also appear to be the most intelligent and quickly tamed of the white cockatoos (I strongly suspect that there is a link between the attributes of tameness, intelligence, and speaking ability in parrots).

The Greater Sulphur-crested Cockatoo, and all of its subspecies as well as the other white cockatoos, such as the Moluccan and the Umbrella, can learn a small number of words. As with the macaws, these are usually spoken in extremely loud voices, but, unfortunately, the sounds are frequently distorted; the speech rating is significantly lower if the parrot's owner has to translate what the bird is saying.

The Palm Cockatoo and the various Black Cockatoos are all quite rare and will normally not be available as pets. As it happens, none of these is highly rated as a talking parrot.

When working with any parrot, body language, such as the erected crest of this cockatoo, is an important signal for the trainer. S. Green

Eclectus

This attractive group has grown in popularity. Unlike most parrot species, there are very obvious differences in appearance between males and females. Their fur-like plumage is beautifully colored, and in this genus it is the females who have the more colorful feathers. They do not develop large vocabularies but are capable of learning a few words that they will repeat freely. Their natural calls are quite interesting, particularly those of the males during the breeding season.

Conures, Caiques, and Pionus

None of these parrots are notable talkers. The conures lead the other two groups in terms of limited speech, but if a speaking bird is a primary goal for you, choose an African Grey or an Amazon. On the other hand, these small parrots (as well as other nontalkers) can give their owners a great deal of pleasure with their friendly manner and clever acrobatic behavior. To some people this can be more important than the ability to speak.

4

PARROT NUTRITION

This dexterous Goffin's Cockatoo will not drop a bit of his tasty peanut. Joan Balzarini

The panic-stricken phone call from upstate New York came at a very early hour. The breeder had purchased two pairs of Sun Conures from a lady in Florida and both females had arrived with bone fractures, one with a fractured lower leg and the other with fractures in both the wing and lower leg. The airline disclaimed any responsibility, as the well-built shipping box showed absolutely no sign of damage. The breeder asked if I would contact the seller. I knew both individuals and had recommended the Florida parrot fancier as someone who wished to travel and relax and who wanted to give up two proven pairs of Suns. Telephone research indicated that both hens were prolific layers and that the Florida breeder had not been aware of the acute need for calcium supplements for her birds. Even though they were producing eggs with properly hardened shells, their own calcium needs had gone largely unmet and decalcification of their bones had taken place. A monetary adjustment was made and prompt surgery repaired the damage. It took months, however, for the hens to be returned to normal health, which was achieved with a well-planned diet including all necessary and appropriate supplements. Happily, these pairs went on to breed again and as far as I know they are still producing beautiful Sun Conure chicks on a regular basis.

Birds, just as all other animals, need a diet that meets certain requirements. They must have proteins for tissue growth and replacement, carbohydrates to provide energy, and fats to maintain normal body temperature. When the supply of these nutrients falls short, the body will substitute other nutrients, using fats and proteins for energy and carbohydrates and proteins for generating heat. Since the body cannot substitute any other nutrient for proteins, the use of protein for energy or warmth shortchanges the bird by interfering with its normal function of tissue-building. Birds also need the proper amounts of vitamins, minerals, and trace elements (minerals needed in minute quantities but still crucial to normal health).

If you keep birds either as pets or for breeding, you are responsible for providing them with a healthy and pleasing diet that will keep them fit and happy and allow them to reach their potential life span. Many otherwise unexplained losses can be traced directly or indirectly to nutritional disorders. Birds that are to be bred require an even more carefully planned diet that changes during certain times of the year. Although some of the information on proper nutrition can be obtained by experience, it is certainly more humane, as well as economically more efficient, to benefit from the experience and research of others. New bird buyers should be made aware of the importance of a proper diet, and breeders should consider providing them with a good book on diet and nutrition. The cost can be built into the selling price of the bird, and breeders will be giving the chicks they breed and sell a better chance for a healthy life.

A proper balance should exist between the nutrients, as excesses of some can do as much harm as deficiencies. Many birds are attracted to seeds and other foods with a high percentage of oil, but an excess of fat can cause liver problems or diarrhea. Birds in the wild as well as those kept in outside flights in colder regions require more oil-rich foods, but consistently feeding comparable proportions to the same species in an indoor flight or aviary may cause liver damage, symptoms of which include drowsiness, ruffled feathers, and increasing inactivity. Serious liver damage can result in death, and necroscopy will show lesions,

discoloration, and enlargement of the organ. Fortunately, the progress of the affliction can be reversed by vastly reducing fat intake.

Birds are particularly dependent on the minerals calcium and phosphorous, as these are the main constituents of bones, and calcium plays a very important role in the formation of egg shells. The need for these minerals is always there, but it is particularly important in young, developing birds and egg-laying females. Birds should also be provided with supplementary vitamin D_3, without which a calcium/phosphorus imbalance can occur. Birds with sufficient exposure to sunlight can manufacture their own vitamin D_3, but, obviously, not all captive birds have this opportunity.

BALANCED DIETS FOR PARROTS

A basic seed or pellet diet (some people prefer to mix the two and serve a combination seed/pellet ration) should include a variety of seeds such as safflower, sunflower, oat groats, and millet. Nuts such as peanuts, pine nuts, or almonds should also be included, but be sure to limit the amount of nuts you feed. Even though it is amusing to watch a parrot shell a nut while grasping it with one foot, eating these rich, tasty items will diminish the amount of other foods a parrot is willing to eat. Fruits and vegetables should also be provided (preferably in the morning and then removed at night). The fruits and vegetables you feed are largely determined by what the birds will eat. Some people report that their parrots will not eat vegetables or fruits, but you may be able to alter this by wedging pieces of apple or slices of orange high in a corner of the cage. The stubborn and curious parrot will investigate these new objects and in doing so may discover that he likes their taste.

Supplements in the form of cuttlebone for minerals and powdered or liquid vitamins should be given daily. I prefer the powdered vitamins in warm weather or in the case of birds that will not drink their water if a liquid vitamin has been added. Powdered vitamins will adhere to fruit and vegetables instead of falling to the bottom of the feed dish.

The above suggestions are very broad and do not take into account the special needs and preferences of certain species. Kenton and Alice Lint, in *Feeding Cage Birds, A Manual of Diets for Aviculture* (1988), list many such items, including

Brazil nuts for macaws, eucalyptus seeds for Gang-gang Cockatoos, macadamia nuts for the Black Cockatoo group, and papaya and sweet potatoes for the Eclectus.

Sprouted seeds are favored by almost all birds but are of particular delight to canaries and finches. Sprouting is a fairly simple operation that requires about three days; you can purchase a sprouting jar with full information in any health-food store. It is imperative that the instructions on washing the seeds at several intervals be followed. You will be alerted to this need by your own nose during the first stages of sprouting, but follow through with the washing instructions to the end. Sprouted seeds are delicious and most people steal a few handfuls for themselves. The vitamin content of the seeds increases dramatically during sprouting, and it is also an excellent test of the viability of the seeds, since only live seeds can sprout. Old, dead seeds have very limited nutritional value and should be avoided. Good seeds to sprout that are easily obtainable from health-food stores include radish, rape, lettuce, mung beans, and milo.

FOOD HINTS

Certain items seem to be almost universal favorites among parrots. I have never seen a parrot turn down a piece of graham cracker, and when I distribute fresh corn on the cob, within minutes every resident of the bird room is chewing away. Certain flavored dog biscuits are also received with pleasure by every bird in my collection.

This is far from true, however, with many other food items that one would assume all parrots would love. Often, after having gone to a great deal of trouble to obtain a particular fruit or green, I am rather disappointed to find the special treat lying on the bottom of the cage with hardly a beak mark on it. Most bird keepers have failed at some time to get a parrot to try something considered important to his diet. In these cases you should use some ingenuity. For example, if you have a particular fruit you want the bird to try and he has been dropping it out of his dish untouched, wedge or spike the fruit at the top corner of the cage. The curious parrot is guaranteed at least to examine it and may pleasantly surprise you by nibbling on the fruit he had previously flung from his dish.

Indian nuts are another favorite, but they are sometimes difficult to obtain, which has something to do with the fact that they are not an annual crop, as well as the high price (almost five dollars a pound!). Parrots, without exception, love this sweet, delicately flavored nut, and if you can locate a pound or two, they make an excellent treat and a fine training device. They are rather rich as a steady diet, but try them as a lure with a timid bird and his reaction may surprise you.

When selecting food items, remember that although parrots have a poor sense of smell, they do have a remarkably well-developed color sense that significantly affects what they choose to eat. I used to think that the wild birds took a perverse delight in attacking the small number of apples, peaches, and cherries that our fruit trees yielded. They would ignore the trees until the fruits were ripe and then swoop down to enjoy the best of the lot. Of course, they made it a point to ignore those fruits that were not ripe. Several years ago I realized that this was not malice, discovering that with their marvelous sense of vision, so necessary to an animal that hunts for food from the sky, birds can spot ripened fruits by their colors, naturally choosing these over the unripened ones. Parrot owners who have had difficulty getting their independent little friends to eat certain foods can take advantage of this capacity. Experiment with various bright natural food colorings, which are quite harmless, and, by changing the color of certain foods, get the parrot to try them. A parrot who has rejected natural safflower or oat seeds may consider trying blue or red versions. Ultimately, when the bird discovers that he really like these items, it may be possible to put away your food-coloring equipment.

A graham cracker or dog biscuit fed during the evening will probably be dipped into the water by your bird; you may be assured from this that he is getting some of the vitamins that you have put in the water.

When buying seed in bulk you have a right to expect that it is reasonably fresh. Most bulk seed comes in bags that are dated, just as grass seed is. Don't hesitate to ask if the seed is fresh. A merchant who hopes to keep your business will probably not sell you old seed if he or she knows you are concerned about it.

Very old seed loses part of its nutritive value and is also more likely to be infested with seed moths, although almost all seed is threatened by

these annoying but harmless pests. To diminish the number flying about, you can put up a couple of old-fashioned flypaper strips.

Some treats, such as peanuts, Indian nuts, or cedar nuts, can be taste-tested for freshness. By eating a few yourself you will be able to tell immediately if they are stale or rancid. If your parrot's intake of food suddenly drops, try to determine whether you may have inadvertently made a change in his food, food dish, or living conditions. Parrots are the most stubborn and conservative of animals and the slightest change is enough to cause them to stop eating. I recently had to buy a jar of brewer's yeast that was flavored rather than plain because that was all my pharmacist had available. After a day or two I became aware that the plastic bowl in which I put the previous day's leftover seeds (to feed to the wild birds) was getting rather heavy. Taking out the flavored yeast quickly brought everything back to normal. Of course, failure to eat could also be an indication of illness, but you would probably see other symptoms if such were the case.

FEEDS, SEEDS, AND SUPPLEMENTS

For many years, bird fanciers were content to provide very limited diets for their pets. Mixes of one or two favorite seeds with treats from the family table were not uncommon. In recent years, however, pet owners have become more sophisticated and are fully aware of the link between diet and health, both as it affects their pets and themselves. It is not simply a coincidence that manufacturers are modifying their products and advising the public of the merits of their various feeds through detailed and informative advertising.

Although all producers of seed mixes, food pellets, and vitamin and mineral supplements agree on the need for a complete and balanced diet, many use different strategies to achieve this result. Some impregnate the seeds with additives, while others claim this breaks down the protective seed coat, possibly shortening shelf life. Some prefer to coat the outside of the seeds with supplements, but others believe that the bulk of this material will never be ingested in any case. Birds have a remarkable

An ideal parrot diet includes grains, beans, vegetables, and fruits (opposite). Larry Willet

A Cockatiel and a Green-cheek prepare to examine the vegetables offered to them. Dr. David Henzler

color sense, which has led some manufacturers to use bright food coloring on seeds with the expectation that a bird might more willingly select a brightly colored sunflower than one of normal color.

Bird food in the form of pellets has the advantage of uniformity. There is no picking and choosing of seed favorites with healthful but unwanted seeds left over or swept to the bottom of the cage, but birds that are currently fed seeds do not generally make the transition to pellets willingly. To make pellets, nutrients, vitamins, minerals, and amino acids are blended and then extruded in pellet form in appropriate sizes for different birds. Those who prefer pellets cite the ease of feeding, resistance to spoilage, and freedom from messy seed hulls.

Most pellet manufacturers are addressing the critical needs of young birds and breeding birds, as well as helping to avoid obesity in older birds. One cannot assume that a single diet will be suitable for all parrots, as sedentary birds do not require the same amount of protein as active breeders or birds in large flights that engage in much more vigorous physical activity.

Regardless of the type of diet you feed, there is always the concern that it may be lacking in one or more of the essential vitamins, minerals, or trace elements. Although only minute quantities of these are required for normal health, the continued lack of one or more of them can have a markedly negative effect on fertility, feather condition, longevity, and vigor.

For quite a few years the hottest topic under discussion in the nutrition field was in regard to the relative merits of liquid supplements as opposed to those in dry powder form, along with whether to use the bird's water or food as the vehicle for the supplement. There are also two subgroups, favoring oil-based vitamin solutions and water-based preparations, respectively.

Lambert-Kay produces Avitron, a multivitamin supplement that is fairly pleasant tasting and leaves no oily residue in the water cup. The manufacturer has also come out with Avimin, a mineral supplement in water-soluble form.

Nekton is a more recent arrival on the supplement scene. It is an import that is used in seven different products to provide color enhancement, fertility and plumage improvement, and an anti-stress vitamin mixture. The water-soluble powder can be sprinkled on food or dissolved in the drinking water.

Mardell Laboratories, well-known for their antibiotic, Ornacyn, has added to their line Ornacyn-Plus, which includes vitamins and amino acids that could benefit an ailing bird that is using the antibiotic. The company has also recently brought out an anti-stress compound consisting of electrolytes, trace elements, and vitamins in a fruit-flavored powder.

There is also a large class of additives that are used by color canary breeders to enhance color. Nutritional Research has been providing flamen oil and other color enhancers for many years.

During the last few years a new additive has begun to gain favor, the Lactobacillus organism

At thirty days, this hand-fed Goffin's Cockatoo chick weights 275 grams. It is part of the highly successful breeding program at the Hagen Avicultural Research Institute. Rolf C. Hagen, Inc.

that normally flourishes in the intestinal tract of healthy birds. An animal that has been ill and heavily medicated may have lost many of these organisms and could benefit from having them replenished. This is also recommended for birds suffering from diarrhea. Quite a few firms, including Mardell Laboratories, offer this product, which comes in both powder and liquid form. There is also some variation in the particular strains of the organism used. The other new additions to the nutritional scene are spirulina and wheat grass. Spirulina is an alga that adds many trace elements when dried and sprinkled on food. Wheat grass is a powdered form of the wheat plant that purportedly enhances health by introducing elements not normally found in standard bird diets.

As indicated above, individuals who take on the responsibility of owning a pet must commit themselves to providing an appropriate diet. This is particularly true in the case of captive birds since, in the wild, these creatures generally have the opportunity to fulfill their requirements for nutrients, minerals, vitamins, and trace elements by choosing from a wide variety of fruits, seeds, and insect life.

5 GROOMING PARROTS

Good grooming for anyone, animal or human, improves appearance by highlighting attractive features. Most people feel at their best when properly groomed and it is quite possible that birds respond in the same manner. When you see an array of properly groomed birds on a show bench you cannot help but notice their impressive stance and confident manner.

Grooming is also an important health issue, as, for example, excessively long nails can cause a bird to become trapped if a toe is wedged into a tiny opening. Unclipped nails also tend eventually to grow into deformed shapes that may bend at odd angles or even begin to resemble a corkscrew.

A parrot that does not use his beak for chewing bits of wood or other hard objects may develop an overhanging upper beak, which is not a normal situation. It can be difficult for a parrot with such a beak to crack small seeds or even to hold them. Although nail clipping can be done by most any bird owner, I do not recommend that you attempt to trim your bird's beak yourself; if you cause the beak to bleed it is very hard to stanch the flow.

Wing clipping is usually done with new birds to facilitate taming. By clipping the first five to eight primary flight feathers on one or both wings, you limit flight and cut down on the amount of bird chasing you have to do during the training period. Some owners enjoy taking their tame birds out of doors, but if their wings are not clipped they may fly away, become disoriented, and never return. Most parrots are expert climbers and jumpers, so even a parrot with clipped wings can elude capture if you take him outdoors and he decides to escape. You should play it safe and restrict all outdoor activity to outdoor cages or flights, even if your bird's wings are clipped.

There are various schools of thought on wing clipping. Some people want to limit the bird's flight but are anxious that he retain the ability to flee from an aggressor or to break his fall if he should lose his balance while on a perch. For these reasons, such people generally clip only one wing. A bird clipped in this manner will fly in a circle very much like an aircraft with one engine disabled. He will not look as attractive with only one wing clipped, but the wing feathers will eventually grow out and at that time the owner can decide whether or not to clip again. Another method is to clip both wings but avoid any of the secondary wing feathers.

In the wild, birds such as this Greenwing and Hyacinth Macaw engage in grooming activities that keep their feathers, beaks, and claws in top condition. When such birds become our pets, that responsibility becomes ours. Robert Pearcy

You can also clip alternate feathers on both wings, but this may leave certain birds still capable of flight.

The first time you try clipping your parrot's wings, get a friend to work with you as a holder while you act as the groomer. If there is danger of biting, you may have to resort to gloves or wrapping the bird in a towel.

Begin by laying out all of your equipment: gloves, towels, scissors, nail file, and hydrogen peroxide or other coagulant to stop bleeding if a nail or wing feather is cut too short. Have your helper use one hand to hold the bird around the neck in a loose grip with a finger and thumb; holding the head too tightly will only cause the bird to resist more. With the other hand the helper should get a firm grip on the body of the bird across his midsection. Encourage the parrot to hold onto your hand with his feet as this will keep him from clawing at you. The wing not being clipped should be held close to the body with the helper's thumb and fingers.

To trim, extend one wing as if you were opening a fan or an accordion door. If all feathers are present, you will find that there are ten primaries on each wing. The primaries begin in the middle of the wing. You will see that they begin next to the secondaries, whose tips turn back toward the bird's body. Cut the last five primaries farthest from the bird's body. You should cut them off about half way up the shaft, just under the line formed by the tips of the primary covert feathers. While the holder maintains a grip on the bird, the groomer moves from side to side to clip each wing.

You may wish to repair the tail if it has been damaged in transit or because the bird may have flown wildly while being moved to his new home. Check to see if the tail has all of its twelve feathers. If any are broken, the shaft that remains should be pulled out so that a replacement can grow in. Remove a broken feather by tightly grasping the shaft of the feather close to the tail and pulling straight out with a rapid and firm movement. If you wish to make the removal of a broken feather easier, you can spray the area of the feather with warm water for several days prior to pulling out the damaged shaft.

A broken feather is easy to spot since it dangles at an odd angle. A new feather looks like a bit of straw sticking out of the bird with a small feather being pushed through it. A feather that has been removed will replace itself in about six to eight weeks, but a broken feather will not be replaced until the next molt.

Feather regeneration is a demanding body activity. If many ragged or broken feathers have been removed, close attention to the parrot's diet is necessary. Give ample nourishing food as well as an appropriate vitamin supplement.

NAIL TRIMMING

Many parrots will wear down their nails while others will actually chew off the sharp points. In an older, inactive parrot, nails may become excessively long and sharp. This is uncomfortable for you when you hold the bird and also risky, as the parrot may catch the long, thin nail in any small opening.

To cut the parrot's nails, one foot should be kept exposed for nail trimming while the other foot is held under the palm of the assistant's hand. The holder grasps the leg joint to prevent the bird from jerking his foot, while the groomer then easily trims the nail.

A guillotine-type dog nail clipper is recommended for trimming. The clipper must be sharp, as a dull instrument will crush rather than cut. Hold the nail firmly with one hand and slip the clipper under the nail with the other.

Trim off excess nail, but leave enough curve for gripping. A good rule of thumb (or claw) is to cut too little rather than too much. Cut off a bit of each nail at a time until you approach the live "quick." If you accidentally cut into this area, be prepared for some bleeding. Hydrogen peroxide, styptic powder, or styptic pencil will stop this bleeding.

TRIMMING THE BEAK

Beak trimming should not be attempted by an inexperienced individual. Although the beak is made of a material similar to that of nails, it has a richer supply of blood vessels that are closer to the tip. Improper trimming can therefore cause serious bleeding that is very difficult to stop. A file or emery board is suggested for use in rounding the tip of the beak instead of trimming it.

Let beak trimming be done by your veterinarian or a thoroughly experienced bird groomer. This individual should hold the beak while his or her associate restrains the bird. With a thumb under the lower beak, the groomer's upper fingers are used to bring the two parts of the beak, or mandibles, together. Parrots have tremendous jaw power and caution is advised. A secure grip must be maintained on the bird to counter any strong resistance. The bird's tongue must be kept out of the way, and covering up the bird's nostrils with the fingers should be avoided. The expert should now carefully and conservatively trim the excess beak and then file the rough edge until it is smooth.

BATHING PARROTS

Baths may be given with plain water or water with a few drops of glycerin. Use a misting sprayer. You will find that most parrots enjoy and welcome a spray bath and will generally extend their wings to catch as much of the liquid as possible. To avoid chilling the bird, use fairly warm water; if you spray it on your own hand first you will see that the spray cools as it passes through the air and it should reach the parrot at a comfortable temperature. If you are in doubt about engaging in any of these procedures have it done first by your vet, an expert at your bird shop, or an experienced friend.

6 AVIAN MEDICINE

The history of veterinary medicine is long and honorable. Early Babylonian and Egyptian records speak of veterinary practices with specialists in oxen and doctors of fowl. It is interesting to note that the medical advances for humans and animals have followed almost parallel paths of development. When George Washington was treated with leeches or had his famous dental prosthesis made of wood, his farm animals were suffering equally unsophisticated care, and today's doctors of veterinary medicine are using virtually every type of diagnostic tool and treatment that may be found in a modern physician's office. In fact, in the area of preventative medicine, veterinary medicine may even be several steps ahead of human medicine, as the preventative techniques or immunization for farm and home animals are a crucial part of well-animal care.

At the turn of the century, veterinary medicine centered on the horse and farm animals, which were the mainstays of agriculture and transportation. Henry Ford's invention changed all that, and with the horse's loss of prominence, veterinary medicine changed direction. Currently there are more than 55,000 veterinarians in the United States, approximately one-half of whom specialize

in small animals and 3,400 of them engaging in a mixed small and large animal practice. Many school districts offer courses in large and small animal care, with some graduates going on to become veterinary assistants or in some cases to veterinary school.

The large growth in numbers of exotic birds kept as pets has also had an effect on veterinarian specialization. As medical help for birds became increasingly necessary, many vets began to develop expertise in this previously limited field. Dr. Robert B. Altman of Franklin Square, New York, was an early avian practitioner, and his father, Dr. Irving Altman, surely deserves to be called a pioneer in the field. In an interview, the younger Altman described sophisticated blood tests for birds in which little more than a drop of blood can provide information on liver and kidney functions, blood-sugar levels, red-cell count, and other important avian health indicators.

Another veterinarian whose name has come to be synonymous with bird care is Dr. Ted Lafeber of Niles, Illinois. Dr. Lafeber's nutritional research has had a wide-ranging effect on the way in which pet birds are fed in the United States.

William D. Sumner, D.V.M., of Greensboro,

Tremendous advances have been made in avian medicine over the past fifteen years. Techniques and procedures that were once unheard of are now routine. It is exciting to contemplate what will be accomplished in the future. Courtesy American Animal Hospital Association

North Carolina, a past president of the American Animal Hospital Association, encourages compassion for pet owners as well as ailing pets. He believes that the veterinarian should put him- or herself in the pet owner's place and recognize the depth of the owner's attachment. Such a doctor would be loath, for example, to suggest that the pet owner might purchase several new budgies for the cost of treating a sick one. Not surprisingly, Dr. Sumner has owned and maintained a variety of pets, including birds.

Veterinarians are also active in research. Dr. Gary L. Butcher worked at the Department of Veterinary Microbiology & Parasitology at Texas A & M, and has done research on the problems of French Molt, Avian Gout, and Psittacosis. Dr. Greg Harrison of Lake Worth, Florida, is a specialist in avian hysterectomies as well as nutrition. Dr. Robert Phillips, a veterinarian at Colorado State University, was the first veterinarian in space on a 1986 shuttle flight, where he conducted a battery of biomedical experiments to determine the effects of weightlessness on animal functions. Dr. David Graham, formerly of Cornell University and now at the Schubot Research Center at Texas A & M, has been deeply involved with the problem of feather maturation syndrome in cockatoos. Dr. Bran Ritchie's name is closely associated with the effort to develop a parrot vaccine against this deadly syndrome, which has been a problem for so many breeders and pet owners.

The veterinary profession has made and continues to make vital contributions to the field of medical knowledge, for as Sir William Osler, the founding father of modern medicine, put it: "There is only one medicine."

PROBLEMS WITH ILLNESS AND ACCIDENTS

The average bird owner should not experience serious health problems with his or her bird if common-sense rules are followed. Take note of the following causes and many problems can be avoided:

Drafts: Birds can tolerate reasonable changes in temperature quite well. They do not, however, fare well if subjected to drafts. Avoid open windows during cold weather in early spring, winter, and late fall. Never keep a bird in line with the cold air issuing from an air-conditioning unit. If your bird does catch cold, he can be treated with an over-the-counter antibiotic or one prescribed by your veterinarian. Injected antibiotics work faster, but these obviously must be given by a veterinarian.

Poor hygiene: This is the cause of most illness in otherwise healthy birds. It includes feeding spoiled or suspect food such as wilted greens or fruit, and leaving easily spoiled foods in the cage for many hours. Failure on the part of the owner to wash his or her hands before feeding or working with the bird can also be a problem as can handling or feeding a healthy bird without thorough hand washing after working with a sick pet.

Carelessly providing access to toxic materials such as paint or chemicals is a common cause of illness. Another is exposure to birds who are carrying

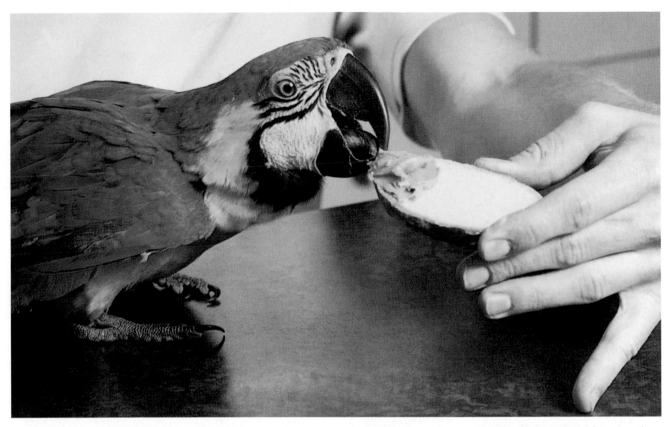

Sometimes the most effective way to administer medication to a bird is through a treat. This Blue and Gold patient has had something added to his peanut butter hors d'oeuvre. Courtesy American Animal Hospital Association

communicable disease. Any bird is suspect if you are not certain of its health, and newly purchased birds are doubly suspect.

Re-emergence of pre-existing conditions takes place when a bird is subjected to stressful situations or poor diet for any length of time, thereby lowering his resistance.

Accidents: Bleeding nails and blood feathers are frightening because of the splattering of the blood droplets as they hit the floor of the cage. Cut nails carefully and avoid the impulse to cut as much nail as you can. If you just nip off the tips of the nails on a frequent and regular basis you will avoid bleeding. Bleeding from the feathers is usually caused by the breaking of a feather with blood vessels in it. Both nail and feather bleeding can be stanched with hydrogen peroxide, styptic pencil, or styptic powder. The bird should then be kept as quiet as possible until a blood clot forms. I prefer the peroxide method, and either dip the bleeding nail or feather into a capful of peroxide or soak a clean cotton ball with peroxide and apply it to the bleeding area.

Flying into windows or obstructions can be dangerous or fatal to your bird. If he is a new arrival and you permit him to fly in the house, be sure that blinds are down over windows and drapes are drawn over large glass doors. You can also temporarily cover mirrors with a towel.

Pets: Dogs and cats can pose a serious threat to your parrot. Many will enjoy peaceful coexistence with birds but on occasion their natural predatory instincts can take over. Play it safe and keep birds protected from these animals.

Keep several good books on avian medicine available so that you can intelligently describe symptoms to your veterinarian if you think your bird is ill. Read a chapter on "the well bird" and learn to recognize abnormal behavior when you see it.

WARM WEATHER–CARE HINTS FOR PARROTS

The summer months are a delight for most people, as we plan leisurely days away from our jobs and, in some cases, away from home for weeks or months at a time. Everybody deserves a vacation, but being away from home always poses the problem of arranging for care for our parrots during a season when special attention must be paid to sanitation and cleanliness.

This pair of rare Blue Princess of Wales Parakeets is maintained under broad spectrum lighting. Courtesy Wingsong Aviaries

Our pets are most vulnerable during warm weather, as this is a time when bacteria, molds, and fungi thrive, so it is crucial for you or those who care for your birds to keep their seed and water dishes as well as their cages scrupulously clean during this period. Good hygiene will avoid many health problems and you should choose your surrogate birdkeepers with this in mind.

Not everyone is willing to care for a parrot. Their size and nature make them considerably more difficult to tend than a cage or two of canaries or finches or a tank of fish. Therefore, some special

thought must go into planning for your temporary replacement.

If you have only one or perhaps even two parrots, you might ask a friend or a relative if your bird can stay with him or her while you are away. This type of care keeps the bird in a functioning household, which can be more pleasant than being alone other than for daily visits by someone to renew seed and water. Before making such an arrangement, be sure that you know the household and any of its potential hazards. The presence of a cat or other animal, for example, may be a good reason not to ask a particular person to take care of your bird.

For safety reasons, the toy shown here was not a wise choice for this Red-fronted Macaw. Joan Balzarini

If possible, try to develop a reciprocal arrangement with another parrot owner—he or she takes your bird when you go on vacation and you do the same in return. This type of plan has immediate benefits, as, theoretically, such an individual will have some knowledge of parrot care as well as a liking for these birds. Food and care should be a cut above average (for birds) in such a household, which can help make up for the temporary separation. If it is the first time you've made such an arrangement with the individual, it would not be out of line to visit the home and check on the cleanliness of the cage and food dishes of the resident parrot. If the potential caretaker's bird shows any obvious signs of illness, such as listlessness or clogged or running nostrils, drop that home from consideration.

If you do not know any other parrot owners, check your local pet shop or seed supply store, and ask if you can tack up a notice offering exchange parrot sitting. The parrot subculture has always kept a low profile for reasons of security. We worry about theft and vandalism because parrots are valuable and enticing possessions, and in some parts of the country, such as south Florida, theft has become endemic. You should, however, be able to locate kindred spirits whom you deem trustworthy at bird club meetings, pet shops, veterinarians' offices, and similar places.

You can also consider fanciers who keep budgies, finches, cockatiels or canaries. Basic care is the same, and these fanciers may also wish to exchange services with you.

Children and other household residents should be evaluated before committing your pet to any arrangement. Very young children pose no problem unless their parents object to the morning and evening screaming at which parrots excel. However, any child capable of walking (but not yet fully able to reason) may be a threat to your pet or to him- or herself. Fingers thrust into cages or the opening or tipping of cages can all have disastrous results.

A somewhat simpler approach to summer care would be to have the pet sitter come to your home. In this case you obviously have to choose someone you know and trust both with your bird and your possessions. The parrot is kept in familiar surroundings and you need not worry about threats to his safety from children or animals. Of course, as mentioned at the beginning of this section, when using this approach, the bird will have less contact with people and may suffer from loneliness. A clock radio that goes on in the morning and off at night along with a timer for the lights are a must for this type of arrangement. To have the lights and radio on constantly will interfere with the parrot's sleep.

Another possibility would be to have your bird cared for by the local pet shop. Lots of contact with people and care by knowledgeable individuals may, however, be outweighed by exposure to other birds that might be unhealthy. In addition, while your parrot may return home with new words in his vocabulary, he may also have added loud screams or other unpleasant sounds.

Try to simplify the routine for anyone who cares for your parrot. A limited variety of seeds or pellets can include the bird's favorites and will make for easy feeding. Remind the host that the seed dish should be refilled every day, even if it looks full, as some parrots eat the seeds at the bottom first. Vitamins and other additives can be skipped for a week or two without any harm to your pet. This will help to prevent his water from becoming foul if the weather turns warm and your replacement is a bit slow to change it. Using a hooded water dish will help to keep water clean.

Don't hesitate to remind your caretaker about problems with air conditioning or the danger of drafts. If you've chosen the right person, he or she will appreciate all input, and a healthy bird will greet you when you return.

SOME DO'S AND DON'TS OF SUMMER CARE

Give your parrot a light spraying with water several times a week; a plant mister filled with tepid water is ideal for this purpose. The first time you shower him, be slow and gentle in your approach, a good idea in any case when dealing with parrots. If he shows any fright or discomfort, stop and try again later. Most parrots will react with delight and show it by extending their wings and twisting their bodies to provide the largest possible surface to catch the most water. Spraying should always be done early in the day so that the bird has a chance to dry his feathers thoroughly before bedtime. If necessary, a quick spray can even be given while the bird is in his cage.

Cleanliness, cleanliness, and more cleanliness is the key to summer parrot care. In hot, humid weather, failing to wash a food or water dish is really begging for trouble. Use a dish-washing liquid and thoroughly clean and rinse all food and water dishes every day. Summertime is also a good time for a complete cleaning of cages and perches. Pay particular attention to the openings for food and

Dangerous Plants in Home and Garden

If your parrot has the freedom of the house, he may be attracted to the colorful plants you use for decoration. Not every part of a dangerous plant is poisonous; in some cases it is only the seed, leaf, or stem. When in doubt, consider the entire plant a risk.

Apricot and peach seeds, morning glory seeds, and four o'clock seeds contain a precursor of cyanide. The actual flesh of apricots and peaches is harmless.

House plants such as narcissus, hyacinths, daffodils, and lilies are poisonous. The greatest concentration of poison is in the bulb, and eating that part of the plant may result in nausea, vomiting, diarrhea, and convulsions and can ultimately be fatal.

Some cactus species are poisonous, as are castor beans. Diffenbachia, a popular household plant (also called Dumbcane), and its relative the Elephant's Ear, are both poisonous.

Save mistletoe for stealing kisses. All parts of the mistletoe, especially the berries, are poisonous.

The seeds and pods of wisteria are poisonous, as are the leaves, bark, and berries of the yew shrub.

Some parts of plants we grow for food are dangerous, including the leaves of the rhubarb plant, any green part of the potato plant, and the stems and leaves of the tomato plant. Large quantities of these can be fatal.

Beware of the beautiful and colorful laurel and its relatives the azalea and rhododendron; all three are poisonous. English Ivy is another culprit, with poisonous leaves and berries.

The ever-popular philodendron can be dangerous if the leaves and stems are eaten in large amounts.

All parts of the popular Christmas poinsettia are poisonous, as are the berries of the holly plant and leaves of hydrangea.

Beware of the Lily-of-the-Valley plant. Even the water from a vase that has held this plant can be toxic.

---

water dishes, as material tends to accumulate in these areas. The cage tray should be thoroughly scrubbed, and this is also a good opportunity to scrape the perches clean and wash and dry them in the sun. A linoleum knife makes an excellent tool for this purpose. Perches that are worn or very dirty should be replaced.

There are various sprays on the market that can help rid the cage of mites. These should be used after the cage has been cleaned and while the bird is elsewhere. A total housecleaning of the bird room is in order at this time, and you will probably be amazed by the quantities of seeds and bits of fruits and vegetables you will find under cabinets and tables. Warm weather also brings an influx of pesky seed moths, which, as discussed earlier, are a problem to anyone who keeps stores of seed. I have found that simple flypaper works very well in keeping the moth population down. Hang it where birds will not fly into it, as it is very sticky. A variety of types are available, but I find that the old-fashioned ones work best.

7 BREEDING PARROTS

An important change in emphasis has taken place gradually during the last twenty-five years. Increasingly, many serious parrot fanciers have switched from attempts to collect and maintain choice specimens of desirable and, in many cases, rare parrots from the wild to earnest efforts to pair and breed the birds they keep. Indeed, it is rapidly becoming a mark of shame to keep a single representative of an uncommon species without making an effort to reproduce it.

Surely it is a great act of kindness to mature parrots to provide them with mates. I have often been asked why parrots pluck their feathers. The majority of the time it is the result of sheer boredom and frustration. This is particularly true when parrots are prevented from engaging in forms of behavior that are natural to them in the wild. You would never prevent your parrot from digging, chewing wood, preening, cracking seeds, screeching, and other activities that are basic to its nature. Can you in good conscience interfere with a drive as fundamental as reproduction?

Different species have different needs in order to breed. A cockatoo pair, for example, needs a large flight for the most gratifying results. Kendra Bond

A sophisticated incubator provides regulated heat and moisture and will even turn the eggs. Courtesy The Humidaire Co.

In addition to helping your birds to lead a healthier and happier life, breeding parrots is a strong argument for permitting them to be kept as pets. Adding numbers to a species without removing birds from the wild can counteract many of the unfounded criticisms made about aviculturists by animal rights activists.

If you have mature parrots that are free, or at least easy, breeders, then with an appropriate flight, proper food, and a good choice of nest boxes, it is quite likely that the hen will produce fertile eggs. Once the eggs have been laid, however, there are a host of potential problems. First-time parents may fail to incubate or feed. Even worse, they may decide to throw the eggs from the nest and start a new round.

Breeders must step in at the slightest hint of trouble and be prepared to assist in incubation and, in some cases, the final stages of hatching. Until about 1989, your principal recourse at such times was a series of frantic phone calls to experienced friends or sympathetic experts who, of course, might not be very compassionate in the wee hours of the morning. People who are becoming active in breeding today are much more fortunate in that a developing body of accurate and well-written literature dealing with breeding, hand feeding, incubation, and emergency intervention has become available to all in magazine articles and books.

Although the flow of imported birds has virtually ended, it is still possible to obtain a considerable variety of pairs that are or will be suitable for breeding. Some of these birds are recommended because they breed readily, while others should be chosen because their supply is dwindling and we have an obligation to propagate the species.

Moluccan Cockatoos, Umbrella Cockatoos, and Goffin's are all good choices as potential breeders. The aviculturist can locate and pair off older birds

A brooder is useful when parrot chicks are taken from their parents for hand feeding while they still require extra warmth. Courtesy The Feather Farm

that were imported years ago or purchase domestically bred birds and wait for them to mature. Four or five years old is the minimum age for breeding the three species mentioned above.

Blue and Gold, Greenwing, and Scarlet Macaws are very popular. As with the cockatoos, older birds can be found for pairing or you can purchase young specimens and wait patiently until they reach about five or six years of age. These young adults may be surprisingly compatible and bond quickly.

Among the Amazons, Yellow-napes, Double Yellow-heads, Orange-wings, Spectacled, Blue-fronts, Red-lored, and the various subspecies of the Mealy were imported in huge numbers from 1975 through 1990. Unfortunately, only the most popular, such as the Yellow-nape, Double Yellow-head, and Blue-front, were bred regularly, so it may be difficult for aspiring breeders to find domestic birds to purchase. You can, however, seek out older, imported birds; due to longevity of parrots,

even an adolescent bird is a viable candidate for breeding.

Large numbers of African Greys have been imported and bred, and these delightful talkers are plentiful. The so-called Congo Grey commands higher prices than its smaller and less colorful relative the Timneh, but both groups are equally talented and are capable of breeding at about four years of age.

Many of the common conures are available and are considered free breeders. These include the Mitred, Blue-crowned, Half-moon, and Sun Conure. The last of these is currently the most popular, although in earlier years it was the Half-moon that people chose most often.

Australian parakeets (not to be confused with budgies), such as the Rosellas and the Ringnecks from Asia and Africa, are gaining in popularity but as yet they play a secondary role to the more common parrots described above. Now that importation has ceased, these two groups should gain in

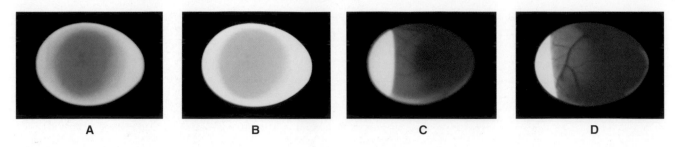

A	B	C	D

Developmental stages of a parrot embryo as viewed during candling. Photo A shows the initial blood spot that indicates a fertile egg. The network of blood vessels continues to develop throughout incubation and is particularly evident in Photo D. Bill Wegner

Intervention by the breeder may be required to save chicks in trouble. Crimson Star

popularity since many breeders are now successfully working with them. They also offer the advantage of being ready for breeding at ages as young as two years.

Unless you have unlimited funds and vast space at your disposal, deciding which birds to begin with can be a difficult question. Any decision should be based on a combination of factors. Unless you have some special affinity for a particular species, choose the most mature pairs you can find. This does not mean looking for an aging parrot like the late, lamented King Tut (the former official Moluccan Greeter at the San Diego Zoo), but if breeding is what you're after, a four- or five-year-old pair of Blue and Gold Macaws is a better choice than a pair of ten-month-old Blue-fronts.

Second, choose birds that have a reputation for easy breeding, and save your efforts with more difficult birds for a later date, after you have had success with a less challenging species. Also, at least one or two of the pairs you set up should be able to provide you with chicks that have a reasonable market value. This will give you a return on your original investment and expenses, enabling you to

buy other pairs (or missing singles) and providing funds for food, housing, and veterinary care.

My personal favorite is the universally popular African Grey, which can breed at about four or five years of age and is reasonably priced. In addition, these birds are still in good supply. The demand for hand-fed babies is relatively constant and it regularly peaks each time Alex the African Grey Genius appears on television or is described in a magazine or newspaper article.

You may not be adding to the supply of an endangered parrot species by breeding African Greys, but the experience and income might encourage you to try your hand at Goffin's Cockatoos or an even more exotic species.

The domestic breeding of parrots is growing rapidly and some hobbyists are fast becoming avicultural entrepreneurs as they breed clutch after clutch of cockatoos, macaws, Amazons, and African Greys. Prospective purchasers have become quite sophisticated, demanding a "domestic hand-fed baby" from the moment they enter a shop or visit a breeder. The increased demand for the offspring of the larger parrots as companion animals has kept prices fairly stable and makes the investment in incubators, hospital cages, seed, housing, and time worthwhile.

There is also an admirable movement afoot to discourage the keeping of rare singles solely as pets. Specialty groups are forming stud lists and facilitating breeding exchanges and other activities designed to help people find that elusive female Scarlet Macaw or male Black Palm Cockatoo for a breeding loan.

DEMANDS ON THE BREEDER'S TIME

Do not assume that you can simply leap into breeding birds as a money-making hobby on weekends. Breeding, if done correctly, can become an almost full-time occupation. It is also not something you can walk away from if you need a vacation or feel the urge to take a long weekend. In many respects I would compare it to being responsible for a large group of children who, while capable of eating and playing on their own, are frequently in need of adult supervision and attention. If you plan to breed your parrots, be sure that you have someone you can count on as a backup for emergencies or for those times when you want to escape. A tradeoff of time with another breeder is an excellent procedure, as you can be fairly sure that such a person will provide reliable and appropriate care for your birds.

HAND FEEDING

If you are a breeder, you quickly learn that not every clutch will be cared for by its parents. Some clutches may appear to be getting excellent care and then one sad day you enter the flights and

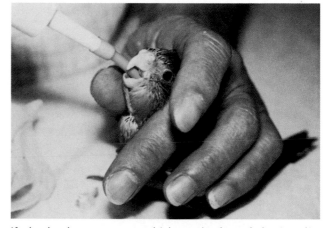

If absolutely necessary, a chick can be force fed using the tube or gavage method. Before trying this, ask your avian veterinarian or an experienced breeder to demonstrate the correct technique.

discover that an immature hen or a jealous male has plucked or possibly injured or killed the chicks. Perhaps you are breeding Hyacinths or Black Palms. Should you risk those valuable fertile eggs to the care of a hen who may, for no reason known to you or anyone else, dump the eggs out of the nest box?

Difficult decisions such as this, of course, are why many breeders offer a much better price for a

Hand-feeding techniques include using a specially designed spoon with turned-up sides to the bowl. Kathe O. Sacco

parrot if you purchase it when it is old enough to be shipped but has not yet been fully weaned. The buyer completes the hand feeding, saving the breeder from at least part of the lost sleep and rushed suppers that go along with hand feeding chicks. Savings of $200 to $300 per bird on chicks worth $700 or $800 are not unusual. A responsible breeder will assist you by answering questions and offering guidance when a chick is not eating well. If you have the opportunity to take advantage of this type of discount, please be aware that if you don't succeed, the tragedy and financial loss are your own.

You might at this point ask why breeders simply do not let the parents feed and care for the birds until they fledge. This is a legitimate question and some breeders actually do this, but the resulting chicks are no more tame than wild birds. Such young, of course, cannot command the same price as tame, hand-fed baby birds.

I know a very successful breeder who had Hyacinths and Eclectus that bred regularly. He eventually gave up on hand feeding and sold the chicks at lower prices, having decided that the extra profits for hand-fed, weaned babies were just not worth the time and effort involved.

A considerable mystique has developed about hand-feeding and its challenges. In reality, it is no different from any other skill involving livestock. A certain amount can be learned from books and magazine articles, but since you are dealing with living creatures, it is important that at some point you watch an individual who is proficient in using hand-feeding techniques. Reading appropriate material can precede or follow your own observations and will enhance your understanding of what you see.

Interviewing an Expert

I recently had the opportunity to interview Mark Marrone, owner of Parrots of the World in Rockville Centre, New York, on the topic of hand rearing. Mark has hand-fed birds for at least fifteen years, and it was delightful to watch him as he went through his morning feeding routine with his many baby parrots. When he began hand feeding there were few if any experts he could turn to for advice, so the skills I saw him display were crucial to his success. Watching Mark feed babies made the job look very easy. Although he hand feeds birds as young as ten days old, he does not recommend that the average purchaser begin with a bird that young, as it may require as many as six feedings a day. If you do a bit of simple arithmetic, you will see that six feedings a day is actually six feedings day and night. In addition, the early stages of hand feeding require the greatest skill. At this time the temperature, texture, and proper quantity of food is critical.

Chicks can be obtained from breeders at ages ranging from six to twelve weeks or even older. Mark indicates that during the first month, hand-feeding requirements should drop down to about four feedings a day. By six to seven weeks, you will probably be feeding only three times a day and by ten weeks, one or two feedings a day. It is perfectly normal, at this stage, for the chick to actually lose some weight. He is eating less formula and chewing some pellets or cracking some seed. The instinct that drives him to eat less at this point helps to prepare him for fledging, when he will need a lighter and sleeker body for flight. Mark cautions against hand feeding beyond eight to ten weeks. If you fail to wean the bird at this stage, it may lose its desire to wean and hand feeding may have to go on for a very long time.

The Art of Hand Feeding

When hand feeding chicks, you should strive to emulate parental behavior as closely as possible. This means that for very young chicks (whose feeding schedule is pretty close to human baby "demand" feeding) you should feed every three hours. Is a 2 A.M. feeding possible for you? It depends both on your devotion to the task and how late you stayed up to feed the chicks during the previous evening. Will the chicks die if they don't have late night or early morning feedings? Probably not, especially if you see to it that feeding the young is the last thing done before you go to bed. Fortunately, this difficult period lasts only for a short time, after which the number of feedings per day drops to one every four hours. The time between feedings will gradually lengthen until you are also offering seed, the young birds begin cracking it, and finally refuse the hand feeding. At this point, they are considered weaned.

Hand feeding baby birds is an effective means of enhancing survival and socializing them at the same time. It also calls for an uncommon amount of dedication and sacrifice on the part of the breeder. Courtesy Eastman Kodak Corp.

There are many available formulas for hand feeding, but I recommend that you obtain the one used by the person who bred your birds and, if possible, a sample of this food to help the chicks make the transition from one location to another. If you are unable to obtain specific information from the breeder, you can check with others who are successfully hand feeding in your own area. This local information is valuable since the materials they are using will also be readily available to you.

Equipment for Hand Feeding

The most commonly used hand-feeding instrument is the syringe. Depending on the size of the bird, you can choose something as small as a medicine dropper or as large as a kitchen basting tool. If you are dealing with a bird that is extremely small or

young, you can put a small-diameter, plastic or rubber tube over the tip of a medicine dropper to make an even smaller feeding device. For obvious reasons, plastic devices should be used instead of glass, and all feeding equipment should be thoroughly cleansed and kept in a disinfectant solution between uses. Pay particular attention to the "O" ring in plunger-type syringes, as well as any part of the equipment with a tiny opening where food may collect.

Hand feeding closely simulates the feeding of the baby bird by its parents. Thus, if you use a spoon, bend the sides of the spoon up so that the bowl of the spoon is shaped something like a canoe. By bending the spoon, you make it easier to retain the food within the bowl, and you also offer a smaller cross-section that will fit more easily into the baby bird's beak. If you are dealing with a very young bird, you will probably have to hold him firmly, as he may not realize your good intentions and try to flee. Get a comfortable grip that will not block the bird's swallowing and hold him as loosely as possible.

Along with all these warnings to be careful, I can offer the following encouragement: If the hand-feeding formula is palatable and at an appropriate temperature, any healthy and hungry chick will cooperate beautifully and practically pull the spoon or syringe out of your hand.

There are many formulas for making up a nutritious mixture for baby birds. The one given in this chapter is recommended for baby parrots, ages six to twelve weeks. It may be modified if you cannot obtain certain ingredients, but try to keep replacements as close as possible to the originals. Also, avoid changing an ingredient once the baby is eating a particular diet, since doing this can put him off his feed. If possible, get the makeup of the formula fed by the breeder or pet shop and, if you consider it satisfactory, continue with the same mixture.

Refrigerate any leftover sunflower meal so that it does not spoil. The formula itself can be frozen in small containers and will keep for long periods. Once defrosted, it should be kept refrigerated, but limit its use after defrosting to three or four days. Starting at about eight weeks, keep a bowl of seed accessible in case you have a precocious individual who wants to be weaned early and can begin to eat seed on his own.

Many breeders find that syringe feeding is the easiest and most effective route to follow. In some cases, the baby bird will cooperate fully by reflexively opening his mouth and tilting up his head when approached with the syringe or baster. You can ensure that the meal you are providing is comfortably warm by using warm water for the liquid portion of the formula. It is also useful to keep the formula in the same type of compartmentalized feeding dish used for human babies; keep it in the center section and put warm water in the other compartments. As you feed, you can use the water in one compartment to clean the baby's feathers when they become splattered with food. If you neglect to do this, the resulting matted feathers may later be lost. The other water compartment can be used for thinning the formula if it gets too thick. Before feeding, use a thermometer, instead of your wrist, to determine the temperature of the formula. The food should be about the temperature of your own body, and a thermometer reading in the vicinity of 95 degrees Fahrenheit is acceptable. •

There has been a common misconception since the 1970s that the feeding syringes must be inserted into the right side of the chick's mouth. The opening into the bird's esophagus, or food tube, is in the center of its body, just as it is in yours. Perhaps a flounder with its flat body design has its esophageal opening on the left or right but not a bird. Squirt the food right in (over the tongue, of course) and be more concerned to avoid messing the baby or yourself with spilled formula than the direction in which to squirt. It is very important that the temperature of the food be kept lukewarm, as food that is too hot can burn the delicate tissues of the mouth and crop, while food that is too cool can cause crop impaction, one of the most common problems with birds fed by inexperienced individuals.

Insert the syringe deep into the bird's mouth cavity and gently squirt food into the esophagus. Be sure that the food enters the esophagus rather than the windpipe, or trachea, which leads to the lungs. You can distinguish the two tubes quite easily: When you look into the bird's open beak, the windpipe comes first, and is normally covered with a little lid, which remains closed except when the bird is taking a breath or producing sounds. It will also close reflexively at the instant of swallowing. The esophagus is behind the windpipe, and its opening

Five conure babies being fed using an "assembly line" technique.

When hand feeding it is imperative to monitor a chick's weight carefully and constantly.

is a horizontal slit. Keeping in mind the swallowing reflex described above, be careful not to squirt food into the bird's mouth when he is squawking and do not feed too rapidly. You will know you have done a good job of feeding when the little bird's crop is plump; this means that it is full and that the food will be moved along to the rest of the digestive tract.

If a newly arrived baby refuses syringe or spoon feeding, you may use gavage (tube feeding) as a last resort. Use a small syringe and extend its length with a small-diameter rubber tube. Have an associate hold the bird firmly. Elevate its head, open its mouth, insert the tube into the esophagus, and gently squirt in a small amount of food. Continue this until the crop is full. It is not a pleasant experience for the bird or for you, but he must eat or he will die. Fortunately, tube feeding frequently results in the bird's adjusting to and accepting spoon or syringe feeding

If you talk to breeders who hand feed, you will soon recognize two great schools of thought—the spoon feeders and the syringe feeders have almost a religious fervor about which technique is the correct one. Actually, both methods are acceptable, and the only real reason for choosing one over the other is to select the method with which you and the chicks are most comfortable. If you choose to use a syringe, select the type with a changeable tip, so that you can modify the flow of food as the chick gets older and capable of handling coarser food. Also be sure that the syringes can be boiled or autoclaved to ensure that they are absolutely germ-free when you use them.

The consistency of the food is determined during its preparation and has a significant impact on whether the bird will get his fill and how well he will be able to digest the food.

If you're not successful at hand feeding, do not wait too long before you seek assistance. A baby bird that goes without food will rapidly lose weight and become dehydrated. If the situation continues for too long, death will result. If you are hand feeding (and I highly recommend it in spite of these warnings), have an avian veterinarian or an experienced breeder in reserve to help you if an emergency arises.

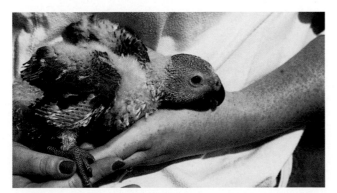

Thanks to hand feeding, this growing African Grey baby will make a marvelous pet for some fortunate person.
Sharon and Ray Bailey

Baby Formula

5 cups water
1 cup quick-cooking oatmeal (not "instant" oats)
1/2 cup raw wheat germ (from health-food store)
1 tablespoon corn oil
1/2 teaspoon salt

Mix and cook the above cereal for 5 minutes, remove from stove, and add one 4 1/2-ounce jar of baby vegetables (strained garden vegetables), a combination of peas, carrots, and spinach. (For cockatoos and cockatiels increase this amount by 1/3 to 1/2.)

1 cup powdered milk
2 cups sunflower meal (from health-food store)

If sunflower meal is not available, purchase raw hulled sunflower kernels and grind them in a blender. Add 2 slices of very dry whole wheat bread mixed with 1 1/2 to 2 cups sunflower kernels, and grind them together in the blender to prevent the kernels from becoming soggy and sticky. The bread will add nutrition to this formula.

Special Notes

Do not expect a baby that has been removed from the nest to accept hand feeding until its crop is empty of the food provided by its parents. This can take eight to twelve hours.

Do not change formulas radically, as the baby bird will become used to a particular taste or flavor. If you can no longer obtain a particular ingredient, try to get something similar. If you sell the baby bird, give the new owners a sample of the formula to get them through the first day and a clearly written recipe so that they can duplicate the food you have been feeding.

Avoid overfeeding. You will know the bird has had enough when the crop becomes plump and rounded.

If possible, avoid hand feeding until the chicks are at least ten days old.

HYBRIDIZATION

In any discussion of breeding, the problem of hybrids must be considered, following a clarification of the term. A hybrid is the offspring of two different species; for our purposes, the definition should be extended to include subspecies. Hybridization can and does occur naturally in the wild between closely related species but not between those that diverge widely. Yellow-fronted Amazons can successfully breed with Panama Amazons and Yellow-naped Amazons, but an Illiger's Macaw cannot breed with a Blue and Gold Macaw. Hybrids produced in the wild are generally unsuccessful and tend to disappear, although in rare cases they have evolved as a separate species. Hybrids produced from birds that are extremely disparate are generally known as "mules." The term *mule*, in addition to referring to a cross between a horse and a donkey, is a generic term for a hybrid that is sterile and, therefore, cannot reproduce. A famous exception to this rule is the offspring that result from crossing the Hooded Siskin with a canary, a popular product of some breeders' desire to produce a red canary.

Some individuals confuse hybrids with mutants, the results of sudden biological changes from parental forms due to alteration of a chromosome. This can occur spontaneously or it can be stimulated by radiation or exposure to certain chemicals, which explains the deformed plant and animal life appearing in the vicinity of those Pacific islands that were used for early atomic testing. Some breeders are quite enthusiastic when a mutation occurs and make every effort to breed the bird back to its parents or with its siblings in an effort ultimately to stabilize the mutation and breed it with predictability. Because mutations often lack the survival ability of normal birds, I can only speculate that some breeders encourage mutations because they represent the possibility of financial gain when sold as rare specimens.

Crossbreeding to produce hybrids was an

When hand-fed chicks are hungry, they make their wishes clearly known. Sharon and Ray Bailey

accepted activity until the late 1980s. The procedure was becoming so common that standardized names were proposed for hybrid macaws to avoid confusion regarding their parent types. The first of these names was given to the cross between the Blue and Gold and Scarlet Macaws. This was called the Catalina Macaw, presumably because it had initially been bred on Santa Catalina Island, near Los Angeles. It may have been the first recognized hybrid among the macaws because Scarlets and Blue and Golds were both familiar species. Crosses between Blue and Gold and Greenwing Macaws are now called Harlequin Macaws. "Shamrock Macaw" commonly refers to a green hybrid resulting from crosses between Scarlet and Military Macaws. Hyacinth and Blue and Gold hybrids are often called Tracey Macaws, in recognition of their origin at the Tracey Aviary in Salt Lake City, Utah.

No other group of parrots has been hybridized as commonly as the large macaws, so there is no comparable group of names among the Amazons and other parrot-family birds. One exception is the Sunday Conure, obviously denoting a cross between the closely related Sun and Jenday Conures.

Much of the strenuous opposition to hybridizing parrots stems from the concern that many of the original species are already rare or endangered and that hybridization further depletes the diminishing pool of breedable birds. Hybrids of the first generation commonly resemble both parents, and are readily identified. Later generations, however, may not show the original traits, and if sold and bred as pure specimens, they will further adulterate the gene pool and pose a threat to its integrity.

In aviculture, purity of the species is vital. We are not breeding birds to enhance their survival characteristics or increase their yield in ways that are done with corn or poultry. Breeding a seedless orange, for example, makes sense both esthetically and economically, but the best rationale for breeding the larger parrots is to obviate the need to import them from the wild and in some cases to produce stock that can be returned to a natural habitat. Hybridizing to produce a more colorful or desirable macaw has no place in the bird fancy.

In a number of cases, the normal balance of males and females seems to have become skewed so that either sex may be more difficult than the other to obtain. This is why Scarlet Macaw females command a higher price than males. In other situations, a particular parrot is so rare that a breeder with only one bird may have little chance of obtaining a mate. Fanciers, particularly those who keep rare birds, are often disinclined to inform others of these possessions, significantly interfering with breeding loans. Some fear theft or vandalism, while others are concerned that the endangered species they own might be confiscated by a regulatory agency. These often irrational concerns have for many years impeded the sharing of birds for breeding loans, which unfortunately has encouraged both crossbreeding when a bird of a particular sex is unavailable and hybridizing relatives to produce stock that is closely related to both species. Adherents of these questionable practices offer as an example the Buffons Macaw, which is a close relative of the Military. The Buffons is extremely rare, and confusion about its identity already exists. It is a mistake to assume that breeding it with a Military is better than not breeding it, when the use of stud registers is growing among serious breeders. It is much more desirable to engage in breeding loans than hybridization, which results in confusion and a loss of genetic integrity. The recent emphasis on stud registers and the efforts of specialty organizations to locate suitable breeders are positive steps in this direction.

Although there is some financial reward for selling hybrid birds, most reputable aviculturists now agree that parrot-family birds should not be hybridized. The thousands of hybrids now in existence should be kept or sold only as pets, and not for breeding.

DETERMINING SEX IN BIRDS

It is obvious from the preceding descriptions of pairing, breeding, and hand feeding that breeding birds is a serious business. It is important to determine the sex of your birds before setting them up for breeding in order to avoid losing vital weeks and even complete breeding seasons.

You cannot assume from their appearance that birds are male or female, even if they engage in behavior that seems like sexual foreplay to you. Traditionally, birds that have had their sex determined by a veterinarian have a tattoo or indelible mark placed under the wing, males under the right wing and females under the left. Unless some form

of proof is offered, have the breeding birds sexed again to avoid the possibly futile pairing-off of same-sexed birds. Even the assurances of the person who sold you the bird must not be accepted without proof.

When dealing in young birds, an accurate knowledge of their sex can be a useful and sometimes crucial selling point. Some people prefer one sex to the other because they believe that birds of a particular gender are more gentle or perhaps more friendly or talented. This may or may not be true, but for those who wish to breed birds, basing sex determination on a hunch that may prove inaccurate can cost a prospective breeder one or more seasons of reproduction.

A concern with sex determination is unique to birds and certain other higher vertebrate groups that in many cases do not show dimorphism, unlike dogs, cats, hamsters, and so forth, that all have obvious primary sexual characteristics. Birds lack such external structures, and unless they possess gender-specific (dimorphic) markings, feather structures, or eye colors, which are related to their sex, other evaluative techniques have to be used.

Only a few species of parrots show dimorphism, including the following:

Eclectus—Males are green and yellow, while females are blue, red, and purple. Males and females differ so markedly that early collectors regarded them as different species.

Cockatoos—Males generally have a dark brown to black eye, and females have a brown to reddish-brown eye. These differences are most obvious in the white cockatoos but do not show up in young birds, all of which have eye colors similar to those of females. Female cockatoos also show a striated design on the undersurface of the tail, but once again this is not a characteristic that can be used to sex young birds.

Cockatiels—Males have bright yellow facial markings, while the face in mature females is gray. Striated tail markings are also visible in mature females but cannot be used to determine the sex of young birds.

Breeding loans are a good way to avoid hybridizing, which produces birds such as this "Shamrock Macaw"— the result of a cross between Scarlet and Military parents (opposite). Joan Balzarini

All the yellow pigment in this Yellow-naped Amazon mutation has been masked, resulting in a blue and white bird, an intriguing rarity. Hans Andersson

These are only a few of the dimorphic traits recognized by aviculturists. In addition to others we have not mentioned, traits are often referred to that may best be described as dubious. These include a flat or "snakelike" head in female African Greys; vigorous display activity and expansion of the pupils in male Amazons; feeding of "female" by "male" in any species; and relatively large size of males. I also suspect that in some cases pelvic sexing, discussed below, may be no more accurate than chance. Of course, in the unlikely event that all of the above factors are present in a single pair, they might prove helpful as a potential indicator of sex.

Recognized Techniques for Sexing Parrots

Pelvic Sexing—Since the egg must pass between the pelvic bones, there is generally a wider space between these bones in females than in males. This is most obvious during the breeding season. The individual doing the test must have sufficient

In view of habitat destruction and population reduction in many parrot species in the wild, reliance on natural breeding is no longer sufficient to ensure the continuation of viable populations. Kathe O. Sacco

experience to have formulated a satisfactory standard of comparison. Ideally, known females and males of the same species should be compared first to ensure maximum accuracy.

For those who disparage this method, I should point out that the late Maude Knobel of the London Zoo and the British Avicultural Society did many postmortems on birds that had been sexed earlier in their lives and found the technique highly accurate in Amazons and African Greys.

Feather Sexing—Sex determination through examination of feathers has been around for a long time. One recognized method of sexing grouse is by comparing tail-feather markings and patterns, and a similar process can be used with woodcocks. In 1984, literature appeared on a technique developed by a student in Utah who, while seeking a way to determine sex through blood fractions, accidentally developed a method of sexing by microscopically comparing the placement of the feather barbules and barbicels at a magnification of ninety-five times. Although it created a stir at the time, nothing more has been heard of this discovery.

Sexing by Hormone Analysis

This technique was originally developed by Dr. Arden Bercovits and associates at the Research Department of the San Diego Zoo. Males and females produce the same hormones, but male birds produce much larger amounts of the male hormone testosterone, while the major sex hormone produced by the female is estrogen. The droppings of birds contain both of these primary sex steroids in relative amounts (referred to as the E/T ratio) that can be a highly accurate indicator of sex in a normal bird. E/T values of birds of known sex were subsequently charted and a sexual difference noted. Later research indicated that unhealthy birds may not show normal E/T values for their species and should not be tested during periods of illness or stress. In addition to accuracy, advantages of this technique include the fact that it is risk-free, and that the bird need not be present for sexing to occur. A number of veterinarians and others are providing this service in different parts of the United States.

Sexing by Laparotomy

This is the method usually referred to when surgical sexing is mentioned. Following anesthesia, a small incision is made in the left side of the abdomen. Several membranes must also be torn so that the intestines they hold in place may be gently moved aside to allow the viewer to determine whether testes or ovaries are present. A two- or three-day recuperation period is recommended before birds subjected to this test are shipped. Although laparotomy is a definitive sexing technique, and is virtually 100 percent accurate, it is invasive and, like any surgery, entails an element of risk. I do not, therefore, recommend it for use with birds that are irreplaceable either for financial or sentimental reasons.

Genetic Sexing

This is a highly recommended procedure, with an accuracy rate approaching 100 percent; the only failures are due to paperwork errors or the highly unusual cases when a laboratory technician misreads a slide. There are other sexing techniques that offer a high degree of accuracy, but most of these have drawbacks: surgical sexing, as noted above, is almost 100 percent accurate but poses a risk if the anesthetist puts the bird too deeply under. In addition, restraining the bird for the anesthesia is stressful and has, on occasion, had tragic results. In the case of surgical sexing, the animal in question must be present, which may require a long trip if you live far from a veterinarian who does this procedure.

Sexing through an examination of fecal hormones is not dangerous but is not always accurate and the results with very young birds or birds that are ill can be distorted. It is also crucial that the sample droppings be properly collected and packaged and then promptly shipped or delivered to the veterinarian or laboratory where the analysis is to be done.

Genetic sexing by blood-feather analysis is not only virtually 100 percent accurate but also meets two other important criteria: there is no danger to the birds being sexed and they need not be present for the sexing procedure to take place. Genetic sexing actually involves the study of bird chromosomes. The work can be done by a genetic specialty laboratory and there are now several of these offering the service either directly to breeders or through veterinarians.

During this procedure, cells from blood feathers (young, replacement feathers in adult birds or new, growing feathers in chicks) are grown in a tissue culture and prepared for microscopic examination by a cytogeneticist, an individual who specializes in the chromosome makeup of cells. There are fresh, living cells available in the pulp at the base of growing feathers. Many aviculturists call them "blood feathers" because they are supplied with blood vessels and bleeding may result if they are broken.

In birds, as in most vertebrates, the sex of an individual is determined by the sex chromosomes in the cells. When the sperm of the cock unites with the egg of the hen, individuals may receive ZZ chromosomes and become males or they may receive ZW chromosomes and become females. The Z and W designations are simply conventions used to indicate the difference in appearance when the chromosomes are viewed under the microscope. These conventions, in birds, are the opposite of those used in mammals. There is no ambiguity with sexing by chromosome observation, as males and females can be clearly distinguished by the size, shape, and staining characteristics of their chromosomes. Since every cell in the body of an animal will have these chromosomes, the cultures used can be made from actively growing feathers.

SPECIES	NUMBER TESTED (CHROMOSOME AND SURGERY)	NUMBER WITH RESULT IN AGREEMENT
Scarlet Macaw	2	2
Blue and Gold Macaw	4	4
Red-front Macaw	1	1
Greenwing Macaw	6	5*
Catalina Macaw	1	1
Golden Conure	1	1
African Grey Parrot	1	1
Moluccan Cockatoo	1	1
Greater Sulphur-crested Cockatoo	2	2
Triton Cockatoo	1	1
Leadbeater's Cockatoo	2	2
TOTAL	22	21

*One Greenwing Macaw was originally misclassified by surgical sexing.

(Chart courtesy of Dr. Carll Goodpasture and Kim L. Joyner, DVM.)

One disadvantage to the technique is that the amount of tissue needed to start a thriving cell culture in the laboratory is fairly large, and thus the procedure is limited to large species such as psittacines, raptors, and water fowl. Excellent results have been achieved with macaws, cockatoos, African Greys, and Amazons. In the case of the smaller parrots, more than one feather would have to be supplied to form the necessary cell culture.

At a time when breeding is assuming ever-greater importance to the successful future of aviculture, the availability of this safe, accurate, and noninvasive sexing technique is truly good news.

As can be seen from the chart, the technique can be 100 percent accurate. In one case (the Greenwing Macaw), a discrepancy occurred between surgical sexing and observation of chromosome constitution. The bird was surgically sexed again and was found definitely to be a female, which was the result of the chromosome study.

part II

THE PARROT FAMILY

AFRICAN GREY PARROTS

A Grey Parrot was used to try to teach a Mealy Amazon to talk. It repeated words to its pupil for a time and when the latter did not learn them the Grey cried out "Blockhead!" and contemptuously turned away. Later, when the Amazon had learned several things, the pair held conversations early in the mornings when they thought they were unnoticed.

—Dr. Karl Russ, The Speaking Parrots

An African Grey has a definite mischievous streak in its personality. This bird looks as though it's sizing up the action outside its cage. Leonard Freud

Historical records on the African Grey are believed to date back to biblical times. Its early importation into Europe made it a favorite of royalty, who were among the few who could afford these expensive imports. The duchess of Lennox and Richmond had a Grey that was a beloved pet; his stuffed remains are on display in the Norman Undercroft Museum at Westminster Abbey in London. In 1956, photos of both the duchess's wax figure and the stuffed Grey (considered to be the oldest stuffed bird in the world) were published in Edward J. Boosey's *Parrots, Cockatoos and Macaws*.

In *Parrots: A Natural History* (1990), Sparks and Soper note reports of handsome gray birds with red tails (obviously African Greys) living in the Canary Islands in 1402. These birds had been imported from nearby West Africa.

You will find that many African Greys are named Jaco. Their owners may have heard the name used for Greys and admired it. They should realize that historically this is a time-honored name for the Grey Parrot, as it is very much like the echo bird's natural call in the wild.

Dr. Karl Russ, in *The Speaking Parrots* (1884), discussing the great speaking and apparent reasoning skills of these birds, describes a brilliant Grey owned by a lady in Germany. This bird could speak in three languages, including Dutch and German. If his German vocabulary failed him he would, without hesitation, substitute the appropriate Dutch word in his remarks. This clever creature lost his home by constant repetition of the phrase "give some to the parrot!" during meals. We all admire and value talking birds, but this was a perfect example of too much of a good thing.

Wolfgang deGrahl, in *The Grey Parrot* (1987), provides a fascinating glimpse of parrot history in a collection of ads offering Greys for sale. One from 1875 read "Grey Parrot 300 marks. Whistles two songs, sings, talks a great deal including one, two, three, hurrah Bismarck!" As the ads go on prices go up and down with economic conditions and availability. One bird that probably did not get sold was described as "Grey parrot, speaks only English, bites women and children."

Konrad Lorenz, in *King Solomon's Ring* (1952), described a Grey that belonged to a friend of his. This parrot was called Geier, which is German for "vulture," because he was badly plucked, everywhere except on the region of his head, which he could not reach. Geier fully compensated for his

The Timneh Grey (left) is smaller and less brightly colored than the Congo Grey (right). Michael DeFreitas

lack of beauty by his ability to speak. He used the phrases "good morning" and "good evening" in an appropriate manner but would only say them when a visitor actually rose to depart; his sensitivity to body language was such that he could never be made to bid a farewell with a staged departure. I experienced the same sort of cleverness with Bill, my Yellow-naped Amazon, who delivered a thoroughly splendid "goodbye" in two different voices—but only for people who actually left the room; pretenders were totally ignored.

The ability of a Grey to reason is also examined by Edward J. Boosey, who describes the scheming behavior of a male Grey he kept at his famous Keston Bird Farm in England. This parrot shared a shelter and flight with his mate. Food for these birds was usually kept in the shelter, but on one occasion it was temporarily placed in the flight, which was separated from the shelter by a sliding shutter. One day, Boosey discovered that the shutter was closed, leaving the hen in the shelter while the male rushed happily around the flight that now held the food and water. Boosey, thinking he might have closed the hen in by mistake, opened the shutter only to find that later in the day it was closed again. He then observed the flight from a hidden vantage point until he actually saw the male slide the little door shut while cackling wildly with laughter.

African Greys are about thirteen to fourteen inches long. Their upper surface is a darker gray than the lower area. This rather monotonous hue is relieved by a bright red tail, which is the last area to develop in baby Greys. They have a black beak and a yellow iris, which is black in chicks but changes to yellow well before the age of one year. A dark-eyed Grey can thus be considered to be a young bird or even a baby, while those with a yellow iris are at least one year old or even older. Smoothness of beak and claws is also an indication of youth in the African Grey and other parrots.

References can occasionally be found to a type of African Grey called "the King Parrot." According to these sources, it is a larger and more handsome version of the standard Grey and has red feathers in its plumage. It is doubtful that such a variation actually exists.

There is, however, a Timneh subspecies that is a bit smaller than the nominate race, with a maroon tail, a pinkish upper beak that becomes darker towards the tip, and a black lower beak. The Timneh parrot possesses all the positive attributes of the nominate species but commands a lower price only because the uninitiated consider it less desirable. There is absolutely no reason to avoid purchasing a Timneh if an appropriate single or pair should become available to you. In the mid 1980s importation of Timnehs was increased, and we now have access to domestically raised young.

Breeding records for the African Grey date back many years, as is to be expected of a bird that has been domesticated for so long a period. According to Prestwich in *Records of Parrots Bred in Captivity* (1951), the Grey may have been bred in captivity in France as early as 1774. The owner of these early specimens had a prolific pair that laid four eggs each spring. Invariably three of these would hatch and the parents would feed the chicks until fledging. Their nest box was a small barrel open at one end and filled with sawdust. In the original account, appearing in Buffon's *Natural History of the Birds*, published in 1779, the author noted that it was wise not to enter the room in which the nest box was kept without wearing heavy boots for protection from the beak of the male bird. In some respects, not much has changed in more than 200 years of aviculture.

Fans of the African Grey should be familiar with the name of Mrs. Gilbert Lee, who was an early and tireless collector and breeder of many types of parrots. She was particularly enthusiastic about rare specimens, and her collection included such uncommon birds as Bauer's Parrot, Forsten's Lorikeet, and Kuhl's Lory. Her specialty, however, was the breeding of a large collection of prolific African Greys. The extensiveness of her African Grey breeding activities led *American Cage-Bird Magazine* writer Edwin John Graham to observe that in 1960 at least eighty percent of the domestically raised African Grey parrots in the United States could trace their lineage back to the original matings of Mrs. Lee's birds.

Mrs. Lee became known as the nation's foremost authority on the breeding and care of African Greys. She was a woman of quiet dignity with a vibrant personality. Her work began with the purchase of a huge bronco, or wild, untamable bird, that had been caught in the wild and never domesticated. He was appropriately named Bronc and, in spite of (or perhaps because of) his unrestrained

"I'll preen your neck if you'll do mine!" Jayne Tansey-Patron

The yellow iris on this bird shows that it is over a year old. Eric Ilasenko

behavior, he was the original source for much of what Mrs. Lee was to learn about the species. Bronc was placed in a flight with two other African Greys of undetermined sex, prompting Bronc to fly into a violent rage that resulted in the death of one of the other birds. Thereafter, he was top bird in the flight. The remaining bird proved to be a hen and in due time produced a nest of four chicks that were all successfully raised. Mrs. Lee eventually owned more than a dozen pairs of reproducing Greys.

Reading Mrs. Lee's articles on the clever African Grey served as my introduction to these parrots and encouraged me as well as many others to purchase this species. I have owned four of them, and my most recent acquisition is Jacosia, a lively nineteen-year-old female given to me by the family of an elderly gentleman who could no longer care for her.

The son and daughter of the owner were quite concerned about who would adopt Jacosia (later renamed Jaco), as they had promised their father that she would continue to receive the love and attention she was used to. Before any arrangements were made, they visited our home and aviary, demonstrating the same care that an adoption agency might show in placing a human child. Jaco talks and whistles and has made a wonderful adjustment to her new surroundings. Her cage is next to that of Tutu, the Sulphur-crested Cockatoo, with whom she appears to engage in acrobatic contests to see who can swing upside down for the longest period of time.

During most of the time that African Greys and other talking birds have been domesticated, it was assumed that their speech was simply mimicry. However, Professor Irene Pepperberg contends that her work with an African Grey has shown that these birds are capable of abstract thought. In 1981, Laurie Jensen, a staff writer for the *Lafayette Indiana Journal and Courier*, was one of the first to cover the beguiling story of Alex. Jensen noted that Dr. Pepperberg had been working with Alex for a little more than four years on a unique experiment in animal communications.

You may at this point ask why the fuss about another talking African Grey. The answer is that Alex's responses to questions and actions went far beyond mimicry; this two-pound feathered wizard could identify colors, quantity, and shapes, for

rewards in anticipation of receiving them, and appropriately use the phrases "Come here" and "I'm sorry" when people entered and left his room. In fact, he was virtually another Polynesia to Pepperberg's Dr. Doolittle.

Alex was purchased in a local Chicago pet shop when he was about a year old. His new mistress was well aware of the studies on communicating with primates such as chimpanzees and gorillas, but little had been reported on communication with birds since an unsuccessful experiment by a well-known psychologist in the late 1950s. Drawn by work going on in animal communication and always interested in birds, Dr. Pepperberg decided, after receiving her doctoral degree, to investigate her suspicion that the limitations of earlier experiments may have been in their methodology, not in the intelligence of the birds.

Her work with Alex began with the identification of certain objects, including keys, wood, and paper, that he could demand at will. She then

Kyaaro and Alo, like all African Greys, are remarkably intelligent. But can they compete with Alex? Maybe. Sisyphus

shifted to the higher level of colors, shapes, and quantities, all the while attempting to establish a form of two-way communication. "Animals have communication abilities," she noted. "They at least have some form of communication among themselves, but the question is how complex that communication is and how similar to our own."

People working with primates are at a disadvantage in that these animals, the most common subjects of studies in animal communication, lack the mechanical ability in their vocal tract to communicate verbally. By contrast, Dr. Pepperberg noted, people can come in and communicate with Alex without learning a special signing method or computer language.

With so many thousands of African Greys being taught by their enthusiastic owners, you may wonder why Alex alone shows these cognitive skills. The answer lies in Dr. Pepperberg's novel teaching techniques, which are markedly different from any other approaches I have heard about or used for teaching a parrot to speak. Her first method is known as the Model/Rival, or M/R, approach, and it requires two people. One individual acts as a trainer, asking questions, giving praise for correct answers, and showing disapproval for incorrect answers. The other person acts both as a model for the parrot's responses and as a rival for the trainer's attention. This latter function is especially interesting in light of the length to which a parrot will go to obtain the attention of someone he cares for.

The second training technique involves only one person and is designed to perfect pronunciation. Dr. Pepperberg believes this procedure encourages direct imitation of a particular human's speech, and she uses it only after the bird already knows a word and is simply trying to say it more clearly.

Alex's training does not involve food rewards for nonfood items; he receives a treat only after he has asked for food. Dr. Pepperberg's objective here is to relate the words Alex says to actual objects rather than merely to evoke responses to bribes.

Alex's vocabulary includes the following words: paper, key, wood, hide (rawhide), pegwood (clothes pins), cork, corn, nut, pasta, eater, scraper (nail file), and walnut. He can verbally identify red, green, blue, and gray objects and can also recognize a triangle, square, and pentagon, calling them "three-corner," "four corner," and "five-corner," respectively. He partially misses the boat on oval shapes, which he refers to as "two-corner" objects. He supplements this repertoire by the functional use of the word "no" and phrases such as "come here" and "wanna go."

Alex has some difficulty pronouncing the final "s" sound, which is ironic in that it means he cannot properly say his own name. During exercises designed to correct his pronunciation, he tended to pick up his trainer's speech patterns, pronouncing "shower" similarly to the way New York–born, Harvard-educated Dr. Pepperberg says "showah." A conversation with Alex is not exactly highbrow, but he does manage to make sense. For example, after eating or drinking he squawks "cork" because he is used to cleaning his beak by rubbing it on pieces of cork after eating or drinking. He is also capable, when perched on a hand, of requesting "wanna go gym" or "wanna go back" to indicate his desire to return to his exercise perch or cage.

After several years of training and having acquired even greater skills, a mature Alex was visited by the press. Bill Brasher of *The Chicago Times*, who had the opportunity to observe him at work and play, described Alex as a two-pound gray parrot with a black, hooked beak, yellow eyes, and a red tail, who used his fleshy black tongue to make noises suggestive of clopping on a coconut shell somewhere in the depths of his vocal tract. This was a pretty good description of the typical African Grey, but as Brasher's narration developed it became obvious that Alex was far from typical.

Brasher recorded the following interchange between Dr. Pepperberg and Alex: "Hi there," says his keeper. "Come here," replies Alex. She places him on a wooden perch and gently blows in his face while murmuring to him affectionately. "You tickle me?" Alex says, massaging his down-covered head. "Gen-tle," he orders. Unlike the everyday African Grey rote verbalization most owners have heard, this appears to be a form of true give-and-take communication.

Early in 1988, Douglas Starr, a Massachusetts journalist, brought readers of *National Wildlife Magazine* up to date on Dr. Pepperberg's latest work with the hardy, ever eager Alex. Starr described how Dr. Pepperberg held a round tray in front of the parrot on which there were five objects, including three keys. "How many keys?" she asks,

"Should I choose it or chew it?" Sisyphus

with Alex promptly replying "Fiiive!" (African Greys are known for their ability to speak in human-like rather than parrot-like voices, and this stretching of the answers is his mimicry of Dr. Pepperberg's carefully enunciated speech.) Dr. Pepperberg corrects this error by reminding Alex that she wants him to give the number of keys, not the total number of objects, and, amazingly, she now gets the correct answer of "Thrrrree!" She proceeds to reinforce this success by complimenting Alex with an enthusiastic "Very good!" Alex is indeed a rare bird, demonstrating a type of mental ability that was once thought to be possessed only by humans.

Skeptics may say that Dr. Pepperberg, like other experimenters working on animal communication, may be reading too much into Alex's actions, but she insists that what she is observing are neither tricks performed by a clever parrot nor language use comparable to that of humans, but are simply demonstrations that even nonprimates can understand abstractions. Her long-range goal is to determine how far an avian species can

Many bird lovers are happy to be on the African Grey bandwagon. Robert Czarnomski

proceed with learning. Since African Greys are easily capable of reaching an age of forty or more, Alex has many good learning years ahead of him.

I have owned African Greys for at least twenty years, and although I have never had an Alex (or a mean-spirited bird such as the spouse abuser described by E. J. Boosey), I have seen some remarkable examples of clever behavior. For example, I kept one pair together in a large cage about four feet long by three feet high. These birds had been obtained when they were fairly young, and since, at the time, I had no intention of breeding them, I never provided a nest box. One morning when I entered the bird room, I was shocked to discover that the birds were apparently not in their cage. Even though the cage door was still closed, I checked the entire area thinking that I might have left them out the previous night while cleaning the cage and then absent-mindedly closed the cage door, leaving the birds outside. While searching, I heard a faint, melodious "Hello, hello." I soon located the source: The pair of Greys had built themselves a nest from torn newspaper, and they were under a large mound in a corner of the cage. Of course, I did not disturb them, but nothing came of this activity, nor did they ever breed for me.

One aspect of the charm of the African Grey is that it will pick up vocabulary without much effort on your part. If the telephone rings and I am told that it is for me I usually respond by saying "okay" and then picking up the phone. When Jaco hears the phone she doesn't wait for me to do anything, but shouts out "okay!" Even though it's a bit out of sequence and the calls are never for her, we all enjoy her skill at linking this phrase with the ringing of the telephone.

Greys are not only vocal, but are also quite dexterous. I provided Jaco with a music-box toy that plays a pleasant tune if the parrot presses the center of it with her beak. Jaco watched me operate it for her but for some reason refused to press the center to make the music play. Instead, she devised a technique of pressing the center of the toy against the end of a bolt that holds her seed dish. It works fine this way, and it leads me to speculate about other possible types of tool-using behavior of which these resourceful birds might be capable.

"Let's write about us." Alan H. Booton

9 AMAZON PARROTS

Amazons, as a group, are extremely popular, and the family consists of more than fifty species. The members of the genus *Amazona* originate in South and Central America as well as some of the Caribbean Islands.

Amazons are green with a variety of cheek, crown, nape, shoulder, and other markings. They vary in size from the small Spectacled Amazon to the hefty Mealy Amazon, but consistent traits can be found in all of them. They exhibit strong curiosity along with a love of play and great agility. These characteristics, plus the fact that many Amazons learn to mimic speech, has helped them to retain their popularity for as long as parrots have been kept as pets.

YELLOW-NAPED AMAZON

During a visit to the aviaries of Alba Ballard, I was introduced to Yuba, a large and heavily marked male Yellow-nape with a delightful personality, outgoing and friendly. He spoke quite well and, in addition, imitated a vocalizing opera singer as he went up and down the scales with a loud "la la la la!" After several visits I became so fond of Yuba that Mrs. Ballard considered letting me purchase

him. Unfortunately, Yuba had developed a strong bond with a Yellow-collared Macaw named Loretto, and I could see the two were virtually inseparable.

An outstanding example of a healthy, well-feathered Yellow-naped Amazon. D. Shaugnessy

I now began to search for a Yellow-nape of my own with great enthusiasm. The year was 1973, however, when parrots were being imported in relatively small numbers. Many importers and shop owners lacked the ability accurately to identify the birds they had, and their ads would frequently offer incomplete information about "Green Parrots," "Yellow-heads," or simply "Amazons" as being available. I visited several pet shops that offered Yellow-napes, only to discover Yellow-fronts and other related species.

It took me about a year, but I eventually located a Yellow-nape that was about one-and-a-half years old. Bill was a fine looking bird, with sparkling green feathers and bright intelligent eyes. His black beak, bristly cere, and nape marking assured me of his lineage and my negotiations to purchase him proceeded rapidly. Keep in mind that in 1973 you could not find many listings for different parrots in the various advertising publications. Importation via quarantine stations was in its infancy, and finding a particular parrot required luck and research. I was fortunate to locate Bill, who was fairly tame and in excellent health. He was also a fine talker, but as I was to discover in the years that followed, virtually every Yellow-naped Amazon can talk and most of them excel in this area.

Amazona ochrocephala auropalliata is a large Amazon that can reach lengths of fifteen inches. The feathers are bright green, except for the yellow marking on the back of the neck that generally appears towards the end of the first year and continues to grow until the bird reaches maturity at about two years of age. The cere and the hairs around the nostrils are black and the beak is dark gray to black.

The Yellow-nape has always been highly prized because of his extraordinary ability to mimic. Of course, you may have also heard this about mynah birds and African Greys, but there is a difference. Only certain species of mynahs, such as the Greater Hill Mynah, learn to speak well and, unfortunately, not every African Grey learns to talk, although those that do become splendid practitioners of this most noteworthy parrot skill. Yellow-napes, however, all learn to speak; some learn much better than others, but none are total disappointments in this

area. The owner of one Yellow-nape once contacted me to seek help in finding a good home for her parrot. The bird talked so incessantly and so loudly that she was being forced to choose between the parrot and her husband. I was able to be of assistance, and this loquacious bird continued his talkative behavior at the home of new owners who were immensely delighted with him.

Descriptions by writers such as Dr. W. T. Greene, who wrote about a Yellow-nape who would use a pitiable voice to say "Please don't go, stay here," served to encourage the enthusiasm of potential parrot owners. As importations increased during the mid-1970s and early 1980s, it became common knowledge that if you wanted a fine talking bird, the parrot to own was the Yellow-nape. Even though shipments of large numbers of these parrots easily filled the demand, prices for Yellow-napes rose quickly as dealers realized that this was the parrot most new bird owners wanted and would pay top dollar for.

In recent years, many bird owners have come to realize that shared affection and a pleasant personality are even more important than the ability to mimic. Young Yellow-napes can be tame and endearing, but they have an unfortunate quirk that appears at about two or three years of age: They become intensely jealous and possessive and can show their displeasure with savage bites. You can avoid some of this aggression if you remember always to greet your Yellow-nape first when you enter the bird room. Also, be sure to feed him first and, if the birds are to be taken out of their cages, make certain that the Yellow-nape is the first bird out. This jealousy may be linked to being "top bird" in the pecking order, but it is not limited solely to other birds. If you happen to be playing with your Yellow-nape outside the cage, be careful not to interrupt the activity by showing affection for your spouse or children, or trouble may follow. This may sound a little like living with Ivan the Terrible. If you intend to keep a number of parrots, perhaps a Double Yellow-head should be your Amazon choice instead.

The subspecies of Yellow-nape, *Amazona ochrocephala parvipes*, which is slightly smaller and more compact than the nominate race, is an occasional source of confusion. It has a red marking at the

The Yellow-naped Amazon is unsurpassed as a talking parrot (opposite). Doreen Gluck

bend of the wing and the beak may be lighter in color. *Parvipes* will often show a yellow marking on the crown, and the nape marking is not yet fully developed in juveniles, leaving their owners to wonder if they have purchased a Yellow-fronted Amazon instead of a Yellow-nape. The nominate species, *auropalliata*, is found in southern Mexico, Guatemala, Honduras, and Costa Rica, while the range of *parvipes* mainly includes the northeastern coast of Nicaragua and islands off the coast of Honduras. Both groups are equally talented talkers, and there is no reason to prefer one bird over the other or to feel that you have been cheated if your Yellow-nape turns out to be of the smaller subspecies.

Bosch and Wedde (*Encyclopedia of Amazon Parrots*, 1984) note that the Yellow-nape has been bred in the United States, Europe, and Australia, and Rosemary Low (*Parrots: Their Care and Breeding*, 3d Revised Edition, 1992) discusses a possible breeding of *parvipes* in England in 1982. The Yellow-nape is currently being bred in the United States. The hand-fed chicks are still in

constant demand and breeders can obtain good prices for them.

DOUBLE YELLOW-HEAD

The Double Yellow-head is one of the favorites of the Amazon family. It has been kept as a pet for well over a hundred years and records of its breeding and maintenance go back even further. Many factors contribute to the popularity of a particular parrot species. In choosing a bird, many individuals express concern that it be colorful and attractive. They also seek information about its potential for speech and its reputation for being a tame, loving pet. Some look to the future and want to be assured that the parrot of their choice belongs to a group that has been successfully bred with some measure of consistency. The Double Yellow-head meets all of these specifications, and, thus, it is no coincidence that it has been a favorite of the Mexicans in its country of origin and was for a time the Amazon most commonly imported into the United States.

A handsome pair of fully mature Double Yellow-heads, a long-time favorite among all parrot fans. Rolf C. Hagen, Inc.

The Double Yellow-head can become an excellent talking parrot. As with most Amazons, your chances for success are much better if you obtain a young bird and work with him regularly. Older parrots will also learn to speak, but not as well. As a guaranteed success in this area, the Double Yellow-head will never rival the Yellow-naped Amazon, which always learns to speak. I do, however, prefer the personality of the Double Yellow-head, as it is a gentler, more friendly bird.

Early writers, such as Charles N. Page (*Parrots and Other Talking Birds,* 1906), indicate that the popularity of the Double Yellow-head was so great at the turn of the century that Double Yellow-head clubs and associations existed to promote it. In his 1884 classic, *Parrots In Captivity*, Dr. Greene describes Rev. Dutton's experiences with three Double Yellow-heads, one of whom the reverend considered the most charming parrot he had ever owned. It had been purchased in France from an elderly couple, and since the previous owner had been a sailor, the bird's language was rather salty. In light of its owner's profession, it is fortunate that the parrot swore only in French.

In choosing a parrot, or any pet, for that matter, you should accept with caution the opinions of those who make broad, generalized statements on the behavior and personality of a particular parrot species or genus based on one or two experiences with the type of bird in question. This disclaimer aside, I truly believe that certain traits of personality and behavior are common to almost all the larger Amazons.

I have owned three Double Yellow-heads. My first specimen of *Amazona ochrocephala oratrix*, the most common subspecies of Double Yellow-head, originating in Mexico, was naturally named Blondi. I purchased her in 1972 when, because of a very strict import ban, opportunities to obtain full-sized parrots were extremely limited. Blondi was one of two birds that had been placed on consignment in a pet shop I visited fairly often. On this particular day the owner advised me that he had a Lilac-crowned Amazon as well as a Double Yellow-head available, and that I could have either one of them for $200. Making a choice was not difficult, as the Lilac-crown wanted nothing to do with me and rejected all of my attempts to be friendly by backing into a corner and opening his large beak.

Blondi, on the other hand, seemed to know that we were made for each other. She just couldn't wait to climb out of her cage and travel up my arm to my shoulder. I was also delighted with her ability to speak, which she did in a high-pitched, rather silly voice. Understandable words and phrases were mixed in with some attractive gargling sounds, and once she started talking, it was a while before she wound down. I bought her on the spot and never regretted my decision.

Blondi's behavior was best described as droll. Although her parrot face constantly wore a horrified look, she actually dealt with life from a whimsical point of view and seemed to be as happy hanging upside down as perched normally upright. She also showed a great deal of curiosity and, unlike many other parrots, she could be tempted to try foods that were new to her by the simple trick of wedging them in a corner of her cage. Blondi would take this as a challenge and after an appropriate wait to be sure that the new food item would not attack, she would investigate it and decide if it was worth eating.

About five years after I purchased Blondi, a secretary with whom I worked approached me about selling a Double Yellow-head that had been owned by her late husband. The price was quite reasonable, but I told her I would have to see the bird before I could decide. A brief visit to her home convinced me of my good fortune. José was a large, well-marked, Magna subspecies of Double Yellow-head and, although he exhibited a certain reserve when I attempted to touch him, he was tame and friendly. This bird had an entire bedroom allotted to him, but it was obvious that he got little personal attention. The volcano-shaped mound of sunflower seed shells on the floor of his cage was an indication of both a lack of regular cleaning and evidence of a limited diet. Upon arriving at my home he was immediately introduced to Blondi and from the display behavior, mutual preening, and general showing off, it was clear that these two would be great companions.

I learned something quite interesting about parrot behavior from these birds. They were often permitted to sit together on a large T-stand. If these interludes took place during the summer, José would act in a threatening manner toward me or anyone else who entered his space. The threats took the form of violent shakes of his head accompanied by whining sounds that went up and down the musical scale. Blondi remained passive and seemed equally receptive to my petting or José's preening of her neck. This type of aggression did not occur in the fall or winter. José and Blondi would still sit together on their T-stand, but after the breeding season ended, José reverted to his old affectionate manner, which even included kisses. I have since heard from other breeders that, contrary to popular opinion, tame birds that have been paired remain tame or revert to tameness when the breeding season ends.

My third Double Yellow-head was a gift from a lady whose daughter had asked her to keep the bird for her for "just a few months." These months stretched into years and although the woman liked the bird, there were problems if she wished to travel or had to be away for a weekend. Her daughter suggested that I might be willing to adopt this parrot, and after looking at her I readily agreed. The new Double Yellow-head was named Rocky, but I quickly renamed her Blondi II. Blondi II was about fourteen years old and had been a domestic, hand-fed pet. Her appearance, manner, behavior, and voice are so similar to Blondi I that it is easy to confuse the two birds. Her feathering was not quite as smooth when I got her, but a summer of spraying with tepid water produced an immense improvement in their texture. Her disposition is delightful. She prefers not to be picked up from the top of her cage, as she would rather fly to the floor and then climb onto your hand. Best of all, Blondi II has a large vocabulary. She was rather quiet upon arriving at her new home, although she seemed pleased to be in the company of other parrots. Later that evening when my son and his family arrived, the new Blondi became extremely vocal. I remembered at that point that her previous owner told me of Blondi's fondness for her grandson, whom the parrot addressed by shouting "Robert!" My grandson, Richard, was with the group, and it was obvious that Blondi's enthusiasm was generated by his arrival. She did not call "Richard!" but she did scream "hi guy!" and later that evening, after a lot of silly laughter and imitation crying, she began to repeat "shut up!" Apparently this was a command she often heard when she carried on in this manner in her former home.

Blondi became similarly enthusiastic when visited by an adult who was not very tall and had short hair. She obviously thought that Richard, or Robert, had returned and again went through her complete routine. She is a charming bird and a welcome addition to my collection.

The nominate species of the Double Yellow-head, *A. o. oratrix*, ranges in length from about fourteen to fifteen inches. They are well-built, husky birds whose short, blunt tails emphasize their stocky figures. Their upper surface is dark green, while the tail feathers and undersurface are of a much lighter shade of green. Many specimens also show an interesting red marking at the bend of the wing. The crown and forehead of young specimens are dappled with yellow, but as the birds mature, these areas come together, eventually resulting in the yellow head marking we associate with this parrot. They have yellowish white beaks and blazing yellow-orange eyes that dilate and contract rapidly when the birds are pleased, frightened, or angry.

The name Double Yellow-head does not refer to the amount of yellow on this Amazon's crown, it actually refers to the bird's appearance when excitement or ill temper causes the erection of its head and nape feathers, resulting in the image of a frightening creature with a very large head. Rapid dilation and contraction of the pupils of the eye along with fanning out of the tail heighten this effect, and the entire display probably serves as a protective strategy in the wild. Keep in mind that ninety percent of this display is sham, and the bird's usual reaction if a visitor gets too close is retreat.

Subspecies include *Amazona o. belizensis*, which, according to Bosch and Wedde, is found in

These Tres Mariae are about five years old. Walt Hansen

A strikingly marked Tres Marias Amazon

the country of Belize. It differs from the nominate species in that it has less yellow on the head and, occasionally, has a few green feathers on the throat. In addition, there is the much desired *Amazona o. tresmariae*, found only on a group of islands off the coast of western Mexico. It is a larger bird and shows a great deal of bright yellow even when young. The mature Tres Marias can have yellow completely covering its head and extending down the neck and back. My only experience with Tres Marias was a foolish failure to purchase one. I was shown the bird in 1975 by a pet shop owner who warned me that it was old and nasty. I assumed he was correct about the age, as the yellow feathers covered its head and extended down its nape and back. In my ignorance I accepted his information,

but in retrospect I realize that the bird was probably not more than seven or eight years old and that I stood a fair chance of gaining its confidence. One rarely finds Tres Marias in pet shops today, and the price is about five times the $200 I was asked to pay for the one I saw.

If you are fortunate enough to find a breeder who has Tres Marias chicks for sale you should be able to identify them without difficulty, as even when young they are heavily marked with yellow, and therefore are not easily confused with other Amazons. If in doubt, ask the breeder to show you the parents, which are unmistakable.

In recent years, *Amazona o. magna* has also occasionally been listed as a subspecies, although some express doubt over its validity as a separate group. The Magna group is also found in Mexico, and these parrots are generally described as being larger and more covered with yellow than the nominate species, although less heavily yellow than the Tres Marias.

A smaller number of Tres Marias Amazons are also bred each year, but these are generally snapped up by purchasers who have been on breeders' waiting lists. Because of their great beauty they command a premium price that can be several hundred dollars higher than that of the more common variations. In the case of Tres Marias, again, ask to see the parents, as sometimes hybrid Double Yellow/Tres Marias young are sold as Tres Marias and even though the offspring are heavily marked with yellow, they are not as desirable as the chicks of a true pair of Tres Marias.

An excellent article on breeding the Double Yellow-head appeared in the November–December 1970 issue of the British *Avicultural Magazine*. Charles Smith had purchased his newly imported pair in 1966 as young, lightly marked birds. By 1970, their entire heads and napes were yellow, but Mr. Smith could not discern any color difference between the male and female. The cock did, however, have a broader beak and a wider, flatter head. The difference in head size became more pronounced as the birds matured.

They were set up in a flight that was twelve feet long by six feet wide by seven feet high with a shelter that was six feet by four feet. After the first winter, they roosted in the outer flight and used the shelter only for feeding or an afternoon nap. A nest box similar to the closet of a grandfather clock was introduced in 1969 and by early June the hen had begun to chew wood to produce some filling for the nest. She then disappeared into the box and was only seen for short periods in the evening. The first round of eggs were not fertile, but there was a new attempt at breeding in May 1970. The first egg was laid on May 7, and another three were laid that same week. Incubation had begun with the first egg, and two weeks later, while the hen was out feeding, a quick inspection showed the eggs to be fertile. By June 5, chicks could be heard feeding and by June 14 it was possible to see two chicks and two eggs that had not hatched. The young were covered with gray down but they feathered, grew rapidly, and left the nest on August 5 within an hour of each other. Shortly after that they were feeding on their own, ultimately developing into strong, perfect birds.

There is virtually no legitimate importation of Double Yellow-heads at this time, but domestic breeding continues to provide enough offspring to supply most of the demand. Prices for hand-fed domestic young range from $900 to $1,200. The ideal selection is a bird about three or four months old. If you have the time to hand feed and can find a younger bird, you may be able to buy from a breeder at a lower price. This will enable you to establish a close relationship with the parrot as you hand feed it.

The Double Yellow-head is an excellent choice if you want to own an Amazon Parrot. Unfortunately, there is still a vigorous trade in Double Yellow-heads smuggled across the border from Mexico. While you should certainly resist the temptation to purchase such a bird for ethical and legal reasons, you should also consider the real danger to you and your other birds from the introduction of a potential disease carrier to your flock. If you are offered a bird at a ridiculously low price, check for closed leg bands and ask for references from other buyers before making such a purchase.

BLUE-FRONTED AMAZON

This handsome parrot, *Amazona aestiva aestiva*, has been known to aviculturists and fanciers for well over a hundred years, during which time it has frequently been confused with the Orange-winged Amazon, *Amazona amazonica*.

Dr. Russ notes that the Blue-fronts were highly prized by South Americans because of their suitability for training. They were found everywhere as pets and great numbers were often brought to market.

The Blue-front is a slim, graceful bird reaching lengths of fourteen to fifteen inches. Its green feathers have dark green margins and its forehead is marked with blue. Bright yellow markings appear on the crown and cheeks as well as on the ear coverts and around the eyes. Blue and white feathers also may extend to the crown. The arrangement of head feathers is highly variable. The bend of the

Compare the color of the beak of this Blue-fronted Amazon (opposite) with the beak of the Orange-winged Amazon in the next photo. Everett Webb

wing is marked with red or sometimes a mixture of red and yellow, the beak is black, and the legs are gray. It is found in eastern Brazil, from Pernambuco in the North through the Mato Grosso region of Rio Grande do Sul in the South.

There is a subspecies of the Blue-front, *Amazona a. xanthopteryx*, in the southwestern Mato Grosso and also in Paraguay, northern Argentina, and the Chaco region of Bolivia. Large specimens of Blue-fronts are often referred to as "Chaco Blue-fronts." The term *Chaco* has come to refer more to large size than to place of origin. *A. a. xanthopteryx* is frequently called the Yellow-winged Amazon. It differs from the nominate race in that it usually has less yellow on the head, and the bend of its wing is yellow rather than red. Bosch and Wedde confirm this parrot's popularity in both the United States and Europe, indicating that it was one of the most frequently imported birds.

Rutgers and Norris (*Encyclopedia of Aviculture*, 1972) describe the Blue-front as gregarious, "usually to be seen in large flocks, often associating with other species of parrots." They consider it an excellent cage-bird pet and observe, as do others, that it is a great favorite in its native habitat because of its propensity for tameness and capacity for speech. The authors also commend the bird's hardiness when acclimatized, and the fact that it can be kept in an unheated outdoor aviary throughout the year. I would modify this observation by suggesting that space heating or shelter be provided in the colder regions of the United States during severe winter weather.

I have occasionally seen mutations of the Blue-fronted Amazon that appeared to be almost pied. Dr. Vriends (*Popular Parrots*, 1983) reports yellow, blue, pied, and Lutino mutations in the collection of Dick Topper of California, as well as additional Lutinos in collections in Brazil.

Dr. Greene describes a Blue-front that lived to be at least sixty-seven years old. The family who owned it had had it in their possession for almost forty years. This bird would repeat such endearments as "kiss me" and "hold Polly" at appropriate times but was not considered an exceptional talker. Her death was blamed on a severe cold following accidental exposure to a draft.

Some early records exist regarding the breeding of these popular birds: In 1888, J. Abrahams, a British animal dealer, reported on the breeding of a Blue-front by M. Renouard of France that had occurred several years earlier, and Edward Boosey provided an extremely well-documented record of a breeding at the famous Keston Bird Farm of England in the December 1939 issue of *Avicultural Magazine*. The parents came from the duke of Bedford's collection. He parted with this pair because, although they proved themselves capable of producing live chicks, they refused to feed them and ultimately caused the death of the young. Boosey decided to give these bad parents a one-season trial at Keston. They arrived there in September 1938 and were housed in an aviary that was fifteen feet long, five feet wide, and seven feet high. The pair was provided with a grandfather clock–type nest box at the end of March. The hen entered the nest almost immediately, seldom to be seen thereafter, and the birds were left undisturbed. The male was a ferocious bird, not one to trifle with: Boosey described how this parrot would, if offered an apple by someone standing close to the aviary, hurry down to the fruit and tear it viciously to

It is easy to differentiate between the familiar Blue-fronted Amazon and the Orange-winged Amazon. The upper beak of the latter is horn-colored and has a dark tip. In the Blue-front the upper beak is slate-colored. Michael DeFreitas

pieces just to demonstrate what he would like to do to the finger of a careless visitor who put it in range of the bird's beak.

Eventually, the sound of young emanated from the nest box. Ever mindful of the reputation of these parents, Boosey decided that their bad behavior as parents might have been due to weariness resulting from the limitations of their diet, which was small seeds. He therefore provided them with a protein-rich diet of fish and eggs, along with potatoes, bread, and milk. The eggs had been laid the first week in April, and the first chick left the nest on July 20. Shortly after this, Boosey had an opportunity to peek into the nest box while the parents were feeding elsewhere. What he saw was the aviculturist's thrill of a lifetime—a nest packed with five healthy chicks. In the photo accompanying the article, the group is happily sitting on a perch while the hen peers into the nest box. (The

father was left out of the photo, as he had to be kept locked away in the flight shelter to prevent him from attacking the photographer.)

ORANGE-WINGED AMAZON

I first became familiar with these colorful parrots in 1976. Then, as now, they were plentiful and inexpensive. They bear some resemblance to the Blue-fronted Amazon, but thanks to the abundance of books that have become available in the last fifteen years, fewer people confuse the Orange-wing with its similar but more expensive relative.

Amazona amazonica, about thirteen inches long, is a green parrot (duller green on the undersurface) with a bright blue marking on the forehead that extends around the lores. The front of the crown and the cheeks are bright yellow, while the ear coverts are grass green, and it has a

The Blue-front does not always shine as a talker, but its delightful personality more than makes up for this. Everett Webb

horn-colored beak that becomes almost black at the tip. An orange patch on the secondary feathers is the source of its name. By contrast, the Blue-fronted Amazon has a solid black beak and lacks the ear covert marking found in the Orange-wing. These two variations are sufficient to identify a bird as a Blue-front rather than an Orange-wing.

Bosch and Wedde note the parrot's wide range, which extends from Guyana and Surinam in the north to almost halfway down the continent of South America. The writers speculate on possible color variations based on sex, with males having more intensive blue and yellow head markings while the cheeks of the females are more pronounced yellow. I have not seen this confirmed elsewhere, but it is worth checking if you have a pair that has been sexed surgically or through the newer chromosome technique.

According to David Alderton (*Guide To Cage Birds*, 1980), these parrots are far from popular in their native environment; in large, raucous flocks, some estimated at more than a thousand birds, they can do severe damage to crops.

I once owned an Orange-wing that was, by contrast, an extremely timid bird. Although gentle, Koko did not learn to speak, and comments from other Orange-wing owners indicate that these birds are not particularly skillful speakers.

In an article in the March/April 1973 issue of the British *Avicultural Magazine*, D. H. S. Risdon described his Orange-winged Amazons as pugnacious birds that had to be kept separate from his many other parrots. When he was short of aviary space, he placed them in an open flight, giving them their freedom during the day. In a short time they shed their clipped flight feathers and became excellent free flyers, returning to their flight and nest box each evening.

A fine article on breeding the Orange-winged Amazon appeared in the January 1983 issue of the British *Magazine of the Parrot Society*, in which I. M. Hadgkiss and K. Mitchell recounted the breeding of a pair they had obtained in 1980. Their aviary was quite large, eighteen feet wide by fifteen feet long by eighteen feet high, with an inner shelter that was eleven feet wide by six feet long by ten feet high. A large hollow log, five and a half by two and a half feet, served as the nest box. In addition to their regular diet the birds received lamb-chop and chicken bones as well as sprouted seeds and other greens.

In April 1982, after having rejected several man-made nest boxes, the pair began to show interest in the log nest, both of them sitting on the perch below the entrance. Eventually the hen began to spend time in the nest, modifying it by chewing up the rotted wood that had been placed in its base.

Copulation occurred on May 21 and several times thereafter. By May 29 there were two eggs, but the authors were unable to inspect them because of determined attacks by the parents. After an incubation period of approximately twenty-six days, two newly hatched chicks were found on June 23. A third chick was hatched the next day, but only two survived. Even though the birds were doing a good job of feeding, the authors decided to hand feed these young when it became apparent that the third chick had been killed by the new and inexperienced parents.

The Orange-wing is not a difficult parrot to breed. Tampa's Busch Gardens, for example, successfully raised eleven young between 1967 and 1974. Unfortunately, there has been little incentive to breed this species since so many imports have been available at low prices for the last twenty years. These low prices, of course, offered an excellent opportunity to build up breeding stock of a full-sized Amazon with only a modest investment. Keep in mind that not many years ago, the same could have been done with Scarlet and Blue and Gold Macaws.

GREEN-CHEEKED AMAZON

As I walked near his cage, Little Mexico made lively striking movements with his head. These aggressive motions were accompanied by a rapid opening and closing of his beak. His eyes virtually blazed as the pupils contracted and dilated almost in rhythm with a low, grumbling sound in his throat, comparable to the noise that an infuriated, giant pigeon might make. My visitors were watching; with courage based on long association, I reached into his cage and scratched his neck. The grumbling continued but now it signified pleasure, and Mexico gradually buried his entire head in my hand and held one of my fingers in his mouth. He is a tame and loving Green-cheeked Amazon, and all of his threats were a pretense.

Amazons are generally delightful to observe and interact with, but prospective owners should realize that Little Mexico was originally a hand-fed

Green-cheeked Amazons are also widely known as Mexican Redheads. Either way, this is a popular, personable bird. Rolf C. Hagen, Inc.

baby whose trust and confidence was built up over a number of years.

Amazona viridigenalis, often referred to as the Mexican Redhead, is a typical member of this genus, and although these parrots are not regarded as good talkers, they tend to make pleasant, friendly pets. If I had to choose between a biting bird with wonderful speech ability and a gently, loving nontalker, I'd choose the latter every time.

Although well known for many years, the Green-cheek's popularity has generally been limited to the United States. Since these birds originate in the northeastern Mexican states of Nuevo Leon, Tamaulipas, and Veracruz, there was a steady flow across the border for many years. Only the Double Yellow, with its greater affinity for speech, exceeded them in popularity. If you or one of your relatives remembers Grandma's green parrot of yesteryear, you can be fairly sure that it was either a Green-cheek or a Double Yellow-head.

One hopes this type of border crossing has ended now that there are enough breeding stocks of Green-cheeks, Double Yellow-heads, Blue-fronts,

and Yellow-napes to provide hand-fed domestic babies for all prospective owners.

The Green-cheek is only thirteen to fourteen inches in length. Its dark green upper surface is set off by the lighter green underparts of its body, and the margins of the feathers of the head, nape, and back are dark, giving the bird an interesting scalloped appearance. The bright red crown, forehead, and lores are the source of the parrot's alternative name, and contrast strikingly with the green region of the cheek. A lilac area behind the eyes and ear coverts is similar to that of the Lilac-crowned, or Finsch's, Amazon, but the latter bird is smaller and a much larger area of its crown is covered with lilac-colored feathers. The eye of the Green-cheek is yellowish, and the beak is horn-colored. Most breeders see no difference in color between the sexes, but Bosch and Wedde believe that females have less red on the head, noting that this is also true of immature birds.

There is a charming likeness of a Mexican Redhead in George M. Sutton's *Portraits of Mexican Birds*, published in 1972. The author refers to them as "Red-crowned Parrots" and notes their penetrating call, which he transcribes as "heelo, crack, crack, crack!" I can assure you that the Green-cheek's calls are even more piercing within the confines of a home. When our bird room becomes noisy, as it does several times a day, Little Mexico's screams can be distinguished by their volume from all the others.

These birds delight in chewing, and owners should provide blocks of pine or willow twigs for them to work on. I usually purchase scrap one-by-three-inch pine at a lumber yard and cut it up into 2- or 3-inch pieces. After drilling a hole through the center, I hang the pine block from the top of the cage with an untreated leather thong, making sure that the strip is at least a quarter of an inch wide, so that the bird cannot get tangled up in it. Willow twigs are also greatly appreciated; the parrot will first slip off the bark and then chew the twig to bits.

Comparatively few breeding reports are available regarding the Green-cheeked Amazon. The first recorded breeding appears to have occurred at the Los Angeles Zoo in 1970. A remarkable pair owned by Paul Springman of Brownsville, Texas, produced eighteen young between 1972 and 1977, some of which, in 1976, introduced another generation.

Amazona viridigenalis was first identified in 1837. It quickly became a British favorite, and in 1885 a Mr. C. Martin took first place in the Amazon Division during that year's show at the Crystal Palace. J. M. Forshaw (*Parrots of the World*, 3d rev. ed., 1989) confirms their original habitat as northeastern Mexico, but notes that they have been introduced to urban Los Angeles, southeastern Florida, and possibly southern Texas. In March 1986 he observed a flock of about fifty Green-cheeked Amazons roosting in trees at Temple City near Los Angeles. According to Forshaw, southern Texas is only a possible locale because there is the chance that Redheads being illegally transported across the border may have been released in this area by smugglers in danger of being apprehended; if this is true, they do not constitute a local population.

George M. Sutton visited the Rancho Rinconda in southwestern Tamaulipas in 1941 and describes the Redhead as one of the most common and noisy birds in the region. By mid-March, most of the Redheads he saw were paired, and pairs could be observed in proximity to each other as the flocks passed over the ranch. Sutton observed quarrels for choice nest locations among the pairs, including a battle among three pairs of Redheads, each wanting an abandoned woodpecker hole sixty feet above ground in an old cypress tree.

Bosch and Wedde consider the Mexican Redhead to be only a fair talker and a somewhat loud screamer. I would agree with their evaluation of its speaking ability and have found the birds to be particularly noisy. They are great chewers and, as discussed above, should be provided with chewing material to occupy them during the day. One Redhead I boarded for a friend for several months regularly destroyed most of his perches and would wind up clutching the side of the cage until I rescued him.

LILAC-CROWNED AMAZON

The pleasingly colored Lilac-crown is small and stocky and reaches lengths of thirteen to fourteen inches. Typically, its upper surface is green with the lower surface a lighter, almost yellowish green.

A Finsch's Amazon in perfect feather. Michael DeFreitas

The neck and abdominal feathers have very dark margins, giving the feathers a scalloped, ruffled appearance. Since the bird also has a tendency to raise its neck feathers, it sometimes seems to be pretending to be a Hawk-headed parrot. There is a deeply colored maroon band between the eyes covering a good portion of the forehead, while the fore-crown and nape are lilac, and the beak is a light horn color.

The Lilac crown is also referred to as Finsch's Amazon, *Amazona finschi*, in honor of the man who first recognized it as a species distinct from the Blue-front. According to Bosch and Wedde, the range of this parrot is central to southwest Mexico. They consider the female to be smaller than the male by a few millimeters, but, of course, one would have to have a sexed male and female available to make such a comparison. These authors charmingly describe the flight of the Lilac-crowns as often ending in "a wave-shaped . . . wide curving arc to the earth." Beautiful!

Karl Aschenborn (*Keeping and Breeding Parrots*, 1990) notes the strong resemblance between the Green-cheek and the Lilac-crown but points out the most obvious differences between the two species, including the brighter green cheeks of the former and its distinctive green ear coverts, as well as its red crown and forehead. In addition, the Green-cheek is a larger, huskier bird.

In *Parrots, Lories, and Cockatoos* (1982), David Alderton reported seeing large flocks of these birds, with over two hundred per flock, in the early 1970s. Forshaw quotes Ridgely as finding them abundant and common as late as 1977. In a recent magazine article, Rosemary Low notes that the location of their nests in mountainous woodlands affords them some protection. This, along with fairly low importation levels during the 1970s, probably accounts for their continued numbers in the wild. However, according to Mark Hagen, speaking before the International Aviculturist Society early in 1993, the habitat of the Lilac-crown and many other Amazons continues to be threatened by human encroachment.

Authentic breeding records on the Lilac-crown go back to 1949, when longtime California aviculturist Dave West, writing in *Avicultural Magazine*, credited Mrs. W. S. Riley of Chino, California, with a breeding pair that was raised in that state. Mrs. Riley reported in the same publication that in 1950 the pair produced two infertile eggs, although a friend of hers, Mrs. Mercer of Bell, California, was successful in breeding them.

R. E. J. and Patricia D. Mann of England described a successful breeding of these parrots in an article published in the October–December 1978 issue of the British *Avicultural Magazine*. Large numbers of Lilac-crowns and other Amazons from Mexico were fairly common in England beginning in the early 1970s. The Manns initially purchased a single Lilac-crown of unknown sex, a second bird a few weeks later. Judging only by the difference in size between the birds, they hopefully set them up as a pair. A hollow log nest box was ignored by the birds for several years, but in May of 1978 they began to breed in a smaller nest, measuring six by eight by twenty-seven inches. Copulation was observed several times during the month of May, when the male was also seen to occasionally feed the hen. On June 2 the first of two eggs was found; it was incubated by the female with such devotion that she would leave the nest only for

The alternate name for the Finsch's Amazon is the Lilac-crowned Amazon. This study shows why the name is so appropriate. Courtesy the San Diego Zoo

about five minutes during the early evening. On June 9 a second egg was discovered. The Manns checked the eggs at the end of June and determined that only one was fertile. On July 3, they discovered a fairly large chick that apparently had hatched several days earlier. The chick grew quite rapidly. By July 15 its eyes were open, and by August 5 it weighed twelve and a half ounces, had gray down on its chest along with a number of green feathers, and was actually beginning to look like an Amazon. On August 29, when the baby Lilac-crown was sixty days old, it left the nest box and entered the flights, looking very much like a smaller version of its parents. This appears to be the first breeding of the species in Great Britain.

THE MEALY AMAZON

Even though these birds are not extraordinarily colorful, they have a whimsical streak that makes them playful and droll in ways that I find extremely attractive. Of course, to a certain extent this could describe many members of the parrot family, but the behavior of *Amazona farinosa* is exceptionally comical.

The term *Mealy Amazon* refers to a group of birds originating in Guyana, Surinam, Venezuela, southeast Colombia, Brazil, and northern Bolivia. They are large, stocky parrots that reach lengths of fifteen to sixteen inches. Their basic color is green, with a number of variations attributed to different subspecies. Since the validity of several of these is uncertain, we will concern ourselves only with the nominate race and two subspecies.

Amazona farinosa farinosa is primarily green, with a variable yellow marking on the forehead. The feathers of the back have a grayish "frosted" look, making it appear as though the bird's back had been lightly powdered with cornmeal flour, hence the common name "Mealy Amazon." The beak is horn-colored, while the brown eye is surrounded by a bare white ring that results in a clownish look, a good reflection of the bird's personality. The species has an extremely loud call and will not hesitate to use it if there is a delay in providing food or anticipated companionship.

Birl, my Mealy Amazon, was an extremely playful parrot that eagerly joined in most of our games and activities. On one occasion as I was cleaning his cage, I placed him in a small

The Blue-crowned Amazon is a member of the Mealy group. Paolo Tiengo

cardboard box with a clean rag inside that just happened to be at hand. He was delighted with this arrangement and made the box into a play area as he chewed the sides and rolled himself in the rag. Birl had an unfortunate habit of frequently repeating an entire series of variously modulated screams until I or a family member entered the bird room or until he simply tired of doing so. If anyone responded to his screams, Birl would joyfully cry "Hi boy!" or "Hi girl!" If he was particularly excited, he would greet the visitor with the hybrid "Hi Birl," the source of his unusual name. A few years ago, we discovered that Birl was actually a female when informed by her purchaser that she had laid several eggs.

The Mealy Amazon's mild nature may also extend to relationships with other birds. According to Bosch and Wedde, in Guyana they can be seen flying and even roosting with Yellow-crowned and Orange-winged Amazons. Werner Lantermann (*Popular Parrot Species*, 1986) housed a pair of Mealys with two young Double Yellow-heads. Although all of the parrots were of equal size, the

Double Yellow-heads bullied the Mealys, chasing them constantly and even driving them away from the food dishes. Lantermann soon moved the docile pair to an aviary of their own.

A. f. virenticeps is a recognized subspecies of the Mealy whose range is the coast of western Panama, Nicaragua, and Costa Rica. It differs from the nominate race in being yellowish green with very few if any yellow feathers on the head, while the crown and forehead are bluish green. In all other respects, however, it closely resembles the nominate race.

A. f. guatemalae is commonly called the Blue-crowned Amazon. It differs from the nominate race in that its forehead and crown are a distinct blue that extends to the nape, where it becomes a dark grayish blue. It is found in Mexico, Guatemala, Belize, and Honduras. Some experts believe it is rare, but this may be because supposed purchasers of Mealy Amazons may unwittingly be Blue-crowned Amazon owners.

The nominate race, *Amazona farinosa farinosa*, is a stocky parrot that at fifteen inches is among the largest of the Amazons. It originates in Mexico and the northern regions of South America, where it inhabits tropical forest regions.

The Blue-crowned Amazon (*Amazona f. guatemalae*) also appears in Mexico but is more commonly found in Guatemala, Belize, and Honduras. Its beak is black except for a horn-colored area at the base of the upper mandible, and forehead and crown are light blue, blending into a grayish-blue at the nape. In most other respects it resembles the Mealy Amazon.

The Mealy group have been highly underrated as pets, with little recognition given to their docile nature and excellent talking ability. This indifference is probably due to the wide availability and reasonable prices of Amazons such as the Yellow-nape, Double Yellow-head, and Blue-fronted that were much better known when parrots began to flood the country in the late 1970s.

Werner Lantermann (*The New Parrot Handbook*, 1986) reports on what appears to have been the first breeding of the Mealy, in this case the Blue-crowned subspecies, by Wolfgang Burkart of West Germany in 1984. Rosemary Low (*Parrots: Their Care and Breeding*, 1992), in a more extensive report on this same breeding success, notes that Burkart obtained six of these birds in 1980,

and in the spring of 1981 he placed one pair in a separate aviary. The female laid on April 5, 9, and 12, and he first heard a chick on May 2. By May 6 three chicks had hatched. Their eyes opened at eighteen days, feathers appeared on the wings at thirty days, and they fledged at sixty-one days.

YELLOW-SHOULDERED AMAZON

The Yellow-shouldered Amazon, or *Amazona barbadensis*, is an extremely attractive Amazon originating on the coast of Venezuela and the island of Bonaire in the Netherlands Antilles, as well as on two islands off the coast of Venezuela. At one time it was also found on Aruba, but Rosemary Low reports that it is now extinct there. According to Prestwich, the designation *barbadensis* means "of Barbados," but the appellation is incorrect, as the parrots do not inhabit that island.

At first glance, its stocky build, distinctive markings, and outgoing behavior are reminiscent of the Double Yellow-head, although the Yellow-shoulder, at about thirteen inches in length, is an inch or so smaller. It has a yellowish white forehead and lores, while the crown, cheeks, ear coverts, and, occasionally, the upper throat are yellow. There is a blue wash in the lower portion of the cheek that continues down the throat and bright yellow markings at the bend of the wing. The female has a bluish cast to the throat, abdomen, and breast, and is generally duller in color.

As reported by Forshaw (*Parrots of the World*, 1973), these birds were fairly abundant early in the century and large flocks were sighted. Unfortunately, within a short time there was a decline of such magnitude that by the 1930s they were rare and are currently considered endangered.

There is some doubt as to the validity of the subspecies *A. b. rothschildi*, which is very similar to the nominate species but purportedly has less yellow on the crown and a mixture of red and yellow feathers at the bend of the wing. Rothschild's Amazon specimens occur only on Bonaire and two islands off the coast of Venezuela. The subspecies was named for Walter Rothschild of the famous banking family, who financially supported Dr. Ernest Hartert's 1892 expedition to Venezuela and the Caribbean. Rothschild was an avid collector of birds, and his specimens eventually became the foundation of the Tring Museum in England, with a bird collection eventually rivaling that of The British Museum.

Regarding doubts as to the validity of the subspecies, Bosch and Wedde cite K. H. Voous, who indicated in 1957 that the differences between the nominate form and the subspecies are not constant and that there is some overlapping of characteristics between individual specimens studied.

Bosch and Wedde also mention an early breeding effort by Jean Delacour in 1977 that unfortunately ended in the death of the chicks a short time after hatching. However, Rosemary Low reports the 1982 successes of Ramon Noegel in Florida and her own achievement when she prompted the breeding of a previously unsuccessful hen by introducing a new male whose personality appeared to be a better match for the female. The first chick hatched on July 15 and was removed and placed in a brooder when inspection revealed that it had been injured by its parents. By its fourth week, feathers were visible over most of the chick's body. It flew for the first time at seventy-seven days and was fully independent by eleven and a half weeks.

WHITE-FRONTED AMAZON

Amazona albifrons is one of the smallest of the true Amazons. Its conformation is typical of all Amazons, with its stocky body, strong beak, and blunt, broad tail; however, it is only about ten inches long, while most of the other Amazons reach lengths of fourteen to sixteen inches. Its basic color is green, but the combination of red lores, white crown and forehead, and blue hind crown make it a very attractive bird, aptly referred to by the alternative name of Red, White, and Blue Parrot. The White-front is also known as the Spectacled Amazon because of the red mask of feathers around its eyes. This is a potential source of confusion, as *Amazona pretrei* is properly called the Red-spectacled Amazon and using such similar common names for these birds is sure to lead to misunderstanding. The red mask marking in the White-front is less obvious in females and young birds than in mature males. There are two subspecies: *A. a. saltuensis*, which has feathers of a blue-green cast, and *A. a. nana*, which resembles the nominate species except that it is slightly smaller. All three groups generally inhabit Mexico and Guatemala.

In addition to their attractive coloring, White-fronted Amazons can also have a pleasing personality, and most who write about them speak favorably. Young birds can learn to speak, but older imports seem more talented at screeching. I once owned a White-front called Taco, a noisy little bird that did not seem to realize he was smaller than the other Amazons I kept and thought nothing of walking right up to the largest of them for a bit of beak dueling.

Bosch and Wedde report mixed opinions about these birds, but on the whole give them positive ratings. These authors note that females lack the red wing marking found in males, and that it is therefore possible to visually sex adult members of this species.

Werner Lantermann (*The New Parrot Handbook*, 1986) also comments on color difference between the sexes, noting that females lack the red shoulder patches found in males. According to Lantermann, White-fronts are no longer as abundant as in the past and, among those offered for sale, males seem to outnumber the females.

Several references to the breeding of this species appear in the literature, but none is very specific. It is possible that because of their abundance few efforts were made to breed them. Rutgers and Norris report a U.S. breeding in 1949, while David Alderton (*Parrots, Cockatoos and Macaws*, 1982) discusses a pair owned by N. Taka-Tsukasa of Japan that were bred in 1922. Prestwich (*Records of Parrots Bred in Captivity*) also mentions the 1949 breeding and gives credit to Mrs. Gilmer and her associate, Mr. Putman.

Large numbers of all three types of Spectacled Amazon were imported into the United States and their abundance kept their prices quite low. Since they are true Amazons, with all the favored characteristics of the group, they make an excellent choice for those who are anxious to own an Amazon but do not wish to spend a large sum of money. Breeding pairs can also be obtained at nonprohibitive prices, and although attempting to breed these parrots would be a challenge, success is far from impossible.

ST. VINCENT AMAZON

My first opportunity for a close-up view of the rare St. Vincent Amazon (*Amazona guildingii*) took place in 1976 when Alba Ballard invited me to see her newest acquisition. I had previously seen specimens of this large Amazon in photographs and zoos, but nothing is as informative as observing a bird in a private aviary. Alba's St. Vincent appeared to be a youngster, and we estimated his age to be two or three years. He was a good-sized, stocky bird, about fifteen inches long. Although he was a new arrival to the aviary, he was extremely tame, friendly, and confident. In many respects he reminded me of a Double Yellow-head, except that the areas that would have been marked with yellow were, for the most part, replaced with white. Thus, his forehead and crown were white, blending into yellow, blue, and then green feathers from the rear crown to the nape. The rest of his plumage was a yellowish-brown. There is a great deal of color variation among these Amazons.

Bosch and Wedde refer to a yellow-brown as well as to a green type of St. Vincent Amazon, noting that these are variations within the same species. The lores and eye region are white, while the beak is a very light green. According to these authors, the females are slightly smaller in size, but there are no other obvious differences between the sexes.

This parrot is found only on the island of St. Vincent, a small Caribbean island located north of Venezuela, and it is the only parrot on the island. It is also referred to as Guilding's Amazon in honor of Lansdown Guilding, an accomplished naturalist and painter born on the island in 1797.

The St. Vincent Amazon has fascinated all who have had an opportunity to see it. Keith D. Frost, writing in the May/June 1959 issue of the British *Avicultural Magazine*, described some of his experiences with this species. Frost lived in Barbados and had firsthand experience with many parrots, but the St. Vincent Amazon was his favorite. He visited St. Vincent yearly and owned one very large specimen; he was expecting two more at the time he wrote and was hoping to breed them. The price at that time was about $15 per bird. Frost commented that unless something was done to stop the natives, "who destroy them whenever the opportunity arises," the birds would soon be extinct.

Kirby, the first captive-bred St. Vincent's Amazon, was a great triumph for the Houston Zoo. Dr. Robert Berry

The limited population of St. Vincent Amazons suffered a severe blow in the late 1970s when the island's volcano, La Soufriere, erupted. An earlier eruption in 1898 following a severe hurricane may have started the population decline, which now threatens the species with extinction.

When an animal population reaches extremely low numbers, the chances for survival diminish, because not every pair will reproduce and there are always losses, even among those that breed successfully. Captive breeding offers some hope for such groups, but this requires cooperative efforts, such as were made in 1976 when the Brookfield Zoo of Chicago, the Bronx Zoo of New York, the National Zoo of Washington, D.C., and the Houston Zoo pooled their St. Vincent specimens to form a viable breeding group. An excellent article on this venture by Robert J. Berry, then Curator of Birds at Houston, appeared in the November 1976 issue of *Animal Kingdom*. Kirby, a baby St. Vincent

Amazon, resulted from the first captive breeding of the species.

SANTO DOMINGO AMAZON

A few years ago a friend invited me to look at a group of young Santo Domingo Amazons he had just acquired. The birds were delightfully tame and playful and one in particular seemed to like people very much. As I scratched his cheek, which parrots adore almost as much as having the back of their necks scratched, he slyly moved his head until my finger was in his beak and then proceeded to gently taste it. Unfortunately, he was not for sale, or I think I would have taken him home with me.

These small Amazons are less than twelve inches long, but their physical characteristics and behavior are the same as those of their larger Amazon relatives. *Amazona ventralis* is known by a variety of names. It is referred to as the White-headed Amazon, Hispaniolan Amazon, and Salle's Amazon.

These typical Amazons are marked with white on their foreheads and around their eyes (hence the designation *White-headed Amazon*). They are basically green, except that their head and breast feathers have black margins. The back of the head and the upper portion of the cheek are a pale blue, the beak is a light horn color, and the eye is dark brown. The adult has a large red marking in the middle of the abdomen on the lower surface. This ventral marking, which is not found in young birds, may be the origin of the Latin name *ventralis*.

Forshaw (*Parrots of the World,* 1973) indicates that as of 1972, Santo Domingo Amazons were abundant throughout the island of Hispaniola and could also be found on some of the offshore islands as well as in Puerto Rico. He speculates that their introduction to Puerto Rico might have resulted from the release of several hundred Hispaniolan birds to prevent the seizure by authorities as illegal imports. Apparently the birds were released outside the port of Mayagüez and many reached land, where they subsequently thrived.

According to Edward J. Boosey, Salle's Amazon was frequently imported by Europeans. He does not consider it particularly attractive and compares it to the Cuban Amazon, to which he believes it is related. Boosey also mentions that the bird often appeared on the show bench in England.

Sidney Porter, an indefatigable traveler, recounted his visit to Hispaniola in the April 1936 issue of the British *Avicultural Magazine.* In earlier days when the island was covered with vast forests, the Salle's Amazon was present in great numbers in the areas that now comprise the two independent countries, Haiti and the Dominican Republic. In an all-too-common tragedy, as the forest was destroyed the parrots were driven further and further back into the interior. Some were killed for food, and others retained as pets or exported. The birds he saw in Port-au-Prince were kept in small cages made from gasoline cans or, if the parrots were luckier, one wing was clipped and they were permitted the relative freedom of a perch on the patio of a house. The birds owned by natives were perfectly tame, as they had been taken from the nest and hand-reared. Porter could have purchased as many such birds as he wished at that time for about one dollar each.

Dr. Russ provides a detailed description of Salle's Amazon, indicating that it was first described as early as 1760 by Brisson, who mistook it for a female White-fronted Amazon. Russ believes that this bird belongs to a group he calls "Porto Rico Parrots."

Alan F. Gates, of the Parrot Section of the Jersey Wildlife Preservation Trust, examined the first successful captive breeding of this species in the November–December 1971 issue of *Avicultural Magazine.* Gerald Durrell, director of the organization, had brought four young Santo Domingo Amazons back from the West Indies in 1964. In May 1966 they were moved to an outside aviary measuring eight by four by six feet. A thirty-six-by-nine-by-nine-inch nest box was hung in a corner of the aviary farthest from the door. Unfortunately, one of the birds died in November of the same year. Their keepers believed they had been left with one male and two females, and observed copulation between two of the birds in May 1968. At the end of May three eggs were found in the nest, but by June 18 they were determined to be infertile. The unpaired female was removed in 1969, as the two mated birds had became aggressive toward her. Two unproductive seasons followed. In 1971, copulation was observed on March 10 and 31, and by April 20 the female had begun to remain in the nest box. The eggs were checked on April 29 to determine whether they were again infertile and should be removed in the hope of being replaced by a second round. Two of the eggs were indeed infertile, but one was not, so three eggs were left in the nest.

The female sat well during the incubation period with her mate feeding her at regular intervals. On May 15, 1971, Mr. Gates heard the sound of a chick coming from the nest box.

The birds were fed a wide variety of seeds, greens, fruits, and other foods. The female finally left the nest on May 26 and the youngster was seen peeking out of the box for the first time on June 30. The weather became quite warm, and in an effort to cool off, the young parrot often sat in the entrance of the nest box with his head hanging out and his beak open.

He finally left the nest for the first time on July 15. This fine young bird was almost identical to his parents except for a head marking of white, yellow, and green instead of white, blue, and green. The baby also lacked the red abdominal patch found in adults.

VINACEOUS AMAZON

Among the parrots, Hawk-heads and Double Yellow-heads have the ability to form a distinct ruff with the feathers of the rear crown and neck. While it earned the Hawk-head his name, this is a rather rare adaptation in an Amazon, although a similar ability with an analogous function is commonly found in those cockatoos that can erect a crest. *Amazona vinacea* does not quite have the same capability, but as part of its exaggerated display behavior it can raise its neck feathers to the degree that they appear to form a ruff.

The Vinaceous Amazon is a medium-size parrot averaging about fourteen and a half inches in length. Its basic color is dark green; however, the feathers of the crown, mantle, and rear nape are edged in black. This suggests a mournful appearance, but, when combined with the bird's red lores and forehead, burgundy throat and breast, and red beak, the result is a very brightly colored and extremely attractive parrot. Females are similarly marked, but have muted colors, as do immature birds.

Rutgers and Norris advise that the area of distribution for this parrot is southeastern Brazil, Paraguay, and Argentina, where large flocks are common and the birds are favorite pets among local residents despite the great damage they do to orange groves. More recent reports warn that destruction of the forest habitat is a threat to the flourishing parrot communities. This is another example of the many cases where the existence of a species is threatened because of the actions of local land developers rather than bird fanciers.

According to Dr. Russ, this species was known to parrot enthusiasts as early as 1760 but was first described with accuracy by Prince von Neuwied, an avid bird collector, in 1820. Dr. Russ also notes that the German bird collector, Mr. Petermann, reported extensive colonies of this parrot in its native habitat. More recently, Forshaw (*Parrots of the World*, rev. ed. 1973) advises that the local population still maintain the parrot and that it is quite common in southeastern Brazil, where it associates with the Red-spectacled Amazon and the Scaly-headed Parrot.

Rev. Rick Wenneborg's Vinaceous Amazon, aptly named Rainbow, is the subject of an interesting article in the September 1977 issue of *American Cage-Bird Magazine*. She was a charming pet and got along well with a Double Yellow-head that was also part of the Wenneborg collection.

FESTIVE AMAZON

At first glance, this fourteen-inch parrot hardly seems deserving of his joyous name, as the colors one sees in the nesting bird are not unusually bright. *Amazona festiva* has a dark green upper surface and a visibly lighter lower surface. The rump and back are bright red (hence the alternative name "Red-backed Parrot"), but this attractive feature is only visible when the wings are open. A deep red, narrow marking appears on the lores and forehead, the eye is yellow, and the beak is dark brown.

Peters (*Check-List of Birds of the World,* 1937) observes that this parrot was first identified in 1758 and that it originates in eastern Ecuador and eastern Peru. A subspecies, *A. f. bodini*, customarily referred to as Bodin's Amazon, is more yellowish green and has a broader red band on the forehead. It originates in Venezuela and northwestern Guyana.

Rutgers and Norris consider the Festive to be less noisy than most Amazons and a talented mimic that learns to whistle tunes and to speak clearly. These authors note, however, that individual birds vary greatly in their ability and that some may prove to be very bad-tempered and spiteful. These authors also report that the first specimen was seen at the London Zoo in 1865.

Dr. Greene also remarks on the ease with which this species becomes domesticated, going so far as to state that they may be permitted to wander the grounds of a person's home at will, as they will always return to the house for their food. He does warn, however, that they should not be permitted such freedom around trees with ripe fruit because of the damage they can do. Greene also describes a pair of Festives that were said to converse in the human tongue instead of screeching at each other in a manner more characteristic of parrots. Although we may be skeptical, the story is intriguing.

Dr. Russ also enthuses over the speech potential of the Festive Amazon, indicating that earlier authors believed this parrot surpassed even the African Grey as a speaker. He does, however, warn potential owners about some very unpleasant characteristics, claiming that the bird is treacherous and ill-tempered and may even bite while being petted.

C. P. Snow, another early author (*Parrots for Pleasure and Profit*, c. 1900), did not consider the Festive to be a good talker, but speculated that those he had seen were probably imports that were too old to learn readily at the time he obtained them. He believed that a young, hand-reared specimen would make a good talker and pet. This, of course, is true of any parrot that has the capacity to learn to speak.

Jean Delacour kept a Festive Amazon on his estate at Cleres before World War II. The bird had been purchased in South America and was given its liberty to fly freely in 1921. In the March–April 1946 issue of the British *Avicultural Magazine*, which appeared less than a year after the end of World War II, Dr. Delacour informed readers that the Festive was still flying around the property and that if he were a better talker he would no doubt have much to say about the destruction that went on in the area during the war.

Very little breeding information is available on the Festive Amazon. A. A. Prestwich discusses a hybrid breeding involving a Blue-front and comments on a very early record of the subspecies *A. f. bodini*, which was bred in France in 1879. In this particular case, three eggs were laid and one chick hatched. The November–December 1966 issue of *Avicultural Magazine* includes a report of a hybrid cross by W. D. Cummings in 1966 between a Festive and a Jamaican Amazon at the Keston Bird Farm in England.

10

AUSTRALASIAN PARROTS

To the Rosella in the Poinsettia tree
Beautiful Bird . . . your wings as vivid as
a tree, Rosella! Beautiful bird . . . .
　　　　　—James Picot, Birds of Paradox

RINGNECK PARROTS

The Ringnecks are members of the genus *Psittacula*, which includes the Alexandrine Parakeet, Indian Ringneck, African Ringneck, Moustache Parakeet, Plum-headed Parakeet, and Blossom-headed Parakeet, as distinct from a group of Australian birds belonging to the genus *Barnardius*, which are also often referred to as Ringnecks. The Australians include the Mallee Parrot, the Port Lincoln, the Yellow-banded or Twenty-eight (so named for its unusual call), and the Cloncurry. The terms *parrot* and *parakeet* are used almost interchangeably when discussing either group, but I prefer to avoid the Ringneck designation for *Barnardius* birds because of the confusion it can cause.

Ringnecks are typically long and slender with elongated central tail feathers. Some aviculturists refer to them as "the long-tailed parrots," a misleading designation that can be applied equally well to other genera. They are also referred to as parakeets (often with the British spelling "parrakeets").

A Lutino Moustache Parakeet. Gunther Enderle, NEKTON PRODUCTS

97

The genus *Psittacula* is extremely wide-spread and its members can be found over much of Asia and Africa; in fact, the Indian Ringneck, *P. krameri*, is considered to be the most widely distributed of all parrots, occurring in China, India, Tibet, Nepal, Sri Lanka, and Africa. The recorded history of the species dates back to the eighteenth century, and hints and commentary that strongly appear to refer to this bird can be found in even earlier records. According to Sparks and Soper, as Alexander the Great's army returned from India after defeating the Persians, one of his soldiers took some tame parakeets as souvenirs of the campaign. The authors consider this the beginning of the trade in Indian Ringnecks between India and Europe.

The Alexandrine Parakeet (*P. eupatria*), named after Alexander the Great, is a very large Ringneck, reaching lengths of twenty to twenty-two inches, with a wide Asiatic distribution. It is sometimes referred to as the Greater Rose-ringed Parakeet to distinguish it from the considerably smaller Indian and African Ringnecks with which it is occasionally confused. It is considered a better talker than the smaller birds. Because the Alexandrines are prodigious chewers, their flights should be made of heavy wood reinforced with cage wire. Males in this group are green with a blue wash on the cheeks. They have a black marking between the eyes and the nostrils and a wide black neck ring that blends to pink as it moves around the nape of the neck.

The African Ringneck, *P. k. krameri*, is distributed across a wide region of northern Africa. It is fourteen to fifteen inches long, with the tail comprising much of its length, and has a green upper surface and a lighter green underside. The beak is much darker than that of the Indian Ringneck. Facial markings include a black ring running under the chin to the cheeks that blends into the pink collar circling the nape.

The Indian Ringneck is the most popular member of this group, which may be due in part to the fact that it is readily available and moderately priced. Prices for some of the exotic color mutations have been quite high, but now that more birds are being bred, they are dropping to reasonable levels. Although it is taxonomically referred to as *P. k. manillensis*, its country of origin is Sri Lanka.

The Indian Ringneck is a light shade of green that becomes yellowish on the lower surface, with a colorful ring that begins at the throat. The collar markings are more intense than those of the African, and it also has a larger beak, the upper part of which is a very dark red, while the lower beak is black. The eye is also black. Females are smaller and have muted colors. The Indian Ringneck is about two inches larger than the African Ringneck, and most of its extra length is in the tail.

In the October 1990 issue of *American Cage-Bird Magazine*, Linda Greeson shares her experiences with Ringnecks and notes that they make excellent pets. For breeding, she prefers them to cockatiels and budgies.

Color variations in animals occur normally in the wild, where they are generally ignored. Breeders of Ringnecks have been quick to capitalize on these variations, and, as a result, some beautiful strains have evolved. According to Dulcie and Freddie Cooke (*Popular Parakeets*, 1989), the Lutino Ringneck, known for more than 200 years, was so prized that very few found their way out of the country of origin. Apart from the budgerigar, more mutations have been stabilized in the Indian Ringneck than in any other parakeet.

Jaynee Salan, a multi–award-winning breeder from California, has successfully bred eighteen mutations of the Indian Ringneck, including the rare blue variety. The males of this extremely attractive mutation are varying shades of powder blue, most strikingly on the forehead and crown.

In some cases only slight variations in size and markings distinguish one *Psittacula* subspecies from another. David Alderton's *A Birdkeeper's Guide to Parrots* (1989) has excellent photos of nine members of this group that should make it easy for anyone to differentiate them. Included are photos of the rare albino Ringneck and the equally scarce Long-tailed Parakeet, *Psittacula longicauda*.

The Ringnecks are all easy to sex visually at a fairly early age, as only the males develop the actual ring marking; one breeder has described the neck area on the female as looking as though a ring only plans to form there. For the most part, these birds can be considered free breeders, and because of their size and habits, medium-sized flights will keep them happy, healthy, and productive. It is not difficult to obtain domestic young and, occasionally, older birds, and hand-fed chicks bond as readily with their original keepers as with new owners.

Ringnecks are not outstanding talkers, but they can mimic sounds and whistles as well as an occasional word or phrase. In addition, they engage in lively activity in their cages and aviaries, and enjoy displaying their agility to an appreciative audience. Parrot fanciers quickly learn that the ability to speak is only a small part of a Ringneck's charm. Linda Greeson observes that for parakeets they are fairly long lived, averaging twenty to thirty years if properly maintained.

As noted above, historical records on Ringnecks go back as far as the eighteenth century, when P. J. Selby in the parrot volume of *Jardine's Naturalist's Library* referred to them as the "Ring Parakeets of Asia and Africa." He considered them elegant birds and the first and only species of parrots to be known by the ancient Greeks. He is also of the opinion that expeditions by Alexander the Great brought the bird from Ceylon to Europe. Sparks and Soper describe a Greek mosaic dating from the second century B.C. showing what is probably an Alexandrine parrot. They also provide an illustration of a Roman mosaic showing a pair of Ringnecks pulling a small cart.

P. alexandri fasciata, a charming and slightly smaller member of the Ringneck group, is known as the Moustache Parakeet. It is just under fourteen inches long and has a well-developed head and beak. A heavy black band of feathers reaches from eye to eye across the forehead, a marking that appears as early as five weeks of age. The gray head has a wash of pale blue that blends into the bright green nape. The upper beak of the adult male is a bright, coral red while the lower beak is brownish black; females have a dark, slate-colored beak and are relatively muted in color. They are named for the black neck ring that in adult males stretches from the lower beak almost to the ear coverts, giving (at certain angles and if your imagination is vivid) the appearance of an old-fashioned handlebar moustache.

These parrots are distributed throughout India, Nepal, Myanmar, Southern China, and islands off western Sumatra. According to Forshaw (*Parrots of the World*, 1973), they appear in huge flocks above fields of rice and grain.

The Slaty-headed Parakeet takes its name from the bluish-gray coloring of the head feathers. Karen Kelley

The Slaty-headed Parakeet, *P. himalayana*, is another of the commonly kept Ringnecks. Adult birds are about fifteen inches long and show typical green Ringneck coloring. They can be distinguished by their head, which is a smoky bluish gray that becomes much darker at the neck to form a black collar or ring. The upper beak is red with a yellow tip while the lower beak is yellow. Females have a lighter-colored head.

Other members of *Psittacula* that are kept and bred include *P. cyanocephala*, the Plum-headed Parakeet, and *P. roseata*, the Blossom-headed Parakeet.

All these parrots have good potential for breeding, and domestic young and, occasionally, older birds, are easily obtained. If you wish to breed parrots, this is an excellent group with which to begin.

ROSELLAS

The Rosellas are all members of the genus *Platycercus*, a group characterized by four equally long

A young Plum-head male being properly held.

Many Rosella species are justly famed for their brilliant coloring. This Eastern Rosella is a stunning example of these birds' great beauty. Cohen Associates

middle tail feathers and outer tail feathers that become progressively shorter in length. They are also sometimes referred to as the Broadtails. The Australian poet quoted at the beginning of this chapter pays fitting tribute to the beauty of this parrot, inspired by the brilliant coloring that has attracted aviculturists for many years. According to Sparks and Soper, its ornate appearance no doubt contributed to its being the second parrot selected to be painted during Captain Cook's final voyage to Australia in 1777.

The different species of Rosellas can be found throughout the Australian mainland as well as on the island of Tasmania, located off Australia's southeastern coast. Dr. H. D. Groen (*Australian Parakeets,* 5th ed.) locates the majority of the species in the eastern and southern portion of Australia, with the following exceptions: The Stanley Rosella is found exclusively in the west, the Brown Rosellas are restricted to the tropical northern region, and the Green Rosellas of Tasmania are unique to that island.

Dr. Groen observes that all Rosellas exhibit a marked aggressiveness toward other parakeets, especially related species, that becomes more evident as the breeding season progresses. Belligerent behavior brought on by territoriality forces other birds that might otherwise encroach on their area to give them a wide berth, which is particularly important during breeding periods. Sparks and Soper also note the belligerence of this group and their "marked antipathy towards body contact," which is limited between the sexes to fighting and copulation. The authors warn that when breeding

Rosellas, the pairs must be isolated for successful nesting to occur. These are words to the wise for those breeders who may be considering mixed flights or flights of different Rosella species.

Lydekker (*The Royal Natural History,* Vol. IV, 1895) refers to these parrots as "the Broadtail Group" and considers them noisy but well adapted to captivity and active and lively in their habits. He adds that during breeding season, they dance and sing in an amusing manner.

According to Dr. Greene, Rosellas were bred in Europe so often that many people tended to forget their Australian origins and thought of them as European birds. He considered the Rosella a noisy bird, its vanity among its chief attractions; these birds, he noted, were quite conscious of their personal charm, and they never wearied of displaying it. Greene, along with other experts, warns against trusting this group with other related species or with weaker birds.

Charles Barrett (*Parrots of Australasia*, 1949) observes that, with the exception of the budgerigar, no other Australian parrot has become as widely known as the Green Rosella, which is generally referred to as the "Pretty Joey" in its native land. Barrett admired all the Rosellas (which he referred to as "broadtails") and considered them "attractively colored and graceful birds."

The Green Rosella, *Platycercus caledonicus*, is the largest of the eight Rosella species, with males achieving lengths of fourteen to fifteen inches. It has been known and kept in Europe since 1860. Males have a yellow head, golden breast and belly, red cere, and blue cheek patches. Despite this array, they are not considered as colorful as the other species in the group. Females are generally duller in color, with smaller heads and narrower beaks. They are alternatively referred to as Yellow-bellied Rosellas, and, since their normal habitat is Tasmania, Tasmanian Rosellas. Kolar and Spitzer (*Encyclopedia of Parakeets*, 1990) indicate that this species can reproduce as early as the first year and that it was first bred in Europe in 1882. According to Ian Harman (*Birdkeeping In Australia*, 1980), they emerge from the forest areas when fruit crops are ripe, causing extensive damage in orchards. When frightened off by farmers they flee with loud screams that sound like "cossick, cossick, cossick!" Hutchins and Lovell (*Australian Parrots, A Field and Aviary Study*, 1985) have found that parrots inhabiting the mountainous regions are a much duller green, with less evidence of yellow on the breast, than those of the open forests.

The Crimson Rosella, *P. elegans*, is alternatively called the Pennant Rosella, and is often simply referred to as the "Pennant." Its head and body are a bright crimson color with blue cheek patches. The black feathers of the upper back have red margins, a coloration that gives the illusion of large, reptilian scales, which is typical of this genus. They are capable of breeding by about two years of age.

The Adelaide Rosella, *P. adelaidae*, exhibits great variations in color, ranging from birds that are almost as red as the Crimsons to others that bear a great resemblance to the Yellows. Most commonly their markings are light orange, with blue cheek patches, tail, and wing margins. Some authorities have reservations about according separate species status to this group, while others consider it a developmental stage between the Yellow and Crimson Rosellas, and still others see these birds as hybrids resulting from regular crossbreeding between Crimson and Yellow birds in the same range. According to Mark Schmidt, in the December 1992 issue of *Australian Aviculture*, the Adelaide and Yellow Rosellas have been most recently classified as subspecies of the Crimson Rosella.

The striking bird shown here is the Crimson Rosella. Cohen Associates

The Yellow Rosella, *P. flaveolus*, is marked with bright yellow on its head, breast, abdomen, and lower back, and orange on the upper breast. In Australia it is sometimes referred to as the "Murray Smoker" after the river region it frequents. Its range is generally in the South.

The Pale-headed Rosella, *P. adscitus*, is smaller than most other Rosella species. Its head is yellowish white with a white cheek patch bordered with blue feathers. The dark blue feathers around the eyes resemble bruises on the white feathers of the cheek patch. These parrots are frequently referred to as Mealy Rosellas in their native land.

The Northern Rosella, *P. venustus*, is even smaller than the Pale-headed species. Its common name is Brown's Rosella, but it is also called the Smutty Rosella, a reference to its color rather than its character. It is among the less familiar Rosellas and is not commonly kept. The head is jet black with white cheek patches that have a blue border at the lower edge. The range of this bird includes northwestern Australia and the Northern Territory, as well as several islands off the northern coast.

The Western Rosella, *P. icterotis*, is usually referred to as the Stanley Rosella in Europe and in Australia. Its range is in western Australia, mainly the southwest. The Stanley is scarlet on the head, breast, and abdomen, and the cheek patches are yellow. Dr. Groen believes these parrots are popular because they are attractive and more affectionate than other species of Rosellas.

The Eastern Rosella, *P. eximius*, was at one time called the Rosehill Parrot after the area where it was first discovered. It is found in the eastern part of Australia, as well as on the island of Tasmania. The head, breast, and vent region are red, the upper abdomen is yellow, the lower abdomen and back are light green, and it has white cheek patches. Three subspecies are recognized.

In a fascinating article on the language of the Eastern Rosella published by the University of New England, in New South Wales, Professor J. LeGay Brereton indicates that most heterosexual animals communicate with each other in such a way that the behavior of the male and female is coordinated with the goal of having the sperm produced at the right time and in the right place to fertilize eggs. This is vital where fertilization is internal and the male and female must be in direct physical contact with each other. Professor Brereton notes that in some species bodily contact occurs even in the nonbreeding season, but that, generally, bodily contact is limited to copulation and rearing young. He further remarks that in those species that have a high level of coordination a more complex signaling system is required.

The Eastern Rosella communicates by visual and vocal means, and many of the signals involve a combination of visual and vocal activity. Professor Brereton catalogued the various calls of the Eastern Rosella, collecting some on tape using microphones augmented by parabolic reflectors. Of the twenty-four calls, only thirteen appeared to have any recognizable function; most of the others seemed to be corrupted versions of meaningful calls. The significant calls fell into three major categories: warning and distress calls, aggression calls, and location and intention calls. The last of these appears to correlate well with breeding seasons and activity, and may well serve as communication to facilitate breeding preparations in this species.

Charles Barrett observes that all of the broadtails (as he call the genus) are "attractively colored, graceful birds." He describes the Green Rosellas at Adventure Bay in Tasmania and reminds us that one of Captain Cook's party shot a specimen that was later painted by the artist William Ellis, who accompanied the explorers. These birds nest in tree hollows and generally choose the tallest nest site they can find. There are six to eight eggs on the average clutch and an incubation time of about twenty-one days. The chicks remain in the nest for another thirty-six days. At this time there is limited breeding stock available but by making your interest known to likely sources you may be able to locate adults or young.

There is a marked geographical partiality regarding the types of parrots maintained and bred in different parts of the United States. Macaws, Amazons, and African Greys can be found in great numbers throughout the eastern and southern states, while Australian parrots, such as the grass parakeets, are extremely popular in California and other western states, despite the fact that birds have not been imported from Australia for many years. Perhaps it is merely the result of an early pattern that, once set in, will take a long time to change. Easterners and others who may have neglected the Rosellas and other Australians are missing opportunities to work with birds that are colorful, friendly, clever, and in many cases free breeding.

KING PARROTS

This richly colored, eye-catching group of parrots, aptly named given their royal feathering, can be found on the islands of Amboina and Ceram in the Moluccas, as well as in Indonesia and Australia. *Alisterus chloropterus moszkowskii*, commonly known as the Green-winged King Parrot, was named, according to A. A. Prestwich (*I Name This*

Parrot, 1962) by the well-known aviculturist Professor Reichenow for Dr. Moskowski, a German physician and bird collector who traveled widely in Ceylon (now Sri Lanka) and Sumatra at the turn of the century.

The King Parrots are large birds that reach lengths of fifteen to sixteen inches. The colors of the various subspecies vary but generally include red, blue, black, and green. The Green-winged King is bright red on the head, neck, and breast, with a lush, deep blue area on the upper mantle that continues to the nape of the neck. The rump and tail are also blue. Dark green wings with a bright red upper beak complete this King's color scheme. Females are not as vividly colored; the head, neck, and mantle are green while the upper breast is a dull red.

Early writers such as Dr. Greene thought quite highly of this group of birds. Greene notes that at one time the Kings were called King Lories; an examination of the texture and color of their feathers accounts for this misnomer. Greene refers to the female of the species as the Queen Parrot, a term not commonly used. He describes the early breeding of a pair of Kings in England but unfortunately fails to give the date or any other specific information. He considers Kings to be gentle and attractive parrots but bemoans the fact that unscrupulous dealers would keep immature birds, which like the female have relatively muted coloring, in very warm rooms, to force a premature molt and hasten the appearance of their more attractive adult feathers.

E. J. Boosey, who also kept this species, admired their magnificent color and impressive size. His birds reared their young using a grandfather clock–type nest box in an aviary that was twenty feet long; originally, the female insisted on laying her eggs on the floor of the flight but eventually cooperated. Boosey described their call as a rather harsh "crallack . . . crallack!" He cautions breeders to keep a close watch on the male, as some are quite aggressive and may hurt or even kill the female.

These birds are a cross between the King Parrot and the Red-wing Parrot. John Gould painted a picture of such hybrids.
Bernard Olier

Nevill W. Cayley (*What Bird Is That?*, 1948) refers to the Kings by their common name, Red-capped Parrot. He describes those of southern Australia and reports having pairs and small flocks. In the wild these birds feed on seeding grasses, but will also make themselves at home in a farmer's orchards.

Dr. Groen (*Australian Parrakeets*, c. 1960) considers this magnificent bird the "King of the Parrots." He recommends very long flights, preferably thirty feet or longer. Under these circumstances the Kings will engage in rapid, graceful flight, while in shorter flights they appear clumsy and sluggish. He has bred these birds in the cold climate of his native Holland, where they acclimate well and become quite hardy.

A. A. Prestwich contributed a fine article on the Green-winged King Parrot to the September/October 1956 issue of the *Avicultural Magazine*. The accompanying photograph shows a pair of these birds in the wild, with color differences between male and female clearly visible. In the article, Prestwich traces the flow of information about the Green-winged King from 1878, when a report was made by E. P. Ramsay, curator of the Australian Museum at Sydney, describing the newly identified species. By 1909 specimens were to appear in many locations. Alfred Ezra (an early president of the British Avicultural Society) obtained a pair that produced young in 1945, 1951, 1953, 1954, and 1955. All chicks and the parents were doing well at the time of the 1956 article and presumably continued to produce young for many years. Other successful breedings occurred as well.

The Green-winged and Amboina Kings, and others of this group, are available from breeders. This is a good species to consider for breeding; the birds are clever and attractive and are known to reproduce in captivity. Prices are moderate and sales of the young should quickly return your investment.

GRASS PARAKEETS

All the birds in this extremely popular group are members of the genus *Neophema*. These parrots are often bred and maintained in Europe and less frequently in the western United States. They are also kept and bred in other parts of this country, and as importation of the larger South American, Pacific,

and Asiatic parrots comes to an end, these attractive birds will no doubt become even more popular.

Dr. Greene, the dean of avicultural authors, tended to be somewhat opinionated, but he did not exaggerate when he described the Turquoisine, *Neophema pulchella*, as "without exception, one of the most charming members of the parrot family." He goes on to note that it combines the qualities of beauty, hardiness, docility, and amiability in one small package. These truly are high marks for a parrot, and we should add that most of the genus are free breeders that do very well for their owners in moderately sized aviaries. If you have enough space for an eight-by-three-by-six-foot setup, you can probably breed these birds. They are also fairly quiet, an important consideration if you, other members of your family, or the neighbors object to loud screeching.

A pair of Turquoisine Parakeets. The hen is shown at the left. Michael DeFreitas

Neophema pulchella is commonly referred to as the Turquoisine. Normal males are generally dark green with a sky-blue marking on the forehead that extends around the eye. One that we observed was yellow where the body is typically green, with the turquoise markings on the head and wings a lighter blue than in normal specimens, and the red wing bar almost completely gone. Female Turquoisines, in both the normal and mutated varieties, have duller coloring overall. Turquoisines seldom exceed eight inches in length.

Another popular member of this group is Bourke's Parakeet, or *Neophema bourkii*. It is easy to breed, and most who keep it consider it a gentle and pleasant bird. This brown, pink, and gray species may not be as brilliantly colored as some of the other grass parakeets, but it is worth considering for those who are interested in breeding something larger than a budgie or a cockatiel.

Neophema splendida, or the Splendid, is not as easily obtainable as some of the other grass parakeets. The way its brilliant, shiny blue plumage catches the light sets the bird off magnificently from its surroundings, and other markings of red, yellow, and green make this a bird truly deserving of its name. In females, the red marking is replaced with green, and the other colors are muted.

A rose-colored male Bourke's Parakeet. Terry Dunham

The Elegant Grass Parakeet, *Neophema elegans*, is another highly attractive member of this group. Its underparts and crown are a bright olive green that blends to a yellow on the face, and the frontal band is two shades of rich blue.

If you are thinking of keeping or breeding grass parakeets, you should have little difficulty getting started. Although not as colorful as some of the other members of the genus, Bourke's Parakeets are a good way to start and are quite reasonable priced.

Mutations are generally much more expensive. As a rule, you should be able to locate sources of Bourke's and Turquoisines fairly easily, while Elegants and Splendids will require a little more research. Your best chance for success would be to find breeders in your area or, if this a problem, to check the classified ads in various bird magazines. You might also advertise in the classifieds or in a local club bulletin.

THE RED-RUMPED PARAKEET

In Australia, the Red-rumped Parakeet is one of the most popular aviary birds. It is an excellent choice for those who wish to keep and breed a more challenging bird than the cockatiel.

Psephotus haematonotus is a fine choice for any beginner. These parrots are readily available and inexpensive, and can be easily sexed by differences in their color and markings. They are also considered free breeders, which means that a properly set-up pair will breed for you if you give them the basics that they need in the way of flight, nest box, and food, and they are comparatively quiet.

Red-rumps are about ten inches in length, a good portion of which consists of the long, tapering tail. The male is green, with a bluish green back and wings, yellow abdomen, white vent and under-tail coverts, and, obviously, a red rump. The female has an olive-green head and upper region, while her neck and breast are a dull yellow. She lacks the male's yellow markings on the abdomen but has the white vent and under-tail coverts. Females do not have the red rump.

These appealing parakeets from southeastern Australia were originally found in the area of New South Wales. They are sometimes referred to as Red-backed Parrots, and their name translates from Latin and several other languages to "bloodback." Despite this gory appellation, the bird has an excellent reputation in the aviary and is such a good parent that the female Red-rump is often used to incubate the eggs from recalcitrant hens of other species.

Marie Olssen, in her illustrated book *Hookbills I Have Known* (1975), cautions that while they are good breeders, the males often neglect to feed their mates during the incubation period, sometimes even preventing the females from coming out of the nest to eat, drink, and evacuate. She describes

The Bourke's is the least vividly colored of the Grass Parakeets. Robert Pearcy

Note the red margins on the feathers of these Crimson or Pennant's Rosellas. Michael DeFreitas

having lost three hens this way just as their eggs were ready to hatch. Ms. Olssen recommends keeping seeds in the nest box in case a pair includes such a bird.

Rutgers and Norris consider this bird to be abundant throughout its extensive range and familiar around farms, homesteads, parks, and gardens, where it is frequently observed in small flocks. They agree that it is an ideal species for the beginner, as it is hardy, breeds freely, is easy to manage, and has a pleasing, trill-like, melodious call. They warn, however, that it is extremely pugnacious and should not be trusted with other species or even other pairs of Red-rumps.

Joseph M. Forshaw wrote an outstanding series of articles on the parrots of Australia that was published in the early 1960s in the *Avicultural Magazine*. His discussion of the Red-rump Parakeet appeared in the November–December 1962 issue of that prestigious journal. It is clear that the series served as the basis for sections of his later books.

Forshaw offers an excellent example of the highly developed community behavior of these birds: When a hawk was spotted coming within a few hundred feet of a flock of Red-rumps waiting to drink at a nearby dam, the birds left their tree and surrounded the intruder, while screeching constantly. This warlike approach unnerved the hawk, which then fled. Forshaw also notes that it was John Gould who presented the Zoological Society of London with the first identified Red-rumped Parrot on September 26, 1837.

Neville W. Cayley (*Australian Parrots*, 1938) characterized John Gould's 1837 notes on this bird as perhaps the most comprehensive yet recorded about the species. Gould wrote, "I have often seen hundreds perched together on some leafless limb of a Eucalyptus, sitting in close order along the whole length until hunger prompted them to descend to the feeding ground, or the approach of a hawk caused them to disperse."

Cayley stresses that the Red-rump is unsuited to life in a small cage but does quite well in a flight or aviary, with two or more broods a season not uncommon. He observes that in his area the bird was widely referred to as the Grass Parrot, probably due to its habit of feeding on the ground. Since there is a similar name, Grass Parakeet, for members of the *Neophema* genus, I advise against this usage.

Charles Barrett also speaks highly of the "Grassies," as he calls them. Motorists driving along the road could be sure to flush them out every few hundred yards with bright flashes of green and red revealing their identity as they flew away. Barrett provides an interesting photo of a Red-rump female enlarging the opening to her nest in a hollow tree.

N. D. Cooper, the first editor of *The Magazine of the Parrot Society*, offered some interesting insights on breeding in the March 1973 issue of that publication. He recommends a nine-inch-square nest box that is eighteen inches high, and suggests filling it with four to six inches of peat to nestle the eggs safely. Cooper also makes reference to the extremely attractive yellow and blue mutations of the Red-rump.

Consider these parrots if you would like to become involved in breeding, as the lessons you learn in working with them will prove invaluable when you move on to more difficult species.

COCKATOOS

For thirty years he talked in feathered pride
For thirty years he talked before he died
You say that parrots do not really know
The meaning of the words they use? Just so,
I grant you that you may be right—but then
do men?
—Theodore Stephanides,"Epitaph for a Parrot,"
from Parrots, *edited by Amoret Scott, 1982*

After several years, most parrot fanciers decide on a favorite among the psittacines. Their choices are generally based on striking color combinations, outstanding capacity for speech, or clever behavior. Since 1969 I have owned many Amazons, African Greys, macaws, and other parrots. The family that has always fascinated me most, however, is the cockatoo. My attraction is largely due to this group's ability to show interest in and affection for the people with whom they live. I realize that the behavior of animals, even within a given species, will vary, but I have known very few mean or unintelligent cockatoos.

THE GREATER SULPHUR-CRESTED COCKATOO

They are primarily white birds and their speech is usually limited, but Greater Sulphur-crested Cockatoos are outstanding as interesting, affectionate, and intelligent pets. Their pleasing personalities are augmented by great dexterity and acrobatic skills. These qualities, combined with an almost manic need to command the full attention of owners and visitors, result in wonderful displays of

A beautiful pair of Citron-crested Cockatoos. Michael DeFreitas upside-down swinging and whirling. Best of all, these cockatoos are never shy: Many an African Grey or Amazon has embarrassed its owner and disappointed guests by sitting silently and rigidly after being praised to the skies as a paragon of speech and amusement. This never happens with the Greater, which is sometimes outgoing to the point of obnoxiousness.

If you own or visit with one of these birds for any length of time, you will become aware of what appears almost certainly to be an ability to reason; how else can you explain the behavior of a parrot who screams "no biting!" when another bird makes a rapid strike at someone's finger? Unfortunately, this same parrot might scream the identical phrase if a seed dish or canister cover is accidentally dropped in the bird room. The explanation is that the parrot associates this phrase with any form of disruption and equates attempts to bite with noisy accidents.

If you are deciding on a parrot and you want a lifelong companion to share your days and moods, you cannot make a better choice than the Greater.

The Greater, or *Cacatua galerita galerita*, is about twenty inches long. Most of this length is the actual body of the bird, as it has a short, neat tail that seems almost stubby when compared to those of macaws and Amazons. It has a well-muscled breast that, combined with an impressive wingspread, makes it a powerful flyer. The body is a clean white color, except for a yellow marking on the cheeks and ear coverts that looks like a slightly misplaced yellow blush; there is also a light yellow wash on the throat and the undersurface of the wings and tail. The large, feathery yellow crest curves forward, and when erected because of excitement or anger, affords its owner a rather startled look. The beak is black and the eye is a very dark brown in males and reddish brown in females. The term *true Greater* refers to the nominate race that, unlike the subspecies described elsewhere in this chapter, have a blue eye ring. Eye color can be helpful in sexing, but other tests are recommended if you plan to set up pairs for breeding. The best of these and the least invasive is gene examination, which is foolproof when done by an expert.

Tutu, a Greater Sulphur-crested Cockatoo, with the author.

Offspring of true Greaters command a higher price than those of the various subspecies because they originate only in Australia. There are relatively few breeding pairs and singles available, as Australia ceased exports of birds almost thirty years ago. As far as actual differences in beauty or cleverness are concerned, the subspecies are the equals of the nominate race, and if they are more easily available or can be purchased at significantly lower prices, you should not hesitate to acquire them—the only real reason for the higher prices commanded by the nominate race is their relative scarcity.

Cockatoos achieved great levels of popularity when the 1970s television show *Baretta* featured a tough-talking detective who melted with love when he came home at night to his Greater, which reciprocated with visible displays of affection. The series is long gone, but many people still think of "Baretta birds" when someone mentions cockatoos.

Baretta's cockatoo was one of the subspecies that include *C. g. fitzroy*, which is slightly smaller than the *C. g. galerita* and has a faint blue eye ring. Fitzroy, named for the Fitzroy River in northwestern Australia, also has smaller yellow markings and a broader beak.

C. g. triton is even smaller than Fitzroy and has a clearly marked blue eye ring. The Triton is named for the Triton Bay region of southwest New Guinea of which it is a native. In the mid- to late 1980s, most of the Greaters sold in the United States were imported from this source. *C. g. eleonora*, another subspecies, is from Indonesia, and has also been a popular import. Although it is the smallest of the subspecies, it is still larger than all of the specimens of Lesser Cockatoos measured and described by Forshaw (*Parrots of the World*, 2d rev. ed., 1978), which may indicate that the so-called mediums are actually smaller versions of Eleonora. This subspecies has a blue eye ring similar to that of Fitzroy, but a smaller beak. Eleonora is found only on the Aru Islands of Indonesia. Some ornithologists doubt that it is actually a valid subspecies.

As has been mentioned earlier, parrots have always been thought of as long-lived creatures, but the desire to own the biggest, oldest, or strongest of anything can lead to exaggeration. Smaller parrots such as conures can live as long as fifteen to twenty years under ideal conditions. Amazons and macaws can do even better: If properly fed and provided with a reasonable amount of exercise they can reach ages of thirty to forty years or more. Cockatoos are also known for very long lives, with many reaching ages of fifty or sixty years. As suggested above, discussions of cockatoo longevity sometimes get out of hand. Edward Boosey (who should have known better) writes of a Greater who supposedly lived to be 138 years old, overlooking the obvious explanation that the lives of more than one cockatoo had been linked together. Another purported Methuselah discussed in an earlier chapter was Cocky Bennett of the Sea Breeze Hotel in Tom Ugly's Point near Sydney, which was credited with having reached 120 years. Unlike most of the geriatric parrots you read about, Cocky's history was fairly detailed. He presumably started life aboard a sailing ship as the pet of a boy apprentice. I have serious doubts, however, that this was the same Greater who lived for twenty-five years with the proprietor of the hotel, who claimed that Cocky was about eighty-five years old when she obtained him. The only records we can ever be really sure of are those for a bird such as King Tut (a Moluccan Cockatoo), whose long history at the San Diego Zoo has been carefully documented from his arrival to the present. Tutu, my own true Greater, was purchased at four months of age in 1973, so I can vouch for her more than twenty years of fun and mischief.

All subspecies of Greaters have been bred in the United States, and I would rank them as good prospective breeders. A long flight and appropriate nest boxes are vital and, of course, you must have a mature pair to succeed. In recent years, aviculturists have learned more about the breeding habits of parrots and now know that the male cockatoo has a nasty habit of jumping into the nest box to attack the female. Carefully designed nest boxes in the shapes of *T*s and *Z*s give the female a chance to escape an abusive mate and also help to avoid destruction of the eggs when the parents are scurrying about. The birds are considered mature at about five or six years of age, and it is suggested that if possible you choose a female that is a year or two older than the male, as young females tend to destroy eggs or may fail to incubate them.

If you hope to breed any of these cockatoos, adequate space for the flight and distance from your neighbors are a must, as these birds scream very loudly several times a day. This is purely high spirits on their part, but others in the vicinity may resent having to share in these moments of good feeling.

GREATERS, TRITONS, AND MEDIUMS

Until the mid-1970s, if you were fortunate enough to own a Greater Sulphur-crested Cockatoo, there was generally no problem in identifying the subspecies. Australian laws restricting exportation meant that only a relatively small number of these birds could be kept in private collections, and most of these were either true Greater Sulphur-crested Cockatoos from Australia or descendants of these imports. After Australia stopped exporting birds, all Greaters imported into the United States came from Indonesia. When the United States permitted the opening of quarantine stations in 1973, importation of the various subspecies of cockatoos from Papua/New Guinea began in great numbers. This flood of cockatoos, coupled with ignorance of the subspecies on the part of many importers and breeders, caused confusion about the identity of these cockatoos. Hybridization of the subspecies, which resulted in a blending of characteristics, was an additional source of difficulty, and, to further complicate the problem, many importers, sellers, and buyers of birds were not fully aware of the distinctions between the nominate race and the subspecies.

Around 1975, classified ads began calling for cockatoos known as "mediums," presumed to be Medium-sized Sulphur-crested Cockatoos. No such subspecies exists; these mediums were either large Lesser Sulphur-crested Cockatoos, which is a totally different species, or possibly members of the smaller subspecies Eleonora. Fortunately, this dubious terminology is no longer being used.

As noted earlier, the original habitat of this parrot is Australia, where it is widely distributed throughout the southern, eastern, and northern portions of the continent. It is still found in large numbers despite its constant battles with farmers, who despise its tendency, typical of parrots, to select a particularly lush fruit or vegetable and then drop its booty for one that appears even better. This antagonism has resulted in laws that permit drastic and ugly attacks on Greaters and other cockatoos: the farmers can now express their wrath toward the feathered looters by trapping, shooting,

poisoning, and worse. Pleas to ameliorate the problem by exporting cockatoos go unheeded, even though exports would reduce their numbers while supplying income and meeting the demand for these beauties in other parts of the world.

The three main subspecies are very attractive and talented birds. Due to a lack of information it is not unusual for people to refer to cockatoos from any of these subspecies as Tritons, but, of course, this is inaccurate; as is clear from the descriptions above, there are obvious differences between them.

If you must have *C. galerita galerita* (which will be the offspring of an Australian bird), be aware that it generally sells for about one-third more than birds bred from parents that came from Indonesia. This price differential is based on supply and demand and the fact that there are more domestic Tritons available than Australian progeny. As far as cleverness and beauty, however, I find no difference between them.

A few years ago, I kept a young Triton with my own birds for about a month prior to shipping her. The bird, which had been raised locally, was unusually tame and loving. She became fast friends with my *C. galerita galerita*, Tutu, who reverted to all of her silly, childhood ways in the presence of this baby. When it came time to ship the Triton off to her new owners, Tutu seemed to miss her for many days after she left.

Tutu, a domestically born Greater Sulphur-crested Cockatoo, was purchased locally when she was less than four months old. Even though she had been weaned, my wife and I encouraged her to eat various types of baby food that we spoon fed. We hoped by doing this to create a strong bond between us, and there is no question that we succeeded in doing so; Tutu is now more than twenty years old and is one of the tamest, most clever, and most delightful parrots I have ever owned. Her speech is limited to a few phrases, but her wonderful personality and acrobatic displays more than make up for this. She is fully aware of how charming her behavior is when she pretends to peck at my hand with vastly exaggerated head movements or calls to me while hanging upside down from the top of her cage.

Consider the following information if you are preparing to select a cockatoo as a companion. Thousands of these birds have entered the United States between 1973 and 1989, resulting in a fairly large and varied breeding pool. This means that domestic baby cockatoos are easily obtainable. If possible, choose a hand-fed bird, as invariably they are very tame; there is quite a difference between a domestic chick fed by its parents and one taken at an early age to be fed by its breeder. The descriptions below include only those cockatoos available for purchase.

Lesser Sulphur-crested Cockatoo

Lessers are smaller versions of the Greater Sulphur-crested, and for many people who want to own a cockatoo, they are an excellent compromise when space and finances are considerations. Lessers look and act very much like their larger counterparts; in fact, some people confuse the larger varieties of the Lesser with the smaller subspecies of Greater. This can be avoided by comparison of their beaks and crests: in the Lessers the beak is shorter but broader and the crest is thicker. Body coloring is quite similar to that of the Greaters in that they have the yellow crest and

yellow under-tail feathers. The Citron-crested Cockatoo, an attractive subspecies, is larger and has more orange in the markings. The various subspecies of Lessers range from twelve to fourteen inches in length.

Moluccan Cockatoo

Moluccans, or Salmon-crested Cockatoos, originate in the southern Moluccas, formerly known as the Spice Islands. These islands, which are part of Indonesia, contain dense forests and luxurious vegetation. Since Indonesia was a Dutch colony until after World War II, these cockatoos were and still are quite popular in the Netherlands as well as the rest of Europe.

Karl Diefenbach (*The World of Cockatoos*, 1985) discusses the variation in size and coloration among these birds, speculating that, because these variations are so great, at some time in the future the differently colored groups of Moluccans may be treated as distinct geographical races. He also points out that where intense coloring is part of a Moluccan's heritage, even young birds will have the

The broad beak helps identify the Lesser Sulphur-crested Cockatoo. Doreen Gluck

The Moluccan Cockatoo, with its backswept crest and beautiful salmon coloring, is considered by many to be the most beautiful of this large, intriguing family of parrots. Robert Pearcy

characteristic deep salmon color. Moluccans differ from some of the other white cockatoos in that it is not possible to make any determination of sex based on eye color. (In the Umbrella Cockatoo, for example, the eye of the female is reddish brown while that of a male is very dark brown, appearing almost black.)

Moluccans are large and highly vocal birds that are great favorites with parrot fanciers to whom noise does not pose a problem. When Moluccans decide to scream, they can produce loud, hooting noises that may remind you of the warning sounded by a train entering a station. Although they are not consistently noisy, you can count on such loudness in their moments of vexation, happiness, hunger, loneliness, or just a general desire to let you know they are there. I particularly enjoy watching them when they accompany their hooting with impatient stamping of one foot, an unusual activity that is also part of their display behavior.

Moluccans are attractively colored. Their large crest has white outer feathers and deep pink inner feathers. The basic white plumage can have various shades of pink, and birds with deeper colors are the most prized. Breeders who advertise their birds for sale often emphasize this deep rose-pink color.

These large cockatoos grow to a length of nineteen or twenty inches, which, combined with their large beaks and crests, gives them a rather formidable appearance. In spite of this they are generally gentle birds. Domestic specimens are a pleasure to work with, and imports tame well if properly treated.

Rosie, an elegant Moluccan hen, was one of the jewels of the author's collection for many years.

Rosie, my first Moluccan Cockatoo, was a large, nicely colored imported female. I was contacted by her owner, who had to sell her because he was moving from his parent's house to a city apartment. At this point I had fourteen large parrots and the thought of another beak to feed was not enticing, but I can never resist the possibility of obtaining a really spectacular parrot and Rosie's owner raved about her. When I entered the living room where Rosie was kept, I was struck both by her beauty and her composed manner. Ordinarily, tame parrots will react to visitors by showing off much as children do, while a frightened bird will retreat to a corner of the cage and make threatening noises. Rosie merely breathed heavily and stared at me with a solemn expression, as if to say, "What kind of new problem is this?"

For me it was love at first sight, but Rosie was rather standoffish, no doubt nervous about this stranger who was taking her to a new home. On the way, I had her traveling cage on the front seat of my car and talked to her throughout the trip. Her only response was to give me sidelong glances and to engage in what I thought was heavy wheezing. I was quite concerned about this until I discovered that it was actually just heavy breathing, and that because her upper and lower mandibles were slightly parted, the movement produced a whistling sound. I was later to learn that this is typical agitated behavior in Moluccans and other cockatoos.

Her entry into my bird room was met with loud screams followed by mutterings, as if the group wanted to know who this intruder was. Matters improved rapidly, however, and Rosie (what other name can one give to a delicately salmon-tinted Moluccan?) became a happy member of the group.

King Tut dreaming of the good old days.

Several years after Rosie's arrival I became the owner of Fred, a male Moluccan who was even larger than Rosie but lacked her deep pink coloring. Fred arrived by plane on Thanksgiving Day, and because our entire family was gathered for the holiday feast, a friend went to the airport to pick him up for me. Once Fred was in the bird room, I decided to open one end of the large shipping crate in which he had traveled and placed it against the opening to his new flight. I then planned to rejoin my family and let Fred make his way into the flight without any threatening attention from me. My intentions were good, but I could not resist slipping away from the dinner several times to see how he was doing. Moving from the crate to the flight posed no problem, and Fred immediately went to the highest perch in the farthest corner. This behavior turned out to be prophetic, as Fred never did become tame for me. He was afraid of men (apparently his former owner's husband had been unkind to him), and although he would eventually permit me to touch his feet and feed him tidbits, he was never at ease with me. A local schoolteacher who loves parrots became his eventual owner, and she has worked wonders with this timid bird.

The behavior of my Moluccans are quite subdued compared to that of Pretty Cocky, a Moluccan owned by one of Dr. Greene's readers. Although quite gentle with children, women, and most male adults, this parrot became violent when workmen were in or near his room. He would fly at them, and after terrifying or even hurting one of the workers, he would fly away shrieking in simulated agony or pain as if he himself had been the victim of attack.

At first glance, Moluccans may be mistaken for Umbrella Cockatoos, but upon closer examination you can easily see that Umbrellas are slightly smaller and have a somewhat squat appearance. They are white with just a splash of yellow on the underside of the tail and flight feathers. They have a light blue eye ring, whereas the eye ring in the Moluccan is white with just a faint blue tinge.

No discussions of Moluccans would be complete without mentioning King Tut, a huge male presented to the San Diego Zoo in 1925. He was the Zoo's official greeter and oldest resident until he died of old age in 1991. Each morning he was carried from the bird house to his daytime perch near the flamingos' enclosure, where he would whistle, sing, dance, and nap while dreaming of past triumphs.

The Umbrella Cockatoo has a unique, broad-feathered crest. Robert Pearcy

Umbrella Cockatoo

The Umbrellas are large birds from the Philippines, New Guinea, and a series of islands in the Pacific, and they can reach lengths of eighteen to nineteen inches. They are sometimes called Great White Cockatoos, a reference to the crisp, snow-white plumage that covers the entire body, except for a wash of yellow on the tail and flight feathers. Their behavior is very similar to that of the Greaters in that they love highly exaggerated body and head movements, and their look of surprise when they raise their crests is delightful. If no one is observing them when they want attention, a loud scream will generally remedy this lack of respect. Unfortunately, these screams are an integral part of the birds' behavior and must be expected at intervals during the day, so if noise is a problem, this may not be the parrot for you.

In general, these birds engage in behavior that shows intelligence and a fondness for and desire to associate with people. This is true not only of domestically raised birds but also, as many soldiers discovered during World War II, of cockatoos just out of the jungle, which showed an interest in the soldiers and their activities and became unusual pets, although unfortunately they could never be brought home.

Cacatua alba has a pale blue eye ring surrounding an eye that is black in adult males and brownish in females and young birds. Mature females have a reddish brown iris. The crest is quite broad and, when erected, resembles a white Native American headdress. Do not confuse the Umbrella with the Moluccan Cockatoo, a larger bird with a salmon-colored crest.

Umbrellas require a good-sized, stoutly built cage or flight and should be given frequent opportunities for exercise outside the cage. However, they will probably also exercise their vocal cords, and, since they are capable of loud screams, apartment dwellers may want to think twice before purchasing them. If you have the opportunity to see or play with a tame Umbrella, however, you may decide to ignore the potential for noise and give in to the temptation to buy one.

Karl Diefenbach describes the great strength of a Moluccan he kept: After losing its early shyness, it dismantled a large cage by cracking the welds of the bars. When let out of its cage at night, it was friendly to all visitors but immediately sought out its owner for special attention.

David Alderton (*Parrots, Lories, and Cockatoos*, 1982) advises that they are hand-reared as pets in their native land, but older birds may pluck themselves if caged. He characterizes these birds as "wondrous," a fairly accurate description for the movements of most of the large white cockatoos.

Wolfgang deGrahl (*The Parrot Family*, 1984) interestingly categorizes the Umbrella as one of the "Black and White Beaked Cockatoos." He invented this designation for the Umbrella, the Moluccan, the Greater, and the Lesser to distinguish them from the White-beaked Cockatoos, a group that includes the Rose-breasted, the Red-vented, and the Leadbeater's. DeGrahl confirms the popularity of the Umbrella among the natives of its countries of origin and is convinced that no other parrot is as social and affectionate as this cockatoo, an assessment with which I would heartily agree.

Umbrellas have been successfully bred on many occasions. An excellent article on such a breeding appeared in the January 1977 issue of the *Magazine of the Parrot Society*. Ray and Zena Wallwork were the owners, maintaining their pair in an aviary made from a third-floor bedroom in the upper story of their home. The Wallworks provided a flight that was six feet high, eight feet long, and four feet wide. Two other families of parrots (lories and African Greys) occupied flights on either side of the Umbrellas, but this did not cause any disturbance among the birds. Double wiring was used, however, to prevent any toe nipping. Mating occurred in the spring, and two eggs were laid in June. By July 14 faint peeping sounds could be heard, as one egg had hatched and an almost-naked chick had emerged. The parents were amazingly protective, even covering the chick with their wings if the Wallworks came too close. The baby fledged by November and at that point attempted short flights.

Bare-eyed Cockatoo

The Bare-eyed Cockatoo, or *Cacatua sanguinea*, is one of the most common of the Australian parrots. It is a roving species, usually moving to areas where food and water are plentiful. Good-sized flocks are commonly observed in many parts of the continent. In addition to northern and central Australia, this species can also be found in a small region of southern New Guinea. A glance at a map or globe will show you the proximity of the northern tip of Australia and southern New Guinea and leads to speculation as to the possibility that these strong fliers originally migrated from one country to the other.

The Bare-eyed is a small, white cockatoo about fifteen inches long and appears to be solidly built. The bases of the feathers of the head, neck, back, and breast are pinkish orange. Other markings include a splash of yellow under the wings and tail and deep pink feathers on the lores and forehead. They have a small white crest that is normally not noticeable until it is raised, in which event they look similar to people raising bushy eyebrows in surprise. The beak is small and horn-colored and

the brownish iris is surrounded with a lopsided blue eye ring, the largest part of which is located below the eye.

John Gould first described this bird in an article written in 1882, about a specimen collected in northern Australia. Since that time, many names have been used for these attractive birds, including Little Corella, Short-billed Corella, Bloodstained Cockatoo, and Blue-eyed Cockatoo. The use of this last should be discouraged, however, as it also pertains to a much larger white cockatoo, the *Cacatua opthalmica*. *Sanguinea* is Latin for "pertaining to blood," which is, of course, a reference to the parrot's forehead marking.

Karl Diefenbach notes that there are two subspecies, the first of which, *C. s. sanguinea*, is larger than the second, *C. s. normantini*, and also richer in color. According to Diefenbach, the Little Corella has continued to thrive over the years and, in a manner similar to the Galah, has actually benefited from the encroachment of agriculture, as

The Bare-eyed Cockatoo's distinctive blue eye ring has a lopsided shape. Larry Willett

farm regions have afforded new sources of food and water. One flock observed near Wyndham in western Australia appeared to contain as many as sixty to seventy thousand birds. Adding that these birds are often kept as house pets in Australia, he believes them to be affectionate and tame members of the household, with a good talent for mimicry. I would rate them even higher—possibly the most exceptionally intelligent of the white cockatoos.

Another vivid description of these parrots in the wild is contributed by Jack Pollard in *Birds of Paradox: Birdlife in Australia and New Zealand* (1967). In a selection called "The Birds of Cooper's Creek," which discusses an area in central Australia blessed with many water holes and, thus, many birds, Pollard mentions sitting on the bank of a large pool during the hour before dusk and being like a spectator in a theater as "the corellas come in by the thousands, screeching hideously . . . as they settle on one tree after another, never quite able to make up their minds."

Matthew Vriends rates these parrots among the best talkers of the cockatoos. He also considers them highly destructive and warns that they can destroy a wooden flight or aviary in a very short time.

Earlier writers, such as Neville W. Cayley (*What Bird Is That*, 1931), generally have only good things to say about this bird. Cayley once witnessed a huge flock of about 20,000 "as they spiraled upward as though climbing an aerial staircase." He was also amused to watch such a group repair to a communal roosting place and then squabble for hours over the most favored perching spots.

Forshaw *(Parrots of the World,* 1973) sees Bare-eyed Cockatoos as "noisy, conspicuous birds" that usually congregate in flocks that, outside the breeding season, can include hundreds or even thousands. Sindel and Lynn (*Australian Cockatoos,* 1988) recognize only three legitimate subspecies: *C. s. sanguinea, C. s. gymnopsis,* and *C. s. normantoni.* The first of these is the largest, at about sixteen inches in length, with a pale orange-red marking around the beak and a light blue eye ring. *Gymnopsis* is slightly smaller, with a more pronounced orange-red marking and a darker blue eye ring. The third group, *normantoni,* is similar to *sanguinea* but slightly smaller, with a small white crest that is almost unnoticeable until it is raised in moments of excitement or surprise. The blue eye

ring has an odd, lopsided shape, the greater part being below the eye.

The Bare-eyed Cockatoo's crest is almost invisible until it is raised. Cohen Associates

Sindel and Lynn also recall an unforgettable sighting of *C. s. sanguinea* in July 1986 at Foggs Dam, a bird-watching area southeast of Darwin, Australia. It was late afternoon on a hot, sunny day, and, as they approached the dam, they could hear the raucous screams of a flock of several hundred birds, about one hundred of which were busily engaged in digging for marine or insect life in the mud flats exposed by the dropping water level. Apparently this type of behavior is not uncommon; Charles Barrett describes a similar scene along the Daly River in the Northern Territory.

These cockatoos are an excellent choice for breeding, and records of success in this area are extensive, going back as far as 1907, when a pair at the London Zoo produced one chick. The Rudkins of California bred them in the United States in 1928, and in recent years Helen and Larry Willet bred these birds quite regularly. If you attempt to purchase a pair for breeding, try to find birds that are at least five years old, and insist on surgical, cytological, or some other definitive form of sexing, as eye color is not a particularly reliable indicator with this species.

In his authoritative *Australian Parrots in Bush and Aviary* (1981), Ian Harman writes of the Little Corella as an excellent pet that becomes tame and affectionate and is a good talker. Most observers agree, some going even further with their praise.

Although not as impressive as its larger-crested relatives, the Bare-eyed shows a high degree of intelligence. On a visit to Alba Ballard's famous collection, I was intrigued by a young pair that followed her around like puppies, demanding her attention and using every means at their disposal to obtain it.

Goffin's Cockatoo

Goffin's received little attention from collectors and breeders until 1972, when a virtual deluge of these parrots began entering the United States. This was due to a combination of factors, including the establishment of government-regulated quarantine facilities that made it possible for parrots to be imported in large numbers, and a change in the agricultural pattern on the major Tenimbar Islands. The production of corn, rice, and coconuts had, with fishing, long been the major sources of income for the population of about 50,000. Extensive deforesting provided additional land for farming and income from timber, but resulted in habitat destruction and a loss of hiding places for the Goffin's. Many thousands have been exported, and, although the birds were once extremely plentiful, this habitat loss threatens their survival.

Rosemary Low, writing in *Endangered Parrots* (1984), cites a report on the status of parrots from the Moluccas, the island group to which the Tenimbars belong, that lists the bird as "common." She aptly compares the Goffin's to the extinct Carolina Parakeet, a prolific bird at the turn of the century that few believed would ever disappear.

Frank Woolham (*The Handbook of Aviculture*, 1987) considers the status of Goffin's "extremely precarious" for these reasons. He also discusses the comparatively low prices they command and their tendency to destroy wooden enclosures.

Karl Diefenbach reports that Goffin's is common on most of the larger Tenimbar Islands, where it is a forest dweller, but warns against the threat

to its habitat posed by agricultural expansion.

Goffin's is a rather plain bird compared with the larger white cockatoos such as the Greaters or Moluccans. Its crest is so small that when not erected the head looks almost smooth; even when erect it is very unimpressive, more suggestive of a little dunce cap than a cockatoo crest. These parrots are hardly dunces, however. I consider them among the most clever of the cockatoos, a quality that accounts for their reputation as virtual escape artists. Several years ago a breeder in Philadelphia purchased six Goffin's Cockatoos with the goal of setting up a viable breeding colony. She reported that they not only severely chewed the wooden two-by-fours holding the flight wire in position, but they also managed to escape by opening the device that latched the door. Until she resorted to wiring it shut, the breeder would find her Goffin's exploring every corner of the bird room when she came in each morning.

The Goffin's was named in honor of Andreas Goffin, a Dutch infantry officer interested in ornithology who served in West Africa early in the nineteenth century when the islands that comprise modern Indonesia were a Dutch colonial dominion. It is a small white cockatoo, reaching a length of only twelve inches, that is not considered a great beauty because of its tiny crest and bulging eyes. This lack of comeliness, however, is more than made up for by its great intelligence, speaking ability, and willingness to display affection.

Until fairly recently, *Cacatua goffini* was considered by many to be a subspecies of the Bare-eyed Cockatoo, to which it is very similar in size and shape, and was classified as *Cacatua sanguinea goffini*. However, the Goffin's is found on the Tenimbar Islands, which are part of Indonesia, while Bare-eyed Cockatoos are natives of Australia. In the 1968 edition of *Australian Parrots* Forshaw treats the Goffin's as a subspecies, while in the 1972 and subsequent editions of his *Parrots of the World*, he views it from a more contemporary perspective as a separate species. In addition, it is no longer listed as a subspecies of the Bare-eyed in the updated version of *Australian Parrots*, published in 1981.

Goffin's has become popular in Great Britain, and over the last few years a series of articles and commentary on this cockatoo has been published in the British *Magazine of the Parrot Society*.

Ray Turner, one of the authors, considers them

delightful characters with engaging mannerisms and an air of innocence. He warns, however, that their voices are far from musical and when they play, their excited, coarse screeching can be very disruptive. He corroborates the general consensus on their destructive nature and the remarkable dexterity that enables them to escape from their cages, recommending that their aviaries be built like Fort Knox, with perches that are not less than two inches thick.

Although the torrent of importation has come to a halt, a great number of breeding pairs have been set up, and the domestic Goffin's should be readily available. If you would like to try your hand at breeding cockatoos, Goffin's is an excellent choice.

Buying several adults should not be very expensive, and even if you do not succeed in breeding, you will have a wonderful time observing their antics.

THE RED-VENTED COCKATOO

Cacatua haematuropygia is considered to be one of the "white cockatoos," an unscientific designation commonly used for cockatoos with generally white plumage. A native inhabitant of the Philippine Islands, it is sometimes referred to as the Philippine Red-vented Cockatoo.

It is a fairly small bird, with most specimens averaging twelve to thirteen inches in length. Males

The Red-vented Cockatoo takes its name from the characteristic coloring on the underside of the tail. Doreen Gluck

are white with yellowish pink over the ear coverts, a wash of yellow on the underside of the flight feathers, and red under-tail coverts. They have a small, broad crest, which, along with their size, can be a source of confusion with the Bare-eyed Cockatoo. Sparks and Soper make some interesting observations on the way in which the forehead is heightened by the erected crest, causing the face to swell to dramatic proportions. This gesture appears to be designed to frighten off a potential aggressor. Females are marked in a similar manner, although attempts at visual sexing can be based on eye color, as the eye in males is almost black, while in the hen it is reddish brown.

The Red-vented Cockatoo is an interesting bird and is kept by some devoted aviculturists. Doreen Gluck

According to Diefenbach, young birds are extremely tame and affectionate and have morning and evening calls that are not particularly disruptive. He warns, however, that older birds become quite aggressive during the breeding season, with males attacking hens and inflicting considerable damage.

Some writers consider this cockatoo to be delicate, but Allen Kempe of Grapevine, Texas, who has kept them and also seen them in their natural habitat, believes that they may have acquired their reputation for frailty from the large number of post-quarantine deaths that occurred during the great importation era of the mid-1970s, many of which may have been the result of poor treatment. Mr. Kempe, writing in *American Cage-Bird Magazine* in February 1972, insists that this reputation is undeserved, and that at the time of his writing they were quite common in the Philippines and could be found in virtually any bird shop in Manila. His own Red-vented Cockatoos normally winter out of doors

with no ill effects. However, he considers them the most destructive wood chewers of any parrots he had ever kept and emphasizes that wire-lined nest boxes are a must to prevent their being totally destroyed.

Barbara Ruffolo, who works with birds at Parrots of the World in Rockville Centre, New York, describes her Red-vented Cockatoo as a highly intelligent but somewhat "indifferent" parrot. He is not terribly noisy, and his calls have more of a rasping sound than the usual cockatoo screams. He enjoys acrobatics more than chewing and in this respect is far from typical of his race. Mark Marrone, who owns Parrots of the World, advises that Red-vents are regularly bred in the United States. Both Barbara and Mark highly recommend them as pets.

LONG-BILLED CORELLA

This intriguing bird is also known as *Cacatua tenuirostris*, or the Slender-billed Cockatoo. In many respects it resembles the Bare-eyed Cockatoo (frequently called the Little Corella), but as the bird develops, the upper beak becomes remarkably elongated. Its distribution is restricted to isolated areas in the Victoria region of Australia.

The Long-billed Corella is fifteen inches long and has a white body relieved by patches of scarlet and yellow markings on the undersurface of the tail and wings. There is a blood-red patch on the forehead, lores, sides of the face, and neck, and the eye is surrounded by bluish skin.

For decades this parrot was on the verge of extinction, but protective legislation has brought it back to a healthy population level, which a September 1984 census estimated to exceed 250,000. Parrot lovers may greet this news with joy, but farmers in Western Victoria consider the Long-billed Corella to be "a pest of plague proportions."

These cockatoos are among the most clever and destructive of the Australian parrots and are reported to be equally adept at destroying wheat crops, power lines, wooden structures, and grass tennis courts. The composition of their beaks makes them highly effective chewing and digging animals. Their normal year-round food is the root of the onion grass, a weed introduced to Australia from South Africa, but they also do severe damage to young wheat and sunflower crops. One farmer reported that in only a few weeks, a flock of Corellas totally wiped out an eighty-acre crop of young wheat. Many farmers favor a change in the ban on shooting and poisoning these birds, while others advocate relaxing the laws against exportation, since they are highly desired as pets throughout the world.

When you combine a clever animal mind with an outstanding tool of destruction, interesting things can happen. In recent years, the judge's box at the Murtoa Race Course was chewed so badly that it had to be replaced. In addition, the pitcher's mound at the local cricket field was rendered unplayable by a flock of Corellas that, after finishing off the mound, stopped to extract the nails from the galvanized roofs of various buildings.

Restrictions against harming these birds have helped to increase their numbers. The introductions of onion grass has given them a year-round source of food and this, along with an agricultural shift in Western Victoria from sheep farming to wheat production, continues to raise the population. Victoria's Fisheries and Wild Life Bureau officials have been tagging the Corellas and then releasing them. Their studies indicate that the birds tend to remain within just a few miles of their original locations since food supplies are abundant.

Charles Barrett describes the Long-billed Corella as "an ugly bird," but ranks its ability to speak with that of the African Grey and the Indian Hill Myna, which is very high praise indeed. Barrett further states that no other member of the cockatoo family, with the possible exception of its near relative, the Little Corella, can rival it as a talking bird. It also takes kindly to captivity and soon becomes both docile and friendly. In Australia the Long-billed Corella is known as a reliable "water-guide," since it rarely strays far from a permanent source of water.

Forshaw (*Australian Parrots*, 2d ed., 1981) provides a painting by W. T. Cooper of the Long-billed Corella sharing a willow tree with a Bare-eyed Cockatoo. The tree is appropriately located next to a small body of water. This painting reveals the similarities between the two birds as well as the obvious differences in beak structure. Forshaw uses the name *Bare-eyed Corella* for *C. t. pastinator*, but I recommend referring to it as the Long-billed Corella and reserving the other name for *Cacatua sanguinea*.

Prestwich notes a possible breeding of this species in 1854, and a report in a French journal of that era mentions a breeding that may have taken place in a zoo belonging to Prince Demidoff.

Reports of their behavior as pets vary but generally commend this parrot as a good talker that is also highly intelligent. Mark Shepard (*Aviculture In Australia*, 1989) believes they make excellent, docile pets and are probably the best talkers among the Australian cockatoos. He warns, however, that they can be savage toward other birds housed in their aviary and recommends that only one pair be kept in a flight.

Alba Ballard has kept this species for many years and notes that they are "smart, charming, funny and intelligent," so much so that she has named one of her Slender-bills Einstein. This parrot frequently boasts: "Ein-stein, very smart!"

According to Graeme Hyde (*Australian Aviculture*, 1987), these parrots use their specialized beaks to dig out roots, tubers, and bulbs, items of which they are particularly fond. He notes that they can be sexed by eye color since males have a dark, almost black iris while that of females is brown or reddish brown, but not before the birds are at least twelve months old. They are not truly mature until at least four years of age.

Rosemary Low (*Parrots: Their Care and Breeding*, 3d rev. ed. 1992) describes the immature bird as having a much shorter beak and a smaller orange-scarlet marking on the throat than the adult. She lists a fairly large number of well-documented breeding successes, even though many other writers report that this is a difficult bird to breed in captivity.

A complete report on the breeding of a pair of Slender-bills owned by Alan Lendon was published in the June 1969 issue of the British *Magazine of the Parrot Society*. The birds were housed in a flight that was approximately eighteen feet long by three and a half feet wide by seven and a half feet high for nine months before they mated, and they were, as recommended above, the sole occupants. Their nest box was a hollow log that was well hidden by plantings within the flight and was only three feet above the ground. The first and second eggs were laid on consecutive days and a third egg four days later. Incubation began after the second egg was laid, the male incubating during the day and the female at night. Two chicks hatched after twenty-four days, but only one survived. This chick left the nest at the age of seven weeks and was much like his parents at that time except that he was smaller and had a shorter upper beak.

Several years ago an unusual hybridization occurred in northern California: Tony Lizotte of San Leandro owns the offspring of a ten-year-old Slender-bill that had been crossed with a Greater Sulphur-crested. The parrot, Kumkapoo, has the typical long upper beak, fleshy blue eye ring, and short, stubby crest of the Slender-bill, although the crest is the same yellow as that of the Greater. It also resembles the Greater in body conformation, and its personality and speech capability are outstanding.

Contradicting other experts, Ian Harman asserts that both sexes of the Slender-bill have dark eyes, making it impossible to use eye color for sexing. Harman considers this parrot a wonderful pet, but warns that its slender beak is extremely damaging to wood and suggests that it only be kept in all-metal flights.

ROSE-BREASTED COCKATOO

Rosies, as those who love them commonly refer to them, are short, stocky, and attractively colored cockatoos that are only about fourteen inches in length. There are two subspecies, the major difference between which is the intensity of pink in the plumage. N. D. Cooper of Great Britain recently bred a Lutino mutation which converted the pink and gray colors of the normal bird to pink and white. He is currently attempting to establish this strain (*American Cage-Bird Magazine*, June 1993).

Rose-breasted Cockatoos are widely distributed throughout Australia, where they are considered pests by farmers because of their depredations against crops. Ironically, because they are clever and winning animals, they are also widely kept as pets by many, including the very farmers whose crops the wild birds destroy, much as early residents of the American West kept tame wolves as pets.

The short, stocky, and attractive cockatoo *Eolophus roseicapillus* is the only member of its genus and is thus referred to as a "monotype." Forshaw believes it to be a link between the white cockatoos and the Gang-gang Cockatoo, a theory supported by Karl Diefenbach, who, in his book

The World of Cockatoos, notes anatomical and behavioral similarities between the species as well as the fact that the Rose-breasted is the only cockatoo that has been hybridized with the Gang-gang. It has, however, also been hybridized with the Greater Sulphur-crested Cockatoo, as pointed out by Alan Lendon in the March/April 1950 issue of *Avicultural Magazine*. Lendon notes that this hybrid and three Rose-breasted–Leadbeater hybrids were on exhibit in the Adelaide, Australia, Zoo. Perhaps the ability to engage in hybrid breeding is a specialty of the Rose-breasted.

I have seen both subspecies and they are appealing and captivating birds. Male specimens of *E. r. roseicapillus*, which originates in central and northern Australia, are about fourteen inches long and are suffused with pink over the front of the body, the crest, the lores, and the region about the eyes. The wings, back, and tail are gray, while the cheeks, ear coverings, and nape are a deep red. They have a red eye ring, a dark brown, almost black, eye, and a light-horn-colored beak. Females are similar but have a reddish-brown iris. In bright light and with at least one bird of known sex, it is usually possible to sex these cockatoos by eye color once they are about a year old. The subspecies *E. r. assimilis* of western Australia has lighter plumage and more pink in the crest. Its eye ring is almost white where in the nominate race it is red.

As noted by Diefenbach, the birds are widely distributed throughout Australia and are quite common. Travelers will find them in flocks of up to a thousand birds, and unlike other endangered species, they look for new agricultural areas, with the result that their numbers and range continue to expand. Alan Lendon remarks that they are even found in the suburbs and parks of Australian cities, and although there are few more beautiful sights than a flock of these birds wheeling through the air, they are a serious menace to agriculture.

Virtually every expert indicates that Rose-breasteds make clever and winning pets that seem to enjoy human company. I remember how thrilled I was when a friend stopped on her way home from the airport to show me a newly arrived young Rose-breasted Cockatoo. She sang a little song to calm the parrot, Rosa, who immediately responded by dancing to the tune!

As with all the cockatoos, the Rose-breasted can live to a ripe old age. In the March/April 1950

A bundle of pink, white, and gray pinfeathers now, this Rose-breasted Cockatoo chick will mirror all the beauty of its species in the near future. Hans Andersson

issue of *Avicultural Magazine*, the duke of Bedford describes a light-colored male with its albino mate that he obtained at an unknown age and had owned for more than fourteen years. Although the pair were still feeding and functioning well as of his writings, they seemed to have stopped breeding.

Kenton Lint, formerly curator of birds at the San Diego Zoo, points out in the May 1970 issue of *ZOONOOZ* that "few birds, if any, are as satisfactory for human amusement as cockatoos." The article includes some excellent photos of baby Rose-breasteds hatched at the zoo.

In an earlier article for the November/December 1951 issue of *Avicultural Magazine*, Dr. Lint provided practical information on maintaining and breeding these clever cockatoos, which were first described in 1751. He writes enthusiastically about the disposition the Rose-breasteds, considering them wonderful showoffs that readily learn to speak and whistle tunes in a soft, flute-like tone.

Also in this article, Dr. Lint claimed credit for the first successful breeding at the San Diego Zoo of a Rose-breasted chick that hatched in June 1951. This achievement represented fifteen years of effort on his part to induce the species to breed, and he considered it quite an accomplishment. The breeding pair were fed corn on the cob, sunflower, oat groats, peanuts, pine nuts, oranges, bananas, lettuce, and dried bread throughout the year in equal amounts during two feeding periods. The only addition during the breeding season was cuttlebone for extra calcium.

Following copulation, the hen laid two eggs, only one of which was fertile. The incubation period lasted thirty days. Because of concern over proper feeding by the parents, the chick was removed from the nest when it was about ten days old, experience having taught Dr. Lint that, even with the variety of foods he fed them, cockatoo parents tend to stop feeding efficiently after about ten days, allowing their babies either to die or develop rickets.

His concerns proved to have been well founded when he discovered that the chick had an empty crop and was urgently in need of food. This the baby accepted, and a schedule was arranged for feeding at four-hour intervals. After about eight weeks, the night feedings were discontinued. At almost two months, a quarter of an orange was offered and accepted. Dr. Lint cautioned that this species reacts nervously when being handled, and the chick would regurgitate its food if anyone opened a window or closed a door during its feeding. At three months of age, although still a baby, the chick could eat by itself but was still being spoon-fed three times a day.

Collette Matlaga raised some interesting issues in a letter that appeared in the March 1987 issue of the *Cockatoo Newsletter*. She had obtained her pair of Rose-breasteds when they were about two and a half years old, hoping to breed them in 1987 or 1988 using a hollow-log nest box about one and a half feet in diameter. Her birds are fed cracked corn, wheat, oat groats, safflower, teazle, white millet, sunflower, and a variety of fruits and vegetables, but they refuse to eat any form of meat when she tries to add protein to their diet. Vitamins and minerals are added to the food and water. She has been advised that sunflower seeds may cause cysts or tumors but does not wish to deprive her birds of these popular seeds. Joe Lannom, the editor of the publication, responds that tumors and cysts do occur in Rose-breasted Cockatoos, but the high-calorie sunflower seeds have not been identified as the cause.

According to Dr. Greene in 1884, a Rose-breasted had been on display in the London Zoo since 1843. He considers this parrot the second most beautiful of the cockatoos (his first choice is the Leadbeater's) and describes an almost unbelievable incident of fostering in which a pair of Rose-breasted babies whose mother had died and whose father was indifferent were placed in the devoted care of a black bantan hen that had lost her own eggs. Her initial response to these big-headed chicks was a look of horror, but she soon adopted them as if they were her own, providing warmth, although most of the actual feeding was done by human hands. This proved to be a quaint trio as they basked in the sunshine while the hen dusted herself with grit and the baby cockatoos climbed on her body.

Rose-breasteds are in great demand, and if you are lucky enough to obtain a breeding pair your investment could be returned rapidly. With Australian parrots so widely prized and so many of them a problem to Australian farmers, one might question the wisdom of the Australian government's prohibition of their export while, permitting many of them to be killed. Crop destruction by these birds can be immense, with losses of fruit and grain crops estimated in the millions of dollars. A proposed solution would involve the exportation of those birds that are not endangered but that pose a threat to crops, a suggestion to which there seems to be few valid objections. At the same time, Australia has built two avian import facilities in Melbourne and Adelaide for the purpose of facilitating the importation of birds that would be of commercial value or benefit to Australia as well as meeting other community needs. Imported birds could come only from those countries on the rather short Newcastle Virus–free list that includes New Zealand, Ireland, Canada, the Scandinavian countries and the United Kingdom.

LEADBEATER'S COCKATOO

Cacatua leadbeateri, or Major Mitchell's Cockatoo, is one of the most attractive Australian parrots. Although not endangered or threatened, it is quite rare and expensive in the United States and Europe. Fortunately, breeding pairs exist in this country, so there are occasional opportunities for the most avid collectors to obtain a Leadbeater's, but be advised that the price is high, easily approaching the cost of a quality automobile. Although the Leadbeater's is one of the most expensive parrots available for purchase, it sells quite rapidly despite this fact.

This attractive parrot is named for Benjamin Leadbeater, who had a specimen in his collection as early as 1831. Leadbeater was the owner of a natural history, or scientific, supply firm in London and he was highly thought of by many ornithologists. In his famous painting of a Leadbeater's, Edward Lear used this gentleman's bird as a model. The source for the other commonly used name for this cockatoo is Sir Thomas Mitchell, a nineteenth-century explorer who made many trips to the interior of Australia. His book, *Three Expeditions into the Interior of Eastern Australia*, published in 1838, offered an excellent description of this parrot along with an accurate and beautiful illustration.

The Leadbeater's is a fairly small cockatoo that reaches a length of only about fourteen inches, making it smaller than some Amazons and about the same size as an African Grey. But it is coloring that makes this bird so impressive: Its overall color is white with varying shades of pink on the head, nape, undersurfaces, and abdomen. The flight feathers are a deeper pink, and a dark pink band marks the forehead. The beak is horn-colored, the eye is brownish, and the legs are gray. The Leadbeater's crest, its most outstanding feature, is forward-curving when erected, at which time its array of red, white, and yellow feathers becomes visible. The base is red, then yellow, then red again, and the tip is a snowy white. The female is similarly marked, except that the upper abdomen is white rather than pink and the crest has a larger band of yellow than that of the male.

Karl Diefenbach discusses a southwest Australian subspecies, *C. l. mollis*, that is smaller than

the nominate race, with a crest almost lacking the characteristic yellow band. He observes that the nominate species prefers sparsely wooded grasslands in the interior of Australia, which is why they probably were not spotted until Mitchell traveled to the interior, earlier explorers preferring the relative safety of the coastal regions. Habitat destruction has decreased their numbers in recent years, but large flocks may still occasionally be seen.

According to Ian Harman (*Birdkeeping in Australia*, 1980) Leadbeater's Cockatoos prefer to nest in hollow trees, where they usually lay three eggs. Their diet in the wild is largely seeds from trees, grasses, and shrubs, as well as bulbous roots and the seeds of wild gourds. Most of these can be duplicated or simulated by those lucky enough to keep these parrots. Harman further notes that they breed readily, even in a small flight.

A. A. Prestwich (*Records of Parrots Bred in Captivity*) credits W. H. Browning with the first successful breeding of this group in 1931 and 1932. However, a report written by his aviary attendant Michael Obioko in 1941 expresses reservations about the success of this undertaking. Although the pair had eggs on a regular basis from 1922 to 1939, the cock would kill the young as soon as their feathers sprouted. One bird did survive in 1927 to the point at which it left the nest, but it was not a strong chick and died after about one week. Because the pair were more than thirty years old, having been obtained in 1903, these problems cannot be attributed to parental immaturity.

Successful breedings have taken place at the San Diego Zoo in 1935, in the aviaries of Mr. Ezra of the Avicultural Society in 1950, in the flights of the renowned Rudkin family of California in 1949, and on other occasions.

Walton and Smith (*Cockatoos and Parrots*, 1969) note that the incubation period for these cockatoos is twenty-nine to thirty-one days. Their time in the nest box is approximately seventy-five days, and they achieve full independence about sixty days after leaving the nest.

Leadbeater's Cockatoo (opposite) is one of the most beautiful members of the cockatoo family. Also known as Major Mitchell's Cockatoo, this bird commands a premium price when available. Robert Pearcy

There is a vivid description of these birds in E. J. Boosey's *Foreign Bird Keeping*. He considers them the most beautiful of the entire parrot family, noting that they live quite happily in cages. His pair were quite noisy and not very good talkers. The former owners of the male were apparently avid tea drinkers, because in response to amorous overtures from the hen, the male looked at her with a puzzled expression and comically repeated: "Cocky want a cup of tea?" At that point the hen wisely decided to have little more to do with him.

PALM COCKATOO

The Palm Cockatoo's Latin name, *Probosciger aterrimus*, is most appropriate, translating roughly to "one who bears a large, black beak." Although some writers break this monotypic, or single species, genus into five subspecies, Forshaw (*Parrots of the World*, 1973) lists only three, treating the other two as geographical variations. For the most part, the differences among the subspecies are only in size. *P. aterrimus aterrimus*, which originates in northern Australia, measures between twenty-two and twenty-four inches in length. *P. a. goliath*, also known as "Goliath," achieves lengths of twenty-four to twenty-six inches and is found in western and southern New Guinea. The third subspecies recognized by Forshaw, *P. a. stenolophus*, is slightly smaller than Goliath and has a smaller crest.

Karl Diefenbach notes that this bird was identified and named in 1788; however, Dr. Greene supports an earlier date of 1707, crediting this description to the Dutch writer, van der Meuien. Diefenbach describes it as an elegant flier that usually remains, singly or in pairs, in the treetops of rain forests. He insists on the importance of maintaining national parks and reservations, as the natural habitat of these birds is being exploited by commercial interests in lumbering and agriculture. Despite their large beaks, Diefenbach refers to them as the pacifists of the bird world, having held wild Palm Cockatoos without restraining their heads and not been bitten.

I have had exactly the same experience with the gentle and friendly Palm Cockatoos owned by Dr. Judy Schwartz and Alba Ballard of New York. They were the first Palms I ever saw, and I had been expecting giant birds. Instead I was astonished at their relatively small size; their heads and beaks were large, but their bodies were no bigger than that of the average cockatoo.

The basic color of the Palm Cockatoo is grayish black. The wings and abdomen are almost entirely black and the large backward-curving crest is made of many thin feathers, which may be the origin of the name "Palm." This cockatoo has large, bare cheek patches extending from under the eye to the lower beak. When the bird is excited, pleased, or angry, this area becomes suffused with blood and turns a bright red, almost as if Goliath were blushing.

Neville Cayley (*What Bird Is That?*, 1948) recounts the interesting displays and antics he saw when a flock of these birds occupied a tree in an area he was observing, describing what Karl Diefenbach refers to as "intimidation behavior." Diefenbach adds that this is always accompanied by a two-syllable, whistling contact call. At the first note, the bird assumes an erect posture and after a shrill, prolonged second note, spreads its wings and lunges forward. Diefenbach also describes the rhythmic stamping of the feet when these birds consider themselves threatened; it is a movement similar to the display behavior exhibited on occasion by Moluccan Cockatoos.

The marquess of Tavistock, later the duke of Bedford, was highly impressed with the display behavior of the Palm Cockatoo, and in the December 1928 issue of *Avicultural Magazine* he comments on a pair that had been in his extensive collection for about a year. His birds were in a large aviary but were initially so shy and secretive, spending all of their time in the shelter, that he originally compared their behavior with the classic description of the behavior of guinea pigs, which can be described as "no behavior." When they finally entered the main flight, the hen, with her crest partly erect, sauntered up to the male in a jaunty manner, and, when she got close to him, puffed out her feathers. She then began to stamp each foot alternately, while posturing and bowing with head-cocking movements in a most affected manner. She apparently considered this behavior highly attractive. Two distinctly different screams accompanied this display, and the hen's cheek patch become a deep pink.

Bill Gordon of Australia, who is well known to readers of *American Cage-Bird Magazine* for the articles written about his birds by A. B. McNabney, contributed a fine description of Palm Cockatoos in the wild in an article in the March 1978 issue of the American *Avicultural Bulletin*. He believes that hawks, the mortal enemies of many birds, avoid the Palm and other black cockatoos, which are more than a match for them. Mr. Gordon often observed groups of Palm Cockatoos in flight, doing their "physical training" in mock battles and diving and evading imaginary hawks.

Following the Convention on International Trade in Endangered Species (or CITIES) held in Washington, D.C., in 1981, legal importation of these impressive parrots was supposed to cease. In spite of this, in 1983 a shipment was brought into Miami, where it was seized by the U.S. Fish and Wildlife Service's Enforcement Division. Part of the seized booty was sent to the National Zoo in Washington, D.C., in February 1984; twelve members of the shipment were housed at the Bronx Zoo, a group of eight were sent to a breeding project in their Indonesian homeland, and four others went to a similar program at a New York Zoological Society facility in Georgia.

THE BANKSIAN COCKATOO

The Banksian, or Red-tailed Black, Cockatoo was named for Sir Joseph Banks, a naturalist who accompanied Captain Cook on his first journey to Australia. The Latin name, *Calyptorhynchus magnificus magnificus*, is, according to Prestwich, a reference to its size and beauty. *ZOONOOZ*, the publication of the San Diego Zoo, noted in its May 1970 issue on cockatoos that, unfortunately, for many years the Banksian's red-banded tail feathers were used in aboriginal rain ceremonies as well as in other tribal celebrations in central Australia.

The Banksian is one of a group of black cockatoos found on the Australian mainland and Tasmania. Diefenbach points out that, within their range, these birds were once an everyday sight, but field research done within the past fifteen years shows a marked decrease in numbers of breeding pairs, which is, of course, the greatest possible threat to a species. He blames increased land cultivation and the resulting loss of habitat. Since the birds are extremely long lived, the results of a decline in breeding activity have not been observed as quickly as they might be with other types of parrots.

These large birds generally exceed two feet in length. The predominant color in males is black, but the back, breast, and nape are brown, and the tail shows a large red band. Males have a dark slate-gray beak, while the female's beak is a light horn color. Among other differences between the sexes, the plumage in the female is a more brownish black, the crest, head, and neck are speckled with yellow, and the tail is marked with orange and black bars. Diefenbach identifies three subspecies, which differ only slightly from the nominate race.

In an article for *Australian Birdkeeper*, Tony Silva described his visit to the home and aviary of Australian aviculturist Peter Chapman, who has had remarkable success in breeding members of *calyptorhyncus*. Silva also visited John Roberts, whose aviaries included one flight with almost forty Banksian Cockatoos, several of which were so tame that they would land on visitors' shoulders without warning. Most reports on breeding note how savage these birds become toward intruders, but Silva describes looking into a log nest box that contained a Red-tailed chick and having its concerned but tame father land on his shoulder as it gently showed its agitation by fanning its tail and raising its crest.

The marquess of Tavistock, later the duke of Bedford, provides a fascinating description of the Banksians in his collection in the 1929 edition of his book, *Parrots and Parrot-like Birds*. He finds the bird's charm and dignity remarkable, and believes that because they become so tame in captivity, it is difficult to find breeding pairs among these birds, since they center their attention on humans. One of his male Banksians, Teddy, was permitted free flight on the duke's estate. Teddy often lost his way, and when he did, he would confidently perch on a tree at the nearest inn and wait for one of the duke's staff to come and claim him.

E. J. Boosey, who illustrated the original version of the duke's book, later described the same birds in his own book, *Foreign Bird Keeping*, c. 1950. He remarked on their magnificent appearance as they flew from one end to the other of the duke's huge aviaries with a leisurely and buoyant flying technique. Boosey also writes of the power of the Banksians' beaks, evident from the fact that "they were able to deal with Brazil nuts with as much nonchalance as a Zebra Finch shucking millet seed."

Joseph Forshaw (*Australian Parrots*, 2d rev. ed., 1981) offers an excellent illustration of a pair of Banksians that clearly shows the differences between male and female, and he warns that there has been frequent confusion from the beginning between the Banksian and the Glossy Black Cockatoo. He further observes that the species was fairly common in Queensland as recently as 1973, although considered rare in other areas, and quotes a 1979 report that noted a decline in northeastern New South Wales but found the birds still to be common in central Australia, particularly in areas with good water supplies.

Ian Harman confirms the degree of tameness these parrots can achieve and their ability to manage small seeds as well as large nuts. He notes that the natural breeding season is May through September, with the usual nesting site being a hollow as high up in a tree as possible. Clutches are small; generally only one chick is hatched from one or two eggs. Incubation, carried out only by the hen, takes twenty-nine days, and the chick remains in the nest until about three months of age.

CONURES

Parrot owners quickly realize that one of the major delights of owning parrots is being able to watch them at play. Among most psittacines, even older birds are attracted to objects that can be chewed, such as leather or wood. They also enjoy toys that can be flung around to make noise; a good, strong cowbell is ideal for this. Conures are particularly agile and entertaining, and observing one or more at play is like attending a parrot circus.

The conures are an important part of the more than 330 groups of hookbilled birds included under the common name of parrot. Sparks and Soper provide some fascinating glimpses of the unique characteristics of these clever birds. Anyone who has ever watched a parrot knows that it exhibits superbly effective use of its claws in holding or manipulating food or toys. These authors, however, point out that many of these birds also demonstrate strong preferences for the use of one foot or the other and can be considered to be right or left footed. The favorite foot varies among different parrots. In tests with a Black-headed Caique, the subject was strongly right footed, accepting morsels of food with its right foot seventy-six out of 100 times.

Sun Conures. Larry Willett

In an experiment with a group of Brown-throated Conures, half preferred to use the right foot and the other half favored the left, and in a study of cockatoos, three-quarters of the group were left footed. Sparks and Soper's examiners also discovered an Eclectus that had been eating fruit with bright red juice. They realized that an incriminating red stain was found only on the right foot and deduced that this bird was right footed.

Much of the current literature on conures takes the position that restrictions on the importation of the larger parrots means that interest in the conures will grow. Conures, however, are already popular. They have been favorite pets since the nineteenth century, reported on by Dr. Greene as early as 1884. The availability and reasonable prices of some conure species certainly make them a good choice for the prospective parrot owner. In addition, many conures are suitable for captive breeding, and their hand-fed offspring are as tame as any of the progeny of full-size hookbills. Conures can also be maintained in smaller quarters than those required for the larger parrots.

Some aviculturists refer to these birds as parakeets rather than conures, a potential source of confusion. Even the extinct Carolina Conure is not immune to this variation in nomenclature and is frequently called the Carolina Parakeet. In classification scientists try to avoid duplicating the names of species, which change of necessity as scientists garner additional information. The designation *conure* is best applied to most of the wedge-tailed parrots of Central and South America. The most popular of these come from the groups *Pyrrhura* and *Aratinga*, although the *Cyanoliseus*, which contains the single species known as the Patagonian Conure, is also kept.

These smaller exotics look and act more like the larger parrots than do any other diminutive psittacines. The genus *Aratinga* includes conures that resemble the miniature macaws; in a few cases these birds are actually heftier than some of the smaller Amazons. Many breed quite readily, and supplies of domestically bred conures are good and should continue to remain so.

Conures range in length from nine to fourteen inches. Some are good talkers while others have small vocabularies, but they all exhibit the charming behavioral traits of the larger parrots, including

acrobatic displays, affection for their owners, and a willingness to permit physical contact. A downside to this resemblance is the large beak, which is quite capable of biting those who force their attentions on a bird before it is ready to be friendly.

Halfmoon (sometimes called Petz's), Jenday, Peach-fronted, Sun, Mitred, and Gold-capped Conures are among the most popular and available species. They are regularly bred, and hand-fed babies can be obtained from breeders or many pet shops.

Conures have soared in popularity since 1989, a verifiable indicator of which is the publication of at least four books devoted solely to conures from 1991 to 1993.

In addition to its beautiful coloring and attractive contours, the Sun Conure makes an engaging pet and a good breeding bird for the budding aviculturist. Dimension Three *Photography*

SUN CONURE

If I were asked to advise a beginning parrot enthusiast on the factors to think about before choosing a bird, I would suggest that he or she consider availability, price, beauty, tameness, health, and willingness to breed, although not necessarily in that order.

The Sun Conure, *Aratinga solstitalis*, ranks high in all of the above areas, and its popularity in the United States is well deserved. It is a compact and well-formed bird with a body that reaches a length of about twelve inches and is covered with bright yellow feathers that are accentuated with a mixture of orange, blue, and green markings in the wings and tail. The brown iris is surrounded by a white eye ring, while the color of the powerful-looking beak ranges from dark gray to black. In older birds, the areas around the eyes, forehead, and cheeks are reddish orange, a feature most noticeable in males. Sparks and Soper beautifully and aptly characterize the Sun Conure as "well named because of its brilliant saffron plumage, washed here and there with orange to stunning effect—a real splash of golden sunshine."

These birds have a number of qualities in common with the Jenday and Gold-capped Conures, and some taxonomists speculate that they may all actually be variations of the same species. The close connection to the Jenday has resulted in the breeding of a popular hybrid with the clever name of "Sunday." Since males and females of both species are plentiful, I do not encourage this practice, as it serves no useful purpose.

Thomas Arndt (*Encyclopedia of Conures*, 1982) advises that although these parrots were rare as pets or breeders prior to 1973, the period that followed saw a great number of imports. The offspring of these birds have matured, and large numbers of captive-bred Sun Conures are now available. Breeding of these parrots has been so extensive that in some cases third-generation captive-bred Suns are being offered for sale. Arndt also notes that populations in the wild are stable.

These birds are found in Guyana, Venezuela, and northeast Brazil. Their importation has been cyclic, with only small numbers coming into the United States in the early 1970s. After that, large numbers of Suns arrived regularly, providing an excellent reservoir of breeding stock; this is fortunate, as imports are now ended.

Sun Conures breed well in captivity, and since a pair can be obtained for under $1,000 (with their hand-fed offspring selling for almost $400 each), these parrots should definitely be given consideration by those seriously interested in breeding or simply in having an attractive, playful pet.

Dr. Greene refers to these birds as Sun Parakeets or Yellow Conures. He agrees with Dr. Russ, a contemporary German aviculturist, that the Sun Conure is "undoubtedly one of the most magnificent of the many beautiful parrots of America." According to Greene, the Sun Conure was first displayed by the London Zoo in 1862. At the time he was writing, these parrots sold in England for about ten dollars each.

The Sun Conure has an outstanding personality: "Tucker," an extremely tame character, is checking out what might be hiding in a pocket. Brenda-Jean Lawyer

An excellent description of breeding Sun Conures was written by N. Ramen of England and published in the January 1976 issue of the *Magazine of the Parrot Society*. The author obtained his pair in October 1974 but they did not recognize each other as mates until a month later, and copulation did not take place until February 1975. In April of that year, they were moved from their indoor aviary to a larger outside flight, eleven feet long by three feet wide by nine feet high. It

Five happy Sun Conures observing the world from their owner's shoulder. Vivian Rozier

provided an enclosed shelter and both the eastern and western ends of the flight and half of the roof were protected with plastic panels. The birds were given a nest box that was eighteen inches square by four and a half feet high, with about six inches of peat and dried grass placed in the bottom. Both birds slept in the box at night. The first egg was laid on July 6 and three more were laid at two-day intervals. Incubation took twenty-seven days, the first, rather bare-looking chick hatching on August 27 and the others appeared at two-day intervals. The hen did all of the incubating chores and the male assisted in feeding the chicks. Their diet consisted of large amounts of bread and milk mashed with dog biscuit to a cereal consistency, as well as apples and eggs for the first three weeks. A mixture of sunflower seeds and hemp was also provided.

Mr. Ramen inspected the nest box frequently, and as he approached, the male would fly into it and sit by the hen, making noise and looking his most threatening. The four chicks thrived and began to leave the nest box on September 22. They were almost identical to their parents except that they lacked the orange wing markings. They

learned to fly very quickly, and Ramen spent many hours watching them.

Sun Conures are prolific breeders and in recent years there have been many successful attempts to raise them. However, caution should be used with these parrots, as with any free-breeding birds, to avoid the production of too many clutches in one season, which can deplete the hen's body of calcium. Removing the nest box is generally an effective way of controlling this. I know of one occasion where two pairs of Suns were shipped to a breeder who was horrified to discover that one of the females had a broken leg and pelvic bone. Examination by a veterinarian revealed that both females had numerous hairline fractures of the leg bones and that their calcium levels were dangerously low; the previous owner had neglected to supplement their diet with calcium, and, apparently, rough movement in shipping had combined with this to cause fractures.

Thomas Arndt thinks highly of Sun Conures, noting that by nature they are quite sociable, although their speaking ability may be limited. Those I have known have learned to speak when they were obtained as young birds. Arndt also provides guidelines on setting these birds up for breeding, recommending either natural tree-trunk nest boxes or the artificial type. He believes that since Sun Conures are inveterate chewers, it is wise to include a second floor board in the nest box.

These handsome parrots can be bred in fairly small flights or aviaries; provided with a flight that is about six feet long by four feet wide, a pair should do quite well. They generally breed in the spring but can breed throughout the year.

Robbie Harris (*Breeding Conures*, 1983), a breeder of several types of conures, speaks well of the Sun Conure. Ms. Harris gives complete details and tips on breeding, and because her recommendations are based on actual experience with this group, this information is extremely valuable. For example, she notes that almost every pair of conures, regardless of species, have a unique style of incubating. Usually it is the hen that does most of the work, some starting with the first egg and others waiting for the third. Ms. Harris also points out that it takes Sun Conures about two years to attain their full color. She advises breeders not to

panic when they spot babies on their backs with their feet in the air; they are not dead—this is just a typical pose for sleeping conure babies, which will also nap on their stomachs and sides.

Although some describe the Sun Conure as noisy, I consider it comparatively quiet, as well as among the most beautiful parrots in the world.

Dr. Russ (*The Speaking Parrots*, 1884) refers to these birds as Yellow Conures, but he does use the correct (for that time) scientific name, so there is no problem in knowing that he means the Sun Conures. Russ remarks that the Venezuelans call this parrot "Kessi-kessi" and that it was a favorite with the natives.

It meets all the requirements of a desirable parrot: It is available, easily tamed, breeds readily, is quite attractive, and is moderately priced. Consider this parrot if you are ready for a new challenge.

JENDAY CONURE

Although many have noted the resemblance between members of the genus *Aratinga* and the macaws, the Jenday Conure reminds me more of a small Amazon. It reaches a length of twelve inches

The Jenday Conure bears a strong resemblance to a small Amazon parrot. Robert Pearcy

and has a beak that is fairly large relative to the head and body. The head, neck, throat, and abdomen are a bright yellow, the remainder of the body is green, the flight feathers are blue-black, and the tail feathers have blue tips. Jendays may exhibit black, or, more commonly, white eye rings.

Experienced breeders indicate that the young are extremely alert and, when handled, develop into exceptionally fine pets. Their loud voices can be a drawback if noise is a problem, but most of their screaming, like that of their Amazon brethren, will be morning and evening cries.

They are excellent captive breeders, and young birds are regularly available. Some writers link them closely to the Sun Conures, even to the point of classifying them as a subspecies of this group.

HALFMOON CONURE

The Halfmoon Conure is one of the best known of its race and has been kept as a pet for well over one hundred years. This green parrot has an orange marking on the forehead and crown that blends into blue toward the rear. It is also called Petz's Conure, and it is sometimes referred to as the Orange-fronted Conure. The Halfmoon is frequently confused with the Peach-fronted Conure, to which it bears a strong resemblance, but these birds can be distinguished by beak color: that of the Peach-front is black while the Halfmoon's is a yellowish white. The Halfmoon is also about half an inch smaller than the Peach-front.

One reason for their popularity is that these conures are famous for becoming extremely tame when kept as pets. I have known of owners who permitted their Halfmoons to fly without restriction in their homes. I consider this practice to be unsafe, however, as these inveterate chewers think nothing of gnawing at electrical wires or other dangerous objects.

I would normally describe Halfmoons as mediocre talkers, but Kenton Lint, writing in the May 1969 issue of *ZOONOOZ*, the publication of the San Diego Zoo, describes a Halfmoon who was a wonderful talker, with a vocabulary including such phrases as "Bang bang!" and "Stick 'em up," usually followed by either "Merry Christmas" or "Happy New Year."

Many successful captive breedings of this species have been recorded, one dating as far back as 1929 and a second in Germany in 1932.

PEACH-FRONTED CONURE

The Peach-fronted Conure, also referred to as the Gold-crowned Conure, is about ten inches long and is green with an orange forehead and crown. It has an interesting and attractive ring of orange feathers around the eye, a black beak, and brown eyes. These conures have been imported for many years, but it is only recently that interest in breeding them has developed.

An article by I. M. Hadgkiss on this topic appeared in the October–December 1978 issue of *Avicultural Magazine*. The author owned a Peach-front and acquired a mate for it in 1977. He determined that his original bird was a female by using an uncertain sexing method based on the flat shape of the parrot's head. His new bird, with a slimmer, more rounded head, was assumed to be a male. Fortunately, both assumptions later proved accurate.

In June 1977 he housed the pair in a thirteen-by-six-by-three-foot flight with a shelter at one end. A ten-inch-square-by-sixteen-inch-high nest box with two inches of dampened peat moss was also provided. By March 1978 he observed the male feeding the hen, as well as considerable mutual preening. On April 6 one egg was discovered in the nest box, at which time the hen virtually disappeared from view, spending most of her time incubating, while the male became very aggressive, screaming loudly if anyone approached the flight. The hen left the nest on April 21 after having laid four eggs. On May 3, twenty-seven days after the first egg appeared, a newly hatched chick was discovered. Of the three remaining eggs, one was infertile and the other two contained dead chicks. The surviving chick left the nest forty-eight days after hatching. It resembled its parents but had a less extensive orange-yellow marking on the forehead and forecrown, and most of its other feathers were a paler shade of green. By the end of July the chick had weaned and was feeding itself.

Young Halfmoon Conures can become very tame. I remember corresponding with one Halfmoon owner, who sent a photo showing his conure peering inquisitively into his wide-open mouth as if it were seeing a wonderful sight.

The Halfmoon, or Petz's, Conure (opposite) has been kept as a pet for more than a century. Robert Pearcy

GOLD-CAPPED CONURE

This is another parrot regarding which caution, and, when possible, the scientific name, must be used to avoid confusion with other conures that have similar names and markings. The Gold-cap is also called the Golden-headed, Golden-frosted, and Flame-capped Conure. The most commonly used name for *Aratinga auricapilla*, however, is the one used here.

These birds are medium-size conures, about twelve inches long. They are predominantly green with a yellowish tinge to the feathers of the cheeks, throat, and ear coverts. The front of the crown is yellow, providing the basis for two of its names, while the forehead and lores are an orange-red, which accounts for its less-common name. The eyes are brown and the beak is shiny black.

The Mitred Conure takes its name from its vivid crown of red feathers. Michael DeFreitas

Gold-capped Conures are native to northeastern Brazil in the northern and central Bahía regions. A good-sized breeding pool exists and domestic babies are frequently offered for sale. Thomas Arndt (*Encyclopedia of Conures*, 1982) describes them as peaceful and interesting parrots that do well as single cage birds, quickly losing their shyness and becoming quite attached to their

owners. He also acknowledges their propensity for chewing and recommends that twigs and other toys be regularly available for this purpose.

A White-eyed Conure (left) and a Blue-eyed Conure. Michael DeFreitas

A. A. Prestwich (*Records of Parrots Bred in Captivity*, 1951) notes an early success in breeding this parrot by S. J. Wigley. In 1930 the parents hatched three clutches in one season and they bred again in 1931.

Kevin Clubb of the Last Chance Bird Farm in Miami has bred these conures quite regularly. He has worked with fifteen pairs and considers the birds unusual in a number of ways. They have an extended breeding season, virtually year-round. Pairs begin breeding at two years of age, and they are excellent foster parents as well as natural parents; his birds regularly fostered the chicks and eggs of a number of other conures, as well as Amazons. Incubation is approximately twenty-four days, with both parents participating in brooding and feeding, and clutches generally number between three and five eggs.

The breeding successes at the Last Chance Bird Farm have resulted in several generations of conures. Clubb has observed hybridization between various conures and believes that the off-spring of Sun Conures and Gold-caps, or Sun-caps, look remarkably like Jendays. He is of the opinion that backcrossing Sun-caps to Suns could result in offspring so close to Jendays that some interesting speculation on the origin of the Jenday would result.

QUEEN OF BAVARIA CONURE

The Queen of Bavaria Conure is universally regard-ed as one of the most beautiful of all parrots. Frequently called the Golden Conure, its name could refer to its price as well as color: a single bird may sell for several thousand dollars. These birds have always been expensive, and, according to Dr. Greene, were selling for the equivalent of about $125 in 1887. They originate in a comparatively restricted area of Brazil, where a great deal of dam-age to their habitat has occurred. This has resulted in their being added to the CITES Appendix I List. Permits are required to purchase them, and these are generally granted only to registered breeders.

Much of this parrot's plumage is bright yellow, which is dramatically set off by green wing feath-ers. It has a large beak and the typical conure short tail, both features combining to give it a top-heavy appearance. It also has a bare eye ring. If the tail were longer, it would resemble a small and very beautiful macaw. With a length of about four-teen inches, it is actually larger than some of the smaller Amazons.

In *Endangered Parrots* (1984), Rosemary Low refers to these birds as "parrots more precious than gold." Included in her lavish praise for this bird is this description: "Its golden plumage, exceptional intelligence and captivating personality set the Queen of Bavaria . . . apart from all other conures, and indeed from all other parrots." This is high praise from a world authority, and many others affirm her opinion.

The Queen of Bavaria Conure, or Golden Conure, is universally considered one of the finest species in aviculture. Cohen Associates

Thomas Arndt (*Encyclopedia of Conures*, 1982) also commends the lovable nature and character of these birds, noting that many were already tame and talking when they were imported. He refers to these parrots as Golden Conures, a common alter-nate name, and reports on his own Golden Conure, which is playful, curious, and sings aria-like melodies. Arndt also makes the interesting point that size is useless in sexing, since hens are as large as and sometimes even larger than males.

E. J. Boosey (*Foreign Bird Keeping*, c. 1950) describes the male of the species as being of "bar-baric splendor." In his opinion the female is almost as brightly colored but is slightly smaller. He finds their voices loud, a failing he feels may discourage some people from keeping this bird.

Dr. Greene remarks that in terms of color, ele-gant shape, docility, and general intelligence, the Queen of Bavaria is unsurpassed by any parrot. He admires their longevity and, writing in 1884, notes that one specimen has been in the Parrot House of the London Zoo since 1871.

An excellent article on breeding these con-ures by Californian Dave West appeared in the

November/December 1957 issue of *Avicultural Magazine*. The author was surprised at his success with this pair, as they were imperfect birds, but on July 1 he found the female with three eggs. In spite of a very hot summer that year the chicks did quite well, with both parents doing the feeding. The male would spend the night in the eighteen-by-eighteen-by-thirty-six-inch nest box that was hung in the shelter of the flight. Mr. West describes the youngsters as noisy chicks whose calls could be heard at a distance of fifty feet while they were being fed by their parents.

The mainstay of the parents' diet during the raising of the young was fresh corn on the cob, of which they consumed a minimum of three large ears daily. They had previously been fond of oranges, apples, and grapes but now ate much less of the first two items and would fling the grapes, uneaten, to the floor of the flight. Sunflower and millet were also consumed.

The chicks were showing pin feathers at thirty-five days and were almost completely feathered by six weeks. They left the nest at the end of the tenth week, but the youngest chick was not quite ready and usually ended up on the ground, having to be placed back in the nest. It was eventually removed for hand-feeding.

The late Bill Wilson, former owner of Norshore Pets in Illinois, successfully bred these rare birds in 1985. Wilson's first clutch had green on the head, mantle, scapula, and tail, whereas the chicks from a second clutch varied considerably. Such variations are typical of this species.

NANDAY CONURE

Nandayus nenday is the single member of its own genus. This attractively marked parrot originates in Bolivia, Brazil, Argentina, and Paraguay and is known by a confusing variety of names, including Black-headed Conure (the common European designation), Black-hooded Parakeet, Black-masked Conure, and Hooded Parrot.

The upper body surface is bright green, fading to a lighter yellowish green on the undersurface, and there is a light wash of blue on the throat and upper part of the breast. The forehead, crown, and cheek regions are a glossy brownish black, which is the source of the bird's alternative names, and has a black beak and brown eyes. There is no difference in markings or color between males and females, although some breeders claim that males have larger heads and beaks than females.

In the wild these birds favor forest regions, and large flocks can frequently be seen flying in such areas, occasionally sharing airspace with Quaker or Monk Parakeets. There have been reports that the Nanday (unlike many other species) has thrived rather than suffered because of the land cultivation; sunflower and corn crops have afforded them a banquet, with farmers as their unwilling hosts.

Nandays have been kept as pets for well over one hundred years, and, as reported by Rutgers and Norris, they were originally exhibited at the London Zoo in 1870, and bred first in Holland by Cornely in 1881, and somewhat later in England by Mrs. Johnstone around the turn of the century.

Wolfgang deGrahl comments on the ready availability and low price of these birds, noting with interest the tendency of pairs to remain close together while sharing tasks and humorous habits such as bobbing up and down when excited.

Many writers criticize the Nanday for two bad habits, loudness and a passion for chewing, but it should be kept in mind that all healthy parrots chew and the Nandays are not exceptional in this respect. Their screams are quite piercing, however, and this is probably because, like most of the conures and other small parrots, their voices are fairly high pitched.

These parrots are still quite common in the wild as well as in captivity, and are considered to be free breeders; pairs commonly produce four or five chicks if provided with an appropriate nest box. They are somewhat noisy, but hand-fed chicks seem to develop into fairly quiet adults.

PATAGONIAN CONURE

The Patagonian, *Cyanoliseus patagonus*, differs from the *Aratinga* conures in that it has a long, tapering tail that can bring the total length of a full-grown bird to sixteen or seventeen inches. It is olive brown on the head, neck, and back, while the undersurfaces are yellow with an olive tinge and the throat and breast are grayish brown. There is a

A devoted pair of Maroon-bellied Conures (opposite). Joan Balzarini

Compare the size of the Hahn's Macaw (center) with that of the Red-masked Conure (left) and the Sun Conure (right).
Jayne Tansey-Patron

A Patagonian Conure. Robert Pearcy

smaller version that is sometimes referred to as the Lesser Patagonian Conure, but many experts do not consider this a separate species, since the only important differences between the two are size and the superior definition of the white band across the chest in the Greater.

A revealing letter appeared in the January 1973 issue of the *Magazine of the Parrot Society* in which June Davis of Rugby, England, described her experiences with a Patagonian. Her bird was placed with a lory and a cockatoo that both took an instant dislike to him; they screamed at him, and he defiantly replied with his own deafening screeches. Compassion for her neighbors caused Mrs. Davis to move the Patagonian to an outside aviary and later to a flight. At this point all parties graciously accepted each other, but the conversational screams became deafening and the Patagonian was eventually moved to a large cage of his own, where I assume he still resides.

Captive breeding is not a problem, and these conures are well worth considering if you wish to try your hand at breeding a bird larger than a cockatiel or budgie.

In the May 1986 issue of the *Magazine of the Parrot Society*, Paul and Jane Bailey described their own breeding experiences with the Patagonian. They set up six birds in a twenty-foot flight, and, in addition to regular nest boxes, they provided a tunnel dug in a bale of peat comparable to those in which wild Patagonians nest in the sides of sandy river banks. When they did not see results, they replaced the regular nest boxes with eight-gallon wooden barrels. Within just a few days one pair began to breed, producing three eggs from which two lovely chicks were hatched.

13 ECLECTUS PARROTS

These larger species of the parrot tribe are not only clever but mentally and bodily uncommonly vivacious, and together with the large corvines, they are probably the only birds which can suffer from that state of mind, common to human prisoners, namely boredom.
— *Konrad Z. Lorenz,* King Solomon's Ring

Birds in this genus show such a marked degree of dimorphism, or difference between the sexes, that for many years males and females were thought to be different species. It was not until the nineteenth-century biologist Dr. Meyer of the Dresden Museum realized that his green specimens were always males and his red and blue specimens were females that it became clear these individuals of *Eclectus roratus* were actually different sexes of the same species. These differences in color are obvious as early as one month of age, while the birds are still in the nest.

Feather structure in the Eclectus differs from that of other parrots. They have such tightly woven feathers that in healthy, clean birds the feathering gives the illusion of silky hair or fur.

Wolfgang deGrahl provides a considerable amount of information about these parrots. He discussed the importation practices in the late 1970s and early 1980s that resulted in many imported birds arriving in frail condition. Most of these difficulties stemmed from ignorance and a failure to properly feed these rather picky eaters. New arrivals should have been coaxed to eat with offerings of choice food, and those importers who took the trouble to do this had fewer problems. Of course, this is not an issue any longer, as the problem

A splendid grouping of Solomon Island Eclectus, one of the parrot tribe's most interesting families. Debra Duchene

does not exist with the domestic Eclectus. DeGrahl recommends that new imports eat a diet of fresh corn on the cob, boiled corn kernels, and rice that can later be supplemented with sunflower, carrots, ripe fruits, and fresh greens. He notes that although they are basically fruit eaters in the wild, the addition of sunflower to their diet will result in firmer stools.

In addition to great beauty, Eclectus parrots have a number of characteristics to recommend them. They tame readily, showing a great liking for people and pairs do very well together, although deGrahl cautions against attempting to keep more than one female with a single male, as a normally gentle female may attack her rival viciously. He even recalls a case where stuffed females were attacked as pseudo-rivals.

These parrots also need a great deal of attention from and interaction with their owners, a fact brought home to an acquaintance who discovered that his domestic baby male Eclectus was plucking itself during the day when he was at work. In desperation, he eventually placed it with a young woman who specialized in the treatment of injured and abused birds, and within a short time the love and attention she provided ended the plucking.

Neville Cayley (*What Bird Is That?—A Guide To The Birds of Australia*, 1972 ed.) notes that in the wild these parrots favor rain forests, where they feed on nuts, seeds, and fruits, usually nesting in large tree hollows at heights of up to seventy feet. Males have an interesting call, which sounds to Cayley like a casually uttered "Quork!" while females generally emit a piercing whistle.

Breeding records appear very early for these parrots. According to A. A. Prestwich, a successful breeding took place in Germany in 1881, and there are records of breedings from Scotland in 1912 and the United States, by the well-known California aviculturist, Mrs. Bonestall, in 1937.

There has always been discussion and controversy regarding the various subspecies of Eclectus. In the third revised edition of *Parrots of the World*, 1989, Forshaw lists ten groups with differences in distribution, size, and markings. I prefer the more rational breakdown provided by Arthur, Bauer, and Desborough in their 1987 book, *A Complete Guide to the Eclectus Parrots*. Wayne Arthur has maintained and bred four subspecies of Eclectus for almost ten years; Fred Bauer breeds parrots as a full-time occupation; and Laurella Desborough

has bred various species of Eclectus for many years. Their opportunities for intensive observations have been incomparable and their descriptions of the subspecies are uniquely valuable. Our own breakdown of the subspecies follows the pattern devised by these experts.

VOSMAERI

This subspecies comes from the northern and central Moluccas and is approximately thirteen and a half to fourteen inches long. The female's head is bright red down to the nape and the lower beak; it appears to be a brighter orange-red than the heads of other subspecies. Beginning at the neck and continuing to the region of the crop, this color blends to lavender, the nape and mantle also showing a broad band of deep lavender. The back and upperwing coverts are a dark red that is brighter and closer to true red than in any other subspecies. The male *vosmaeri* is a deep, bright green. Laurella Desborough describes this color as almost iridescent and believes that viewing the feathers under a low-power microscope can be very helpful in subspecies identification. This bird also has a bright red patch of feathers above the thigh that continues to include the underwing coverts, and there is a turquoise blue marking at the bend of the wings. The upper beak is orange with a yellow tip, while the lower beak is black.

GRAND ECLECTUS

This is the nominate race and is approximately twelve inches long. The female's red head is duller and darker than that of the *vosmaeri* subspecies, and its marking extends down the neck and upper breast in a pattern resembling a bib. The line of demarcation between the red bib and the color of the abdomen is sharp and definite. Where *vosmaeri* is a deep lavender color on the abdomen, the Grand is a dark, dull purple. It lacks the yellow tail. Instead, the tips of the tail feathers are edged in a dusty yellow-orange. Males have the same coloring as *vosmaeri* males, with slight variations such as mauve edgings on the outer webs of the primaries. The tail is visibly shorter than in *vosmaeri* males, while the beak is paler than *vosmaeri* and more slender than that of any other subspecies. Obviously, the name "Grand" does not refer to the nominate parrot's size or colors.

Note the underwing colors of this male Eclectus. Ginny Haddad

A Vosmaeri Eclectus pair. The red and blue hen is at the left and the green male is at the right. Hans Andersson

GRANDMAERI

Arthur and his colleagues have created this fanciful and unofficial subspecies classification as an appropriate niche for intermediate birds that differ in color and size from both the Grand and *vosmaeri* Eclectus and probably originate on the Moluccan island of Ceram. Females are about thirteen inches long and have a red head color brighter than that of the Grand but not as bright as *vosmaeri*. There is a marked separation at the point where the red bib yields to the purplish blue of the breast and abdomen. Males are smaller than the *vosmaeri* but larger than Grand, and have a light lemon-yellow band of color on the tip of the tail.

ARUENSIS

These parrots are restricted to the Aru Islands. They are somewhat larger and more slender than the New Guinea, Red-sided Eclectus and have longer tails. Females are similar to the Red-sided, but the red on their chests extends to a lower area, and they have brighter red tails that are less blackish toward the base.

RED-SIDED

Arthur and his colleagues have observed two Red-sided groups in the United States, one shorter and stockier (probably from New Guinea), and the other, a longer and more slender type, is probably from the Aru Islands. They are thirteen to thirteen and a half inches long. Females have a bright red region covering the entire head and extending down the nape, neck, and crop region as far as the upper breast. The separation between the red bib and the royal blue of the lower breast and abdomen is clearly defined, and the skin around the eyes has an edging of fine blue feathers. Thighs and under-tail coverts are a bright red, while the beak, eyes, and feet are the same as those of the *vosmaeri*. In males, the overall body color is more of a bright brownish-bronze green than that of *vosmaeri* males. The head, back, and wings are a darker green, the nape is a yellowish-green, and the yellow tail-tip marking is somewhat pale and more narrow.

SOLOMON ISLANDS

This is a short bird, about twelve to thirteen inches long. Both males and females resemble the Red-sided subspecies except that they are smaller and more compact, and the females have a shorter neck. The overall green color has a yellowish cast and the red patch on the side of the body is more elongated and wider than in *vosmaeri*.

MACGILLIVRAY

This subspecies is limited to the Cape York Peninsula of Australia. It is the largest of the subspecies, but both sexes are otherwise identical to the Red-sided. It is named for Dr. W. Macgillivray of Broken Hill in New South Wales, who sponsored collection expeditions in Australia as early as 1910. Macgillivray recounts the discovery in Australia of the subspecies that bears his name in the January 1914 issue of *The Emu*. He is also credited with the discovery of the Red-cheeked Parrot (*Geoffroyus geoffroyi*). It should be noted that the actual collecting and discovery was done by Macgillivray's employee, W. McLennon, a popular Australian explorer of the period who was known as "Mac the Naturalist."

WESTERMANI

The existence of this race is questionable, and Arthur, Bauer, and Desborough express doubts about its validity, indicating that it may only appear in captivity. It has been known since at least 1981 and is the smallest of the subspecies, with a length of about eleven and a half inches. Females are similar to the Grands except for their smaller size and the fact that their abdomens are colored a dull, smoky blue. Males are more bluish than the Grands but duller in color, with less red visible on the sides of their bodies.

In addition to its extreme sexual dimorphism, the Eclectus (opposite) differs from other parrot species in the feel of its plumage. The feathers of an Eclectus feel like the fur of some mammalian species. Debra Duchene

Eclectus parrots are prized for their beautiful colors, and they also make wonderful, amusing pets. This Solomon Islands male demonstrates his acrobatic ability to prove the point. Paolo Tiengo

BIAKI

The coloring of the female in this subspecies is similar to that of the Red-sided, except that the neck, nape, and bib appear to be a bright red; males are also like the Red-sided, but smaller. At twelve to twelve and a half inches these birds are slightly smaller than the Grands. Although some experts doubt the legitimacy of this race, it is unique to Biak Island and thus meets qualifications for subspecies status devised by Arthur and his colleagues.

CORNELIA'S

Eclectus roratus cornelia is native to Cornelia Island in Indonesia and is about fourteen inches long. The female is solid red and similar to the Grand, but longer and with a yellow-tipped tail; the red on its chest is particularly bright, and the back and upper-wing coverts are maroon. It lacks any shades of blue, purple, or lavender. According to Bates and Busenbark (*Parrots and Related Birds*, 1969), males have more extensively red beaks than Grands and their wings show a bright blue color.

RIEDELLI'S

This subspecies is smaller than the Grand and Solomons, with a length of about eleven and a half inches. The female resembles a completely red *vosmaeri* but is considerably smaller and has a broad yellow tail band. Males have less red on the sides than any of the subspecies. Their tail tip is a broad, dull yellow. Bates and Busenbark identify them as originating in the northern Moluccas, the same habitat as that of *vosmaeri*. Forshaw, however, claims that they are restricted to the Tanimbar Islands (home of Goffin's) Cockatoo in the southern Moluccas.

Laurella Desborough has made some interesting observations on the vocalizing of the Eclectus. She believes that threat calls, signaling danger, are virtually identical among all the subspecies, but that when actual communication is going on the sounds are unique for each group.

Early observers such as Dr. Greene admired the Eclectus but apparently knew nothing about the different races. Greene comments that these parrots had been imported since 1750, when male specimens were numerous, but at this time, as was mentioned earlier, importers believed that the two sexes were actually different species.

Charles Barrett describes how the owner of a hotel in Coen, Australia, introduced visitors to a pair of tame Eclectus she had owned for years that had free range of the hotel and were caged only at night. They were called "Rocky Range Parrots," a local name for the Grand Eclectus. Werner Lantermann (*The New Parrot Handbook*, 1985), considers the Grand Eclectus the subspecies most commonly kept as a pet. He describes them as "placid and almost lazy birds" that tame rapidly and seldom bite.

I would disagree with Lantermann, as my own observations indicate that the Solomon Island Eclectus is the most common pet. This is probably due to their relative availability, although some writers consider this the most endearing subspecies. I have seen and played with half a dozen domestic types and can confirm that they are clever, lovable birds with excellent personalities and an air of supreme confidence and calmness that I find very attractive. In light of these characteristics and the great beauty of their colorful, "furry" feathers, they are a highly desirable choice for the home aviary, which, as Lantermann recommends, should have plenty of tree limbs and branches as these parrots enjoy climbing.

Ian Harman considers Sir Edward Hallstrom the most successful breeder of the Eclectus. (Hallstrom is also well known for this work with Black Cockatoos.) Harman cautions prospective owners that when breeding in colonies, Eclectus parents usually stop feeding their young as soon as they leave the nest. The neglected babies must then be hand-reared if they are to survive. However, if only one pair of Eclectus breed per aviary, the parents will complete the feeding and rearing even after the young have left the nest.

It is essential that there be no hybrid breeding of any of these subspecies. If we fail to heed this warning, hybrid parents will eventually produce young for whom no clear lineage can be determined. When purchasing Eclectus, ask if you can see the parents; a reputable breeder will not refuse this request unless the birds are brooding or feeding young chicks.

LORIES AND LORIKEETS

The lorikeets are part of the subfamily *Loriinae*, a race that is extensively dispersed throughout Indonesia and Australia. Their rich colors and glossy feathers, along with a neat, compact, and beautifully proportioned body, combine to make this an eye-catching group. Healthy specimens are curious, active, and agile birds that are a pleasure to watch as they satisfy their curiosity about new objects by twisting and turning into odd positions. Dr. Russ (*The Speaking Parrots*, 1884) aptly describes their movements as "pert . . . odd, hasty and violent."

The lorikeets, along with their shorter-tailed relatives the lories, feed mainly on fruits, nectar, and pollen. Their beaks and tongues are anatomically modified for this diet, with their tongues ending in a dense bundle of hairlike structures suitable for picking up nectar and pollen. This adaptation is the reason they are also referred to as the "brush-tongued parrots."

Their soft, virtually liquid diet results in loose droppings, which at one time limited their popularity. In recent years newer diets have been developed that, although still largely liquid, have improved the situation and this, combined with heavy importing from Indonesia during the 1970s and 1980s, has caused an increase in popularity sufficient to account for the foundation of The International Loriidae Society, devoted solely to lories and lorikeets.

A trio of Fairy Lorikeets. Gunther Enderle, NEKTON PRODUCTS

As pointed out by Stan Sindel (*Australian Lorikeets*, 1987), proper design of housing for these parrots can increase the efficiency with which they are maintained and compensate for their loose droppings. Among other things he recommends eliminating solid walls and replacing them with wire mesh wherever possible; if solid walls must be used, they should be of a nonporous, easy-to-clean material. Food and water containers should be so placed to avoid contamination by droppings. The use of feeding bays attached to the aviary can provide this protection.

A complete diet is crucial for these birds, as deficiencies can lead to health problems called "avitaminoses." Kavanaugh (*Lovebirds, Cockatiels, Budgerigars: Behavior and Evolution*, 1987) notes that a vitamin A deficiency in lorikeets can cause lesions that make the birds susceptible to candidiasis, particularly in newly imported specimens.

One particularly attractive and well-named lorikeet is *Charmosyna placentis*, the Pleasing Lorikeet, which is also known as the Red-flanked or Blue-eared Lorikeet. These five-inch-long beauties are found in many parts of Indonesia and are unique in that they show clear dimorphism. The green males have a streaked blue ear patch with red markings on the cheeks and throat. The blue rump, red sides, and red underwing coverts are also quite attractive. Females do not have the blue or red markings, but do have bright yellow ear coverts that look streaked because of the green feathers beneath them. This species is not commonly bred in the United States, but it does show up on the stud list published in the *Bulletin of the International Loriidae Society*. Because other members of the genus, such as Stella's Lorikeet, are regularly bred, there is no apparent reason why the Pleasing Lorikeet should not be bred as well.

A Striated Lorikeet. Paolo Tiengo

A Red-collared Coconut Lory. Courtesy American Museum of Natural History

The March 1985 issue of the above-mentioned bulletin offered an excellent article on the Pleasing Lorikeet written by the late Mrs. J. L. Spenkelink of the Netherlands. She noted that, because of the differences between the sexes, for many years it was thought that males and females were of different species. Her first pair produced two infertile eggs, but seventeen days later a clutch of two fertile eggs was laid. The chicks hatched two days apart, thrived, and fledged successfully. Unfortunately, one chick, a male, died, but the second, a female, grew up without incident.

Trichoglossus haematodus, the Rainbow Lorikeet, is, in contrast to the Pleasing Lorikeet, a very abundant and commonly kept bird. The Rainbow is also known as the Blue Mountain Parrot and Swainson's Lorikeet. It is the largest Australian lorikeet, reaching a length of twelve inches. It has an orange beak and a bright, deep violet-blue head that blends into a green collar. The rump, wings, and back are green, but the chest is red and yellow, with the lower portion a deep violet-blue. Bates and Busenbark commend the bird's beauty and the personality that rivals it. They describe the Rainbows as cheerful and comical parrots that enjoy playing games with each other in a manner very reminiscent of young puppies.

Forshaw (*Parrots of the World*, 2nd rev. ed., 1978) notes twenty-one subspecies! Hutchins and Lovell point out that Rainbows are the largest of the Australian lorikeets and that there is considerable variation in the size of birds, which inhabit a long area of the western coast of the continent. These authors also remark that the Rainbow is the best known and most widely kept lorikeet. The authors warn, however, that although it is a frequent captive breeder, one pair per aviary is best, because attempts at colony breeding usually result in battles. Their book is heartily recommended if you are interested in learning more about lories and lorikeets or Australian parrots in general.

Although not as easy to care for as cockatoos, Amazons, African Greys, and other more commonly kept species, many lory and lorikeet aficionados believe that choosing a pet from among these species offers an important advantage: Because of their unusual, tight, almost fur-like feather structure, there is less of a problem with feather dust, so individuals who suffer from allergies may do better with these parrots than with any other type.

A Red and Blue Lory chick at thirty-two days. Roger Sweeny

15

LOVEBIRDS

The parrot never had a better friend. His Grace, The Duke, maintained leafy parks at Woburn Abbey, England . . . raised hundreds of parrots . . . studied these birds all his life and put what he learned into a book which is respected by parrot fanciers . . . the world around.

—*John Phillips*, Dear Parrot

The lovebirds are all members of the genus *Agapornis*. They consist of nine species of small parrots ranging in length from four and a half to seven inches and, with the exception of the Madagascar Lovebird, originate on the continent of Africa.

Even though these birds are combative with their own kind as well as other birds at various stages of their life cycle, they always do best in pairs and bonded pairs show deep affection and concern for each other.

Lovebirds are popular with newcomers to the fancy as well as with knowledgeable breeders. The more common species are comparatively inexpensive, easy to breed, and relatively simple to maintain. The attempt to produce and maintain new color mutations is a challenge that makes this group particularly intriguing to breeders.

These parrots all have a basic green body, with each species generally named for differences in facial and head colors. This is obviously the case with the Gray-headed, Masked, Black-cheeked, Red-faced, Peach-faced, and Black-collared Lovebirds, but the Fischer's, Abyssinian, Nyasa, and Madagascar species are exceptions to the rule.

An Abyssinian Lovebird pair. The male is at the left. David Frydrychowicz

A fascinating article by William Dilger on the evolution of lovebirds and the role of heredity in their behavior appeared in the January 1962 issue of *Scientific American*. The author points out that these birds select mates early in life and such relationships may last for a lifetime. Like other experts, he credits their mutual devotion with the origin of their name. Working with his colleagues at Cornell University's Laboratory of Ornithology, Dilger studied a group of lovebirds for five years. Some of the conclusions reached by these scientists are quite predictable, while others appear to be at variance with observations made by longtime lovebird enthusiasts. Regardless of whether or not they conflict with your own opinions, the following notes are extremely interesting.

The Madagascar, Abyssinian, and Red-faced Lovebirds show obvious sexual dimorphism and tend to reject colony breeding. All species of lovebirds engage in courtship feeding, but in the three species mentioned above, the female can often be found feeding the male, a form of behavior not observed in other species, "where courtship feeding is a male prerogative." The females of all species vacillate in their enthusiasm for copulation but all signal it by rearrangements of their head plumage; the more a hen fluffs her head feathers the more receptive she is.

Many bird fanciers have had great success with surrogates when the original hen could not or would not sit on her eggs. However, if lovebirds have reared their own chicks, they will reject the young of other lovebird species that have down of a different color. Females given such chicks at the time of their first egg-laying experience do not hesitate to rear them.

In addition to these observations, there is a great deal of information in this article, virtually all of which would be helpful to the reader. If you have a serious interest in breeding or maintaining this species, I recommend that you try to obtain the original issue of the magazine or write to *Scientific American* for information on purchasing a reprint of the article. You might also try to obtain a copy of the article through your local library retrieval services.

BLACK-COLLARED LOVEBIRD

The Black-collared Lovebird, *Agapornis swindernianus*, is also known as Swinderen's Lovebird. It is slightly over five inches long and is green with a thin black collar on the neck below which there is an orange-to-yellow band. The beak is black or grayish black and the eyes are yellow. There are several subspecies, but the nominate race is found in Liberia. This lovebird is extremely rare in captivity.

The lovebirds described below all show sexual dimorphism, allowing males and females to be easily distinguished.

ABYSSINIAN LOVEBIRD

The Abyssinian Lovebird, *Agapornis taranta*, is among the largest of the lovebirds, reaching a length of over six inches. The male is green with a red forehead, beak, and eye ring, and the female is dull green with a red beak, and no eye ring. Their natural habitat is the evergreen mountain forests of Ethiopia. Forshaw (*Parrots of the World*, 1972) notes that they descend from this region only when the figs, for which they have a special fondness, are ripe. A smaller subspecies occurs from southern Ethiopia to the border of Kenya. Abyssinians have been kept by aviculturists since the turn of the century. Although they are not free breeders, they have been bred by a fair number of fanciers. Helmut Hampe, a German breeder, reports having fostered Abyssinian chicks to budgie parents, which raised them after their young budgies were removed.

RED-FACED LOVEBIRD

The Red-faced Lovebird, *Agapornis pullarius*, is a five-and-a-half-inch lovebird of which the entire forehead, face, and neck are marked in bright red. Because the color does not extend around the back of the eye, the sharp contrast between the green head and the red face gives the illusion of a red ski mask. The body is dark green on top, the lower surface is a lighter green with a yellowish glow, the tail is yellow with a red marking and a green tip, and the bend of wing and underwing coverts are black. The upper beak is a light red and the lower portion is orange-yellow. Females are lighter in color and have an orange face and green underwing coverts instead of black.

These birds originate in Sierra Leone, Cameroon, northern Angola, Uganda, and Rwanda. As noted by Vriends (*Lovebirds*, 1986), they prefer wooded regions, where they live in large flocks, feeding on grasses, figs, leaf buds, and millet. They have unusual breeding habits, and prefer to nest in termite mounds that are still actively inhabited by the creatures that built them; even though the hen modifies the termite mound, the termites, which would normally attack any other animals, ignore the lovebirds. This unusual behavior probably accounts for part of the difficulty of breeding these birds in captivity. The first documented success was by A. A. Prestwich in England in 1956, as reported in *Avicultural Magazine*. Prestwich experimented with various nests designed to simulate those used in the wild and found that the birds responded best to barrels filled with tightly packed leaf mold.

MADAGASCAR LOVEBIRD

The Madagascar Lovebird, *Agapornis cana*, is also known as the Gray-headed Lovebird. It is slightly over five inches long. Males and females can be quickly distinguished: In the male, the head, neck, throat, and upper chest are gray, while in the hen these areas are green. The beak is whitish gray in males and yellow in hens. These parrots originate on Madagascar, appearing everywhere except the central portion of the island. They travel in large flocks and can ravage any crops that attract their attention. According to Vriends, they are seasonal breeders, preferring November and December.

PEACH-FACED LOVEBIRD

At up to seven inches long, *Agapornis roseicollis* is the largest of the lovebirds. The male has a delicate pink-red forehead, cheeks, chin, throat, and upper abdomen, light blue upper-tail coverts, and a brilliant green body. The eye is brown with a narrow, yellowish-white ring. It is not easy to distinguish females. For this reason and because they have a faint eye ring, Vriends considers them dimorphically intermediate. They may be slightly larger than males, and their peach color is somewhat muted and less widespread.

Peach-faced Lovebirds are distributed in Namibia and Angola, southwest Africa. They are colony breeders, often building large nests similar to those of the Quaker Parakeet in caves or under the eves of buildings. This is a very popular species

and an excellent choice for the novice, as they are hardy and breed freely in captivity. Many mutations, such as the yellow Peach-face, the pied Peach-face, and the blue Peach-face have been produced and maintained.

As bird breeders work with species in captive breeding, the likelihood of mutations becomes greater. As with the budgie and the cockatiel, mutations are now increasingly seen in lovebirds. Shown here are two examples of color mutations in the Peach-faced Lovebird (violet–cobalt–pastel blue [left], violet–pastel blue [right]). Johann Kloosterman

The following members of *Agapornis* all have white eye rings of varying sizes:

BLACK-CHEEKED LOVEBIRD

Agapornis nigrigenis is a five-and-three-quarter-inch parrot with a dark, brownish-black forehead and cheeks. The sides and rear of the head are yellowish green, the throat is orange, and there is a pink marking on the chest. It has a white eye ring, brown eyes, and a red beak. The colors of the hen are muted, and the cheek plumage is more brown than black. These lovebirds originate in the southern part of the African continent, in northern Zimbabwe. Vriends notes that they are good breeders but that restrictions on exportations have made it difficult to obtain older birds. Horst Bielfeld (*Handbook of Lovebirds*, 1982) suggests that these restrictions might be justifiable in light of the fact that sixteen thousand Black-cheeked Lovebirds were trapped and exported in just one month in 1926 because of damage to millet and other crops.

NYASA LOVEBIRD

The Nyasa Lovebird, *Agapornis lilianae*, is about four and a half inches long. Its forehead and crown are a bright red, the cheeks and throat are a more orange red, and the body is a deep green. The eyes are dark brown with a white eye ring, and the beak is a deep red. Females are indistinguishable from males, except that their colors are slightly muted. The Nyasas originate in southern Tanzania, northern Zimbabwe, eastern Malawi, and western Mozambique. Because of restrictions on exports and cross-breeding with the Peach-face, true Nyasas are scarce. Given proper conditions, they are good breeders in captivity and it should be possible to build up domestic stocks if fanciers are willing to make the effort.

FISCHER'S LOVEBIRD

The Fischer's, *Agapornis fischeri*, is a popular lovebird about six inches long. It originates in East Africa, in northern Tanzania, where small flocks can be observed at elevations of between 3,000 and 5,000 feet. Its green body is marked with yellow on the neck, while the throat and cheeks are orange, and although the head is a typical olive green, the forehead is bright red. The eyes are brown with a small yellowish-white ring, and the beak is red. This bird is an excellent captive breeder that has been a great favorite for many years. There is also a popular blue mutation.

A pair of Lutino Peach-faced Lovebirds; the male on the right. Darden Vaughn

MASKED LOVEBIRD

Agapornis personatus is another good-sized member of the genus that is about six to six and a half inches long. Its head is brownish black marked with a yellow collar, the throat and chest are orange, and the rump is bluish. It has brown eyes, a large white eye ring, and a red beak. These lovebirds have a distribution similar to the Fischer's and are found in northeast Tanzania. They have been bred in the United States since 1926 and are excellent breeders, producing large numbers each year. The blue mutation is extremely attractive and has yellow and green regions where the nominate race is white and blue. All mutations of this species have a light horn-colored beak.

With the exception of the rare mutations, most of the lovebirds are plentiful and priced quite reasonably. If you are interested in advancing from the budgie or cockatiel to a more parrot-like group of birds, the lovebirds are an excellent species with which to begin.

16

MACAWS

MACAWS AS PETS

Many parrot fanciers start their bird collections with smaller species such as conures or Amazons. This is probably an intelligent decision, as smaller parrots require less extensive facilities and many can be obtained at relatively reasonable prices. Eventually, however, a great number of parrot enthusiasts feel the urge to own one of the large, vividly colored macaws. Perhaps it is their beauty, with color combinations among the most striking in the parrot family, or it may be their impressive size and wild tropical appearance that encourages dreams of ownership. Potential macaw owners may assume, as did certain South American tribes, that some of the power and magic of the bird will, by association, rub off on them.

Macaws originate in Central and South America and, until 1989, were commonly imported in great numbers. However, importation of these parrots is now at an end, but with the exception of the really rare species such as the Buffon's there are many breeding pairs of almost all types in the United States, and a considerable number of chicks are produced each year.

There has always been a high level of interest in these parrots, and their relationships with

The Hyacinth Macaw—in a word, spectacular! Luke Golobitsch

humans date back many years. South American natives valued them for their vividly colored feathers, as well as for food, and some Native American tribes raise them as we raise poultry. Among the Pueblos, it was believed that only households of a harmonious nature inhabited by people of good character could successfully maintain a Scarlet Macaw.

Macaws are strong creatures with great power in their beaks. The larger species, such as the Hyacinth and Greenwing, are capable of flexing fairly thick cage bars until they become deformed or weaken and break. Macaws are seldom vicious or nasty. They seem to expect, and get, respect, since only a very foolish person would tease such a bird. They are well aware of their powers, and tame macaws are gentle with their owners. Frodo, my first Scarlet, had exquisite control of his viselike beak, and although he could crush a twig or pine block in an instant he liked to play the typical macaw game of gently squeezing my fingers while screaming in feigned pain as if he were the victim. Studies of macaw brains indicate that their cerebral region, the site of intelligent behavior, is considerably larger than that of other birds of comparable body weight.

Macaws are not spectacular talkers, but what they do learn to say is usually said clearly and loudly. They are also ideal students for those who wish to teach them to perform such activities as roller skating or bicycle riding, on equipment that is, of course, designed for parrots.

Before making what is a fairly expensive investment and a serious commitment of time and energy, keep in mind that when you purchase a macaw as a companion you can plan on having this bird with you for at least thirty or forty years. Is a macaw the parrot for you? If your neighbors would object to occasional loud screams, the answer is no. If your home cannot accommodate a cage that is at least three to four feet square and preferably larger, you should consider choosing a different parrot. If you are intimidated by size and a bold attitude, think about smaller birds. If, however, you think you'd enjoy a parrot with enough personality and self-assurance to grip your wrist in a tight squeeze when you change his water dish or one that will press his warm, featherless cheek patch against your face while muttering endearments, then a macaw might well be your choice.

Once the decision to buy has been made, you must decide which macaw to choose. The following descriptions are accurate, but remember that with living creatures there are always individual variations as a result of inheritance and early experiences.

BLUE AND GOLD MACAW

One of the first macaws I ever owned was Bluebell, a baby Blue and Gold Macaw imported to New York via Italy. I know this sounds like a roundabout journey, but there is a logical explanation: Bluebell and her adopted Scarlet Macaw brother, Fiorello, had been purchased as imported hand-fed babies by an American veterinary student in Italy. He and his wife returned to the United States each summer, and since they were residents in Italy for most of the year, they were legally able to bring the two birds back with them. When I visited the couple, they let me play with these amusing and friendly birds. I suggested that they consider selling them to me at the end of the summer, telling the future veterinarian that it would be a shame to leave a pair of charmers like these with his parents (rather than go to the expense of bringing them back to Italy and ultimately back to the United States again), who would merely feed and clean up after them, when they could be with someone who would give them much more attention. He was undecided at first, but in late August I received a phone call to come and get them. I was so thrilled that, in addition to paying him, I gave him a copy of the original version of Forshaw's *Parrots of the World* as a thank-you gift, a book that is now worth almost as much as the price I paid for one of the birds.

Ara ararauna, alternatively known as the Blue and Yellow Macaw, a popular name in Europe, is a handsomely marked bird distributed through large parts of Central and South America. Many thousands were imported into the United States during the late 1970s and 1980s, most of which came from northern Brazil, Peru, Bolivia, and Ecuador. They are large parrots that can reach a length of almost thirty inches. The upper surface of the body and much of the tail are blue, while the neck and chest are bright yellow, set off with a contrasting band

Bonded Blue and Gold Macaw pair. Michael DeFreitas

of black feathers that runs around the chin and cheeks. There is a bright green marking on the front of the crown and three distinct rows of black feathers on the creamy white cheek patches. Their feathers have a perceptibly sweet odor reminiscent of baby powder. The beak is black and the eyes are light yellow.

Dieter Hoppe (*The World of Macaws,* 1985) notes that they are among the most widely kept of the larger parrots due to their beauty, good disposition, and "relatively good talking ability." I agree with him on all except the last comment: These birds generally learn only a few words or phrases; they can speak in a loud and emphatic voice, but I would not classify them as good talkers. Dr. Greene is impressed with the Blue and Golds' distinct pronunciation of what sounds like the name "Robert"; I fear, however, that this is not so much the use of a popular first name as it is the instinctive production of a particular sound in much the same way that frogs produce "ribbet!" Of course, if your name or the name of a family member happens to be Robert, then a Blue and Gold will delight you.

Blue and Gold Macaws were among the earliest of the parrots kept as household pets. Dr. Russ's book includes a description and illustration of this bird by the biologist Aldrovandi in the mid-sixteenth century. I can confirm the reference, as a number of years ago I was able to purchase and frame a copy of this lovely print.

Under appropriate conditions, the Blue and Gold is an excellent captive breeder. A flight of at least eight feet in length should be used and the pair you work with should be at least five years old. In the case of the female, an extra year or two will enhance your chances of success, as young females often destroy their eggs or drop them out of the nest. Barrels make excellent nest boxes for these birds, but the first time you attempt to breed a new pair you should offer two different types of nest boxes placed at different heights on the outside of the flight. Most parrots prefer the security of a nest that is high in the flight, but there are always some that may select the lower nest box. Once you know their preference, you can remove the extra nest and use the type they have chosen for future breedings.

This Blue and Gold Macaw enjoys excellent indoor–outdoor housing facilities. Joanne Abramson

A five-week-old Blue and Gold chick. Doreen Gluck

There are abundant records of successful breedings both in the United States and Europe. The earliest breeder appears to have been M. Lamouroux of France, in whose aviaries twenty-five young were produced over a four-and-a-half-year period. More recent breeders include the well-known Erling Kjelland of Chicago in 1974 and Doug Trabert in Florida in 1975. Joanne Abramson, owner of Raintree Macaws in California, has regularly bred these macaws for many years.

In a particularly interesting article from the April/June 1976 issue of *Avicultural Magazine*, Daphne H. Grunebaum of England describes the breeding of her Blue and Golds, which were generally permitted to fly freely. The birds were let out at about 9 A.M. each morning and would return a few hours later for a siesta in their aviary. If the weather was good, they were permitted a second opportunity for outdoor flying in the evening. The pair had reared young in 1971 and laid eggs in 1973 and 1974. The 1973 clutch "disappeared" and the eggs produced in 1974 were destroyed by the offspring that had hatched in 1971. The following year, there were many battles between the parents and their boisterous progeny, and the unmannerly offspring eventually threw the nest box to the ground. This was the last straw for Ms. Grunebaum, who arranged for another home for the two younger birds.

Typical breeding behavior followed within two weeks of the older macaws being on their own. The hen no longer wished to fly, and both she and the cock spent a lot of time in the nest box. Eggs were discovered on June 28, July 1, and July 5. The weather at this time was hot and dry, and Ms. Grunebaum regularly soaked the aviary floor with buckets of water. On July 24, Ms. Grunebaum heard loud honks coming from the nest, and she quickly supplied brown bread soaked in milk with glucose, as well as some banana. This was taken immediately and from then on she provided an almost endless stream of food, including sweet biscuits, fruits, nuts, lamb-chop bones, cheese, and a great deal of corn, which was the birds' favorite.

On August 1 both parents took a short flight; this was the first time they had both left the nest at the same time. Ms. Grunebaum was able to inspect the nest and found two large, pink, noisy babies, one unhatched egg, and a walnut. By August 6 the chicks' black beaks were quite conspicuous, as were quill feathers on their wings and tails tipped with blue, and by August 28 yellow feathers had appeared. They were fully fledged by the end of September and were making clumsy attempts at flight. Their owner wisely decided that she would postpone any free flying until the spring. One hopes that these babies grew up to be less rambunctious than their older siblings.

BLUE-THROATED MACAW

This attractive variant of the Blue and Gold Macaw has been referred to as the Caninde Macaw, which, according to Dieter Hoppe (*The World of Macaws*, 1985), is actually a synonym for *Ara ararauna*, the Blue and Gold's scientific name. Hoppe and other experts prefer "Blue-throated Macaw" as a common name for this bird, whose scientific name is *Ara glaucogularis*, a reference to the bluish-green colors of the throat and upper parts.

The Blue-throated Macaw is slightly smaller than the Blue and Gold, and most of the forehead and forecrown is greenish blue, as is the throat. The cheek patch is smaller than in the Blue and Gold, but the cheek markings are much heavier and more distinct and are dark green rather than black. The pattern of markings in the Blue-throated is four lines of greenish-blue feathers that begin just below the nostrils and cover the upper cheek, whereas the Blue and Gold has only three lines of black feathers.

The native habitat of these birds is southeastern Beni and western Santa Cruz in Bolivia. Having known ten Blue-throats, Hoppe notes that, in addition to being smaller than Blue and Golds, they are also more slender. Hoppe's information on this parrot, as well as virtually all the other macaws he writes about, is based largely on personal observation, the kind of information I value most highly.

Forshaw (*Parrots of the World*, 2d rev. ed., 1978) describes the Caninde Macaw as "mysterious." Speculating about its scientific status, he considers three possibilities: that it is a valid species with the same distribution as the Blue and Gold; that it is a juvenile version of the Blue and Gold; and that it is a subspecies of the Blue and Gold. Based on Hoppe's information, Forshaw's first choice is apparently correct.

Hoppe notes that the estimated population of these parrots in what was then West Germany was only fifteen to twenty. Some were in the hands of private breeders, while others resided at Walsrode Bird Park and several could be found at the Berlin Zoo.

Wolfgang Kiessling, founder of Loro Parque at Tenerife in the Canary Islands, acquired a pair of Blue-throated Macaws in 1981 and described their breeding in the January 1985 issue of the *Magazine of the Parrot Society*. Their flight was approximately twelve feet long by thirteen feet high by ten feet deep. The nest box was quite large, eighteen inches deep by twenty-four inches long by thirty-two inches high, and filled with decayed wood and shavings. The birds had originally been on display at the park, and this was not changed; although many visitors pass their flight every day, the birds at the park are quite secure and confident and do not react negatively to the constant flow of observers.

The nest box was placed in the flight at the time the macaws were introduced, and initially they used it as sleeping quarters. Fifteen days before laying her first egg, the hen entered the nest and remained in the box, except for occasional departures to obtain food. The first egg appeared on July 10 and a second three days later. Although both eggs were fertilized, only the first was viable. The hen incubated this egg for twenty-six days, and a fine chick hatched on August 6. Although the hen took extremely good care of her offspring, leaving the nest only to obtain food, the male had no part in the rearing of the chick and did not even show alarm when Mr. Kiessling checked the nest.

SCARLET MACAW

Ara macao has been among the most popular of the macaws for many years, and its beauty, size, personality, and availability have all contributed to the general esteem in which it is held. Even Dr. Greene, an authority with vast experience with many parrots, was impressed enough to indicate that "this grand bird is, without a doubt, king of all

Young macaws benefit greatly from early socialization. Extensive contact with people and free access to suitable toys contribute greatly to the development of exceptionally well-adjusted birds (opposite). Sue Green

the macaws." Although other members of the genus may be more richly colored and difficult to obtain, as a pet I rank the Scarlet at the top of the list of macaws. Regrettably, I have not been alone in my enthusiasm for the Scarlet, and, as a result, a great wave of importation took place between 1975 and 1985 that seriously depleted its numbers. Since June 1986 it has been on the CITES Appendix I list. Among domestic Scarlets, hand-fed females are costlier than males as fewer female chicks are produced.

Although not the largest of the macaws, the Scarlet can reach a length of thirty-three inches or more. A good part of this length is in its tail, but it is still a massive and powerful bird. It is bright red with blue wings and its shoulders and greater wing coverts are yellow with blue and green tips. The head is a vivid red with a curly fringe of bright red feathers just above the cere. Its commanding, sharply curved upper beak is horn-colored, while the lower beak is slate black. The yellowish eye is surrounded by a large naked area that is rather pink from the blood vessels within the skin. According to Hoppe, the female is marked in a similar manner, but may have a smaller beak and a flatter forehead.

Scarlets are found in Brazil, several Central American countries, and the eastern coast of southern Mexico, where, Hoppe reports, they are rapidly decreasing in number. George M. Sutton (*Portraits of Mexican Birds*, 1972) notes that the macaws are called *guacomayos* by the Mexicans, who generally despise them because they do considerable damage to corn crops. He identifies the Mexican range of the Scarlet as Oaxaca, Chiapas, and southern Veracruz.

I have owned several of these powerful birds and have always been impressed by their lack of malice. Frodo, a gentle giant at almost thirty-eight inches in length, could easily open walnuts without breaking the nutmeat. He would start with a small opening and then extract the contents without damaging them. Frodo had the run of my bird room, where he could wander about and play in empty cages while I attended to the other birds. Passing through one area was a tight squeeze, and if he was in the cage in that corner, getting by him was generally a risky effort unless he was bribed with a peanut or two. Failure to do so could result in a sharp pinch from his big beak.

When I held Frodo on my wrist, he would often flap his wings for exercise. It took great effort to

A young Blue and Gold sharing a perch with a Scarlet friend.

steady my hand against the lift generated by those powerful wings.

The Scarlet's good temper should not be abused or taken for granted, as this bird is capable of doing serious damage. Its cage should be strongly constructed, and all exposed wooden surfaces, including perches, replaced on a regular basis. For the same reason, toys for these large parrots must be carefully selected. Wooden blocks made of pine will be destroyed rapidly. I prefer a block with a tough knot in it that I drill through and then hang in the cage with a chain or leather thong. A macaw will chew right down to the knot and then work at the knot itself for a long time, as it is more than a match even for this powerful bird.

These large parrots have been bred on many occasions. A good description of one such breeding was written by D. F. Norman for the March 1975 issue of the *Magazine of the Parrot Society*. The author describes the pairing early in the year, of a six-year-old male and a nine-year-old female, a promising age distribution, as older females are less likely to damage eggs or injure young when they breed. Their aviary was fifteen-by-ten-by-eight feet with a forty-gallon wooden beer barrel as a nest box. Two eggs were laid in April, which, although incubated, proved to be infertile. Two

Frodo, a venerable, strong Scarlet Macaw, was one of the author's great favorites.

more were laid in July that were also incubated by the female with great diligence, while the male spent most of his time guarding the entrance to the nest box. One chick hatched in August, but, unfortunately, the other was dead in shell. The surviving chick fledged shortly after Christmas and grew into a fine bird.

Hybrid breeding of Scarlet Macaws has occurred relatively often and the results can be

The Green-winged Macaw (opposite) is one of the largest of all macaws, but it is a gentle giant despite its intimidating appearance. Eagles, Hawks, & Buffalo

attractive. Most aviculturists, however, are opposed to such breeding as it does nothing to enhance the race. Since males and females are available for breeding programs, there is no point in hybridizing the Scarlets.

GREEN-WINGED MACAW

These macaws are not as colorful as the Blue and Gold and Scarlet Macaws. They are large, red and blue birds with massive heads and beaks. European authors often refer to this parrot as the Red and Blue Macaw. Prestwich *(Parrots Bred in Captivity,* 1951) cautions that older reports from Europe regarding the breeding of these birds may be confusing, as the name "Red and Blue Macaw" can mislead readers into believing that the report is about the better-known Scarlet.

Ara chloroptera is about thirty-four inches long, with a formidable beak to match its substantial head, resulting in what some consider to be a top-heavy look. Their naked cheek patch has between six and seven rows of bright red feathers, and they have a deep red head, chest, and tail. The red feathers of the mantle blend into one or two rows of green feathers, which are then followed by the light blue feathers of the rump. The Green-winged Macaw's feathers are green in the region of the upper coverts, where the Scarlet Macaw is marked with yellow. The upper beak is horn-colored, except for a black base and tip, and the lower the beak is black. A wild yellow eye, which is brownish in immature birds, completes the exotic appearance.

These parrots are widely distributed throughout South America, but exportation and deforestation has diminished their numbers in recent years.

H. I. Gregory of Texas is credited with the first captive breeding of this bird, on which he reported in the December 1972 issue of the *Magazine of the Parrot Society.* He traveled to South America in 1966, where he purchased a supposed pair of Greenwings that he later discovered were both hens. After buying a male from a friend in 1967, he had a true pair, ideal for breeding. The pair produced young for him in the summer of 1972.

A pair of bonded Green-winged Macaws. Karen Kelley

At eight weeks, these Greenwing chicks already strongly resemble their parents. Joanne Abramson

MILITARY MACAW

The Military is the least colorful of the large macaws, but many still consider it attractive.

Ara militaris is a large macaw that commonly reaches lengths of twenty-seven to twenty-eight inches. Much of its feathering is a deep olive green that becomes lighter on the head and almost brownish red on the throat. It has white cheek patches marked with a tracing of greenish-black feathers.

These Military Macaws display preening behavior typical of bonded pairs. Brian Kenny

Its most obvious marking is a mass of vividly colored, fluffed-up red feathers that look almost as if they had been added to the forehead and around the lores as an afterthought. Full-sized Military Macaws are not only among the largest parrots, but are also contenders for the title of heaviest, with body weights ranging from 800 to 1,500 grams.

The Military Macaw originates in northwestern Mexico, Venezuela, Colombia, and northeastern Ecuador. According to Sutton (*Portraits of Mexican Birds*), they are the most northward-ranging of the larger New World parrots. This designation, however, should really be accorded the Thick-billed Parrot, which, with the help of groups such as the Wildlife Preservation Trust and the U.S. Forest Service, is attempting a comeback in southeastern Arizona.

Sutton observed flocks as large as sixty to eighty macaws in Mexico in 1938 and 1941. He describes the thrill of watching these birds in flight, as when they raised their wings, the seldom-seen yellow feathers on the undersurface of the wings were clearly visible. I fear that exports and habitat destruction has depleted their numbers drastically and that such sights are no longer possible in this area. Rosemary Low (*Endangered Parrots* 1984) confirms that their population has declined and includes road building to the interior and forest destruction among the major causes.

Reference to early breeding of these birds is made by A. A. Prestwich (*Records of Parrots Bred in Captivity*, 1952), who ascribes the probable first breeding to Emile Dupont of France in 1887. He also mentions several hybrid successes between Militaries and Scarlets, including one in 1950 by F. S. Scherr, the original proprietor of Miami's famous Parrot Jungle. In addition, a contemporary record exists that credits Paul Springman of Texas, whose breeding successes took place in the late 1970s.

Hoppe (*The World of Macaws*, 1985) recognizes two subspecies, *Ara mexicana mexicana* and *A. m. boliviana*, that differ from the nominate race mainly in that they are larger and have different ranges. *Mexicana* is generally found throughout central Mexico, while *boliviana* has a much smaller range in southeastern Bolivia, extending across the border into northern Argentina. Hoppe provides a highly detailed breakdown of the members of this group.

These young Military Macaws are well on their way to complete independence. Joanne Abramson

The Military has been known as a pet and breeder for many years. C. P. Arthur (*Parrots for Pleasure and Profit*, c. 1900) wonders why the parrot is called "Military" when it lacks any resemblance to a military uniform. Others have speculated that this macaw first became well known to Europeans at a time when Mexico had been invaded by a foreign army or perhaps (and I like this reason better) because the first specimens brought to Europe arrived courtesy of the military.

I had the opportunity to see and admire a Military on one of my regular visits to Alba Ballard's magnificent Long Island aviary. She encouraged me to hold a twenty-seven-inch-long macaw she had named Major. Major, a handsome bird, was calm and gentle and startled me by making efforts to preen my hair when I tried to examine his cheek patch markings. It was almost a "tit for tat" reaction on his part.

BUFFON'S MACAW

There is also a considerable body of information about *Ara ambigua*, a macaw similar to the Military, although classified separately because of its range, size, and unique markings. Also called the Great Green Macaw, Buffon's can be as large as thirty-four or thirty-five inches, and its territory extends from northeastern Nicaragua to Colombia.

Joanne Abramson of California has raised these parrots along with the nominate species and describes them fully in the July 1988 issue of *American Cage-Bird Magazine*. She considers them stockier and larger than the Green-winged Macaw, with a more massive beak, lime-green coloring, and a tail that is a "rainbow of color progressing from . . . red orange to turquoise."

In the same issue of the magazine, Geoffrey Gould, who, with his wife Barbara, has bred and maintained many of the larger parrots, warns that feather color can be distorted by lighting and instead suggests using eye color as a definitive identification test. Gould notes that the Military has a black pupil with a primary yellow ring followed by a second yellow ring, and the Buffon's has a black pupil with a large, steel-gray ring followed by a darker color and then a single yellow ring. He insists that once one is able to compare the eyes, the difference will be clear thereafter, even from a distance.

Hoppe treats the Buffon's as a separate species but hedges by acknowledging that the question has not yet been fully resolved. He remarks that if *A. ambigua* and *A. militaris* are actually the same species, their range encompasses a tremendous land area from central Mexico to Ecuador. Rosemary Low (*Parrots, Their Care and Breeding*, 3d rev. ed., 1992) takes a more straightforward approach and treats it as a subspecies. She believes that studies of the DNA sequence, a relatively new technique, could provide a definitive answer.

In an article written for *Watchbird* magazine in 1983, Florence Gale of California recounted how she and her husband raised two Buffon's chicks in 1982 from a pair that had been hand-fed pets. This was the first breeding of Buffon's in the United States.

She also described the Buffon's, indicating that it originates in a territory ranging from northwest Nicaragua southward to Choco, Colombia. Large size seems to be regularly associated with the Choco region by importers and others, who frequently refer to large specimens of the Blue-fronted Amazon as "Choco Blue-fronts."

Several years ago, Bob Egbert, a high school teacher then living on Fire Island, which is just off the coast of Long Island, showed me a huge specimen of a "Military Macaw" that was about six inches larger than the one I had seen at Alba Ballard's aviary. After a careful (and respectful) examination, I realized that I was looking at a perfect specimen of Buffon's Macaw.

HYACINTH MACAW

In 1979 I was offered the opportunity to purchase a young, hand-fed domestic Hyacinth. The owner, who lived in Michigan, bought and sold birds but had become captivated by this large, richly colored macaw and decided to keep it as a pet. Shortly after he made this decision, economic pressures forced him to sell the bird and I bought it for about $3,500. (Remember, this was in the late 1970s.) Unfortunately, just before he was to ship the parrot the weather deteriorated, and the low temperatures and snow postponed the shipment by two weeks.

When he did arrive, however, he was everything his former owner had said he would be. Blue was beautifully feathered, extremely confident, highly vocal, and remarkably friendly. I marveled at the fact that absolutely no time was needed for him to adapt. I opened the top of his badly chewed wooden shipping case, and Blue popped right out.

I have always suspected a connection in parrots between great size and strength and a high degree of confidence, with an attitude that says, "I'm peaceful but I'm also quite big and strong, so don't mess with me." Big Blue was typical in this respect. Unfortunately, his friendliness became a problem, as, whenever I entered the bird room, he insisted on being let out of his cage and riding on my shoulder. This was far from an ideal situation; it prevented me from playing with any of the other parrots and also became rather burdensome, as Blue was anything but a lightweight. Even when I washed the food and water dishes at the bird room sink he demanded to be on my shoulder, from which vantage point he would gently groom my hair and mutter into my ear as I struggled to finish my chores.

Eventually I sold Blue to a woman in California who had a strong desire to own a Hyacinth. The night he arrived in his new home, she phoned me to let me know that all was well, which I knew myself as I could hear him screaming happily in the background. Since then I have often wondered if his new owner also carries him about on her shoulder.

A pair of Hyacinth siblings enjoying some togetherness in the nesting tree. Hans Andersson

Hyacinths in flight over the Brazilian jungle. Dr. William Clark

The Hyacinth is the largest of the parrots, with mature males easily reaching a length of forty inches or more. Their feathers are a rich blue except for the under-flights, which are a steely gray. They have a large, bare, bright yellow eye ring, with a similarly colored stripe of yellow skin at the base of the lower beak. The head is massive and the large black beak extremely powerful. The overhanging upper beak is sharply pointed and works as an efficient tool when crushing nuts or wood against the anvil-like lower beak.

Dieter Hoppe (*The World of Macaws,* 1983) describes a group of twelve Hyacinths he saw at an importer's establishment. The birds had totally destroyed their massively built enclosures and were hard at work on the wall of the quarantine station, where they dug out wall tiles and then damaged the concrete beneath it to the point that the steel reinforcing rods could be seen.

The late Len Hill, owner of the Birdland Sanctuary in England, had a pair of Hyacinths that became Birdland's trademark. He obtained Leah and Mac from a zoo when Leah broke a zookeeper's finger during a slight altercation.

Anodorhynchus hyacinthinus originates in southern Brazil, from which large numbers were imported between 1977 and the mid-1980s. During that period, a sufficient number of breeders acquired pairs so that domestic, hand-fed Hyacinths are now available even though these birds are no longer imported.

They are the largest and most beautiful of the full-sized macaws. Their rich blue bodies and bright yellow cheek markings give the illusion that you are looking at a stuffed toy version of a parrot. Even recent imports appear calm, and domestic, hand-fed specimens make ideal pets. Their voices are extremely loud, and because they develop a deep affection for their owners, their screams for attention are tantamount to disturbing the peace. Keep in mind that buying one of these parrots is a major commitment of money, time, and energy.

An exquisite pair of Hyacinths keeping a close watch over their nesting tree (opposite). Hans Andersson

LEAR'S AND GLAUCOUS MACAWS

Several years ago I received a packet of material from a photographer in Germany. When I put his slides in the viewer I was startled to see what appeared to be a Hyacinth and a Glaucous Macaw sitting next to each other. The reason for my excitement was that, while I had seen drawings and paintings of the Glaucous, I had never seen the living bird or even a photograph. The completely green head, however, as well as its size and the structure of the upper beak, convinced me that it could be *Anodorhynchus glaucus*. Some experts consider the subspecies extinct, while others report evidence of very small populations, but all sources agree that if it still exists, it is among the rarest of the rare.

A phone call to the photographer was disappointing. He was pleased that I wanted to purchase his photos but could only say that he had photographed the bird in the zoo in Basel, Switzerland, several years earlier. He remarked that he was not a bird enthusiast and had taken the photos only because of the interesting way in which the birds were posed.

It took several days to contact the curator of birds in Basel, but when I eventually reached him he was quite helpful. He informed me that the bird, a female, had been donated to the zoo in 1975 by an individual who wished to remain anonymous. He considered it to be a Lear's Macaw and told us that it was currently on breeding loan at the Mulhouse Zoo in France.

We made contact with the veterinarian and curator of birds at Mulhouse, whose first response to my question regarding the classification of the macaw was hearty laughter. He had also believed it to be a Glaucous, but had discovered that the colors of the head and body shifted dramatically with differences in lighting. Changes in humidity also had an effect on the color. In his opinion, as well as that of Thomas Arndt, a German aviculturist and author of several excellent books, the macaw was a Lear's. The curator reported that his zoo had had the macaw from Basel since July 1987 and that they had recently obtained a male from the Paris Zoo with whom the bird was now set up in hopes of breeding.

The green head in the photo continued to trouble me, as did the sharp curvature of the upper

At the turn of the century, Theodore Roosevelt, Jr., was a famous parrot enthusiast. He is shown here in the White House Conservatory with his Hyacinth Macaw, Eli. Could Eli have been considered the "first bird"? Courtesy Library of Congress

beak, which strongly resembled that of the illustration of the Glaucous in Forshaw's *Parrots of the World* (2d rev. ed., 1978), so I decided to make further efforts to clarify the situation and contacted Dr. Donald Brunning, curator of birds at the Bronx Zoo in New York City. It was either luck or fate that the day I called was the last day that Dr. Carlos Yamashita, a Brazilian wildlife authority and field biologist, was to be in New York, and he was at that moment visiting the Bronx Zoo's sister institution, the Central Park Zoo. Dr. Yamashita is among the few people who have seen and studied the Glaucous. When we spoke he also commented on the color shifts mentioned above, observing that these shifts occur both with changes of light and in the early morning, when moisture from dew has dampened the feathers.

Lear's Macaw, *Anodorhynchus leari*, is about twenty-eight inches long and, thus, considerably shorter than its Hyacinth relative. Names used for this parrot include Little Hyacinth, Lear's Ara, and the Indigo Macaw. The head and neck are blue, although not the rich cobalt blue of the Hyacinth, and the undersurface is grayish blue. The brown

A Hyacinth Macaw on the left and a very rare Lear's Macaw on the right illustrate how changes in lighting accentuate the difference in the color of the two birds. Luke Golobitsch

eye is surrounded by a naked, orange-yellow ring with a matching rounded patch of orange-yellow skin at the base of the lower beak. The corresponding marking in the Hyacinth is a much brighter yellow and is shaped like an elongated crescent.

Although the Lear's had been identified as a subspecies in 1856, its habitat was still unknown as late as 1978. At that time Dr. Helmut Sick, a German ornithologist who had worked in Brazil for almost forty years, published an article on the origin of *A. leari* in the German publication *Gefiederte Welt* (Feathered World). A copy of the article was brought to my attention by Henning H. Jacobson of Denmark, and following an interesting correspondence, Dr. Sick gave permission for a translation of the article to be printed in *American Cage-Bird Magazine*. Sick and his assistant, Dante M. Teixeira, located the natural habit of these birds after three expeditions through extremely rugged territory in an area of Brazil called the Raso de Caterina in northern Bahia. They saw flocks of as many as twenty-one specimens of Lear's flying

together, and located their sleeping and nesting areas in inaccessible caves in the side of canyon-like dried river valleys.

Tony Silva (*A Monograph of Endangered Parrots*, 1989) describes the Glaucous Macaw as twenty-nine inches long and generally greenish blue, with greener underparts and a graying green cast to the head and neck. He quotes Sick and Teixeira on the distribution of the subspecies, which originates along the eastern margins of the Uruguay River and at one time also existed in Argentina. According to Silva, specimens were occasionally offered for sale in 1983 and 1984. He tells of one American collector who refused to purchase a chick that was offered to him because of its "abnormal" color and malnourished condition. It was not until several days later that the collector realized it was a Glaucous, but he returned too late—the undernourished nestling had died.

Sidney Porter, writing in the October 1938 issue of *Aviculture Magazine*, recounts his tour of South America, which included a visit to the Parrot

House of the Buenos Aires Zoo, where he saw a Glaucous Macaw for the first time. The specimen had been in the collection for over twenty years and was known to be as least forty-five years old.

Comparative illustrations of the Lear's and Glaucous Macaws can be found in Elizabeth Butterworth's *Parrots, Macaws and Cockatoos*, published in 1988.

MINIATURE MACAWS

Because of their brilliant colors and expansive personalities macaws have been perennial favorites. Not everyone can own a macaw, however, and some parrot enthusiasts may have to consider alternatives. Although the miniature macaws may not be as impressive as the full-size versions, there is much to recommend them: They are more readily available, their prices are generally lower, they are not as loud as the larger species, and they require less space and maintenance.

A pair of Yellow-collared or Yellow-naped Macaws.
Michael DeFreitas

The Yellow-collared Macaw

A popular alternative name for this parrot is "Yellow-naped Macaw." It was one of the first of the mini-macaws to be bred with regularity, and many breeding pairs have been set up during the past ten years. As a result, a fairly steady supply of hand-fed domestic specimens is available for sale.

Ara auricollis, a typical member of the dwarf macaw group, is also known as Cassin's Macaw and the Gold-naped Macaw. It reaches lengths of sixteen to seventeen inches and is a rich green color, with the cheeks and forehead a much darker green. The feathers of the crown blend from blue to black, becoming darker towards the rear of the crown, and the prominent beak is black except for a light-colored tip. As in the full-size macaws, the Yellow-collar has a large eye and cheek patch that in this case is almost pure white. The distinguishing yellow nape, or collar, is a bright, vivid yellow that, unlike the similar marking in the Yellow-naped Amazon, appears fairly early in the parrot's development and quickly reaches maximum size and depth of color.

Yellow-collars are relatively easy to tame and have some talent for speech, although macaws in general are not outstanding talkers. Those kept by Dieter Hoppe (*The World of Macaws*, 1985) became tame very quickly; his flock, numbering ten and sometimes more, took food directly from his hands. One particular Yellow-collar tamed so quickly that after one week it could be laid on its back to be scratched.

The range of these parrots is wide, including Brazil, western Paraguay, northeastern Bolivia, and northwestern Argentina. A pair of Yellow-collared Macaws was on display in the Parrot House of the London Zoo as early as the 1920s, and they were the first of their species to be seen in England. Apart from this reference, there was very little information about them in the avicultural literature until the 1970s and early 1980s, when a wave of importation resulted in a rapid increase in their popularity.

Rosemary Low (*Parrots: Their Care and Breeding*, rev. ed., 1990) quotes Ridgely, who studied the distribution of Macaws in Mexico and Central America. In 1981 Ridgely observed that the Yellow-collar is "common, conspicuous and ecologically adaptable." Hoppe cites a local expert, who reports of seeing flocks of up to 500 congregating in trees and preparing to spend the night: As groups of birds arrived, quarrels and shrill screaming developed over the most desirable sleeping perches.

Werner Lantermann credits the Bristol Zoo in England or Walsrode Park in Germany with the first breeding of this species in 1976. The late Don Matthews and his wife, Pat, of Allison Park, Pennsylvania, were pioneer American breeders of these parrots. In an article written for *American Cage-Bird Magazine* in 1977, Don Matthews describes them as inquisitive, intelligent, and frolicking little clowns. One of his chicks, a master escape artist aptly named Houdini, baffled his owners by opening all varieties of snaps, latches, levers, and catches until he was finally stumped by a large padlock. By 1974 the Matthews had obtained six pairs that they considered suitable for breeding. They kept them in separate flights with individual nest boxes for two years without results. In August the birds were moved into a large common flight, and after some minor squabbling over perches, two of the pairs exchanged partners while the third pair remained faithful to each other.

Allowing this "natural selection" paid off; by October the birds were back in individual flights, and three fertile eggs had been laid by the end of December. The breeders suspected that the parents might fail to incubate or feed the new arrivals, so they pulled the first egg and placed it in an incubator at 99.6 degrees Fahrenheit and a relative humidity of sixty to seventy percent, manually turning it three times a day. Early on the morning of January 16, they heard a faint peeping sound coming from the incubator room and by noon the chick had hatched. "Boots," as he was called, was hand fed every two hours around the clock until he was fourteen days old, and he rapidly developed into a handsome and lovable young bird that, except for a lighter-colored nape marking, closely resembled his parents. Pulling Boots for incubating and hand feeding turned out to have been a very wise move, as although the two other chicks hatched the parents stopped feeding them after just a few days and they failed to survive.

Yellow-collared Macaws meet all the requirements for those who are interested in breeding the larger birds. Domestic pairs are available that are challenging but not impossible to breed, and their offspring are highly desirable.

The reddish-brown marking above the beak is the source of the alternate name, Chestnut-fronted Macaw, by which the Severe Macaw is sometimes known. Everett Webb

Severe Macaw

In Europe, this parrot is often referred to as the Chestnut-fronted Macaw. Although not especially colorful, it has the bare cheek patch typical of macaws, with a sprinkling of feather tracings. The reddish-brown forehead marking does not develop fully until about two years of age, which is important to keep in mind if you are seeking older birds for breeding. They are about eighteen inches long and intelligent as well as affectionate. Dieter Hoppe finds them to be excellent pets that become quite attached to their owners, and he considers at least one of his own a gifted talker.

The nominate race, *Ara severa severa*, ranges from northern Venezuela to Guyana and then south to Brazil. The subspecies, *A. s. castaneifrons*, is larger and can be found in Panama, Colombia, Peru, and Bolivia. Unfortunately, very few importers have distinguished between the nominate and the subspecies, so individual specimens may be difficult to identify unless known Severes are available with which to make a comparison. Of course, it can be very helpful to know the region from which the parents originated.

Illiger's Macaw

Although less common and somewhat smaller than the other miniature macaws, Illiger's is more brightly colored, with a red forehead and crown, blue-green abdomen, and an attractive red marking on the belly. Breeders indicate that they tame readily and are fair talkers. Pairs that breed do so regularly and can produce between three and eight young during a two-clutch breeding season. Current literature indicates that they are still abundant in their Brazilian habitat, where good-sized flocks have been observed near rivers and in forests. Ralph Small of Illinois was one of the first people to breed the Illiger's in the United States. Mr. Small has had many other breeding successes, including the giant Hyacinths at the opposite end of the macaw spectrum.

Noble Macaw

These are the smallest of the dwarf macaws, with a maximum length of thirteen to fourteen inches. They are actually exceeded in size by some of the larger subspecies of conures. This small green macaw has a blue crown and a tinge of blue on the lower edge of the wing. A subspecies, Hahn's Macaw, is often erroneously treated as a separate species. Both these birds are good captive breeders and potential talkers, and are amenable to taming. The Noble originates in Brazil, and although there is no exportation, some domestically bred birds are available from breeders in the United States.

Red-bellied Macaw

This native of Venezuela, Trinidad, Peru, and Colombia is an attractive green mini-macaw with a blue forecrown and a deep red marking on its belly. It should not be confused with Illiger's Macaw, which also has the red marking on the belly. To distinguish between these birds, remember that the Illiger's abdominal marking is V shaped and the yellow cheek marking on the Red-bellied is much more obvious. Importation of these birds began rather late, probably because of their reputation for delicacy. Rosemary Low (*Parrots: Their Care and Breeding*, 1986) reports on a pair belonging to Candy Mills of England that nested in 1983.

Although somewhat more difficult to breed than some of the other miniature macaws, the Red-bellied is still an excellent choice as a pet. It should not be ignored as breeding stock as the demand for it is steep.

In recent years, restrictions on exports of exotic birds from most of the Central and South America have been imposed along with U.S. laws that ended imports. This has made it increasingly difficult and expensive to obtain larger macaws such as Scarlets, Blue and Golds, Hyacinths, Greenwings, and Military Macaws, since most of the birds available are domestically raised and cost more than twice as much as the macaws that were imported in the 1980s. As more breeders learn

A Noble Macaw (opposite). Courtesy the San Diego Zoo

their skills and take advantage of new developments in avian medicine and pediatrics, the supply of the larger macaws will increase and prices should stabilize. For now, however, if you are eager to own a bird that looks like a macaw and has all the spirit and playful personality associated with these colorful, large-beaked parrots, you should consider the mini-macaws.

17

A VARIETY OF SMALLER PARROTS

So green his feathers, they dimmed the cut emerald; scarlet his beak, with saffron spots. No bird on earth could copy a voice more closely or sound so articulate.

—*Peter Green (translator),* Amores *by Ovid*

MAXIMILIAN'S PARROT

Maximilian's Parrot is part of a group of South American parrots of the genus *pionus*, which consists of eight species that are fairly easy to recognize by their stocky build and short, squared-off tails. Although they are several inches smaller than most of the Amazons, a large Pionus and a small Amazon, can be confusingly similar unless you remember that most Amazons have green under-tail coverts, while those of the Pionus are red. In addition, Pionus parrots have a deep notch in the upper beak and a prominent, naked cere.

Pionus m. maximiliani is typical of the group. This parrot is sometimes called the Scaly-headed Parrot because the overlapping of its head feathers is highlighted by their dark gray edges, giving the illusion of scales. Their basic coloring is the rather subdued olive green of the chest, wings, and abdomen. The tail is also green, but the under-tail coverts and vent are red. These birds have a yellowish-brown upper beak that becomes lighter at the tip, and the lower beak is lighter in color.

The species originates in northern Argentina, as well as eastern and southeastern Brazil. Rutgers and Norris recognize two subspecies, including one

The color of the throat patch will intensify and the red of the head will be lost as this young "Ruby" Pionus matures. Isabelle Français

called *P. m. siy*. According to Prestwich, this odd name is native in origin and resembles the shrill cry the bird produces in the wild. Maximilian's Parrot was originally named *Psittacus cyanurus* by the German prince, Maximilian of Neuwied, but in 1820 the name was changed in his honor when the biologist M. Kuhl discovered that the earlier name was already being used. Prince Maximilian had a large ornithological collection and had explored the interior of Brazil in 1815–17 as well as traveling in North America in 1832–34.

Forshaw (*Parrots of the World*, 2d rev. ed., 1978) indicates that these parrots were inhabitants of lowland forests and open woodlands, appearing to be fairly common. He cites his own observations of these birds in 1971, and includes many reports by other observers.

Johan Ingels of Belgium is closely associated with the Pionus parrots. Writing in the October–December 1978 issue of *Avicultural Magazine*, Dr. Ingels refers to these birds as attractive and medium-sized, with reddish feathers on the forehead that disappear after the first molt. Describing a typical Maximilian's reaction to stress, Ingels noted that the bird would walk up and down its perch with cheek, neck, and mantle feathers puffed out and the tail fanned and lowered until it brushed the perch. The head was also held quite low, with the beak almost touching the perch. I have seen very similar behavior in Amazons such as the Double Yellow-head. The article is comprehensive and includes photos as well as a list of additional references. I recommend it highly to those interested in these birds.

In January 1981 issue of the *Avicultural Bulletin*, there is an article on breeding the

A Blue-headed Pionus at one year of age. Isabelle Français

Maximilian's Parrot by Morris D. Sale. His first selection from the genus was a quiet, friendly bird that he named Max. The bird became tame in a matter of weeks and was a fine house pet. In 1979 a friend informed him that Max was a female and provided a young male as a mate. Within a year, copulation and mutual feeding were taking place. The birds thoroughly investigated the nest box already belonging to a pair of Peach-faced Lovebirds, even opening the lid used by the lovebirds for access. At this point, they were given their own nine-by-ten-by-fourteen-inch box lined with about four inches of damp garden mulch, of which they promptly threw out half. When the nest was adjusted to her satisfaction, Max attempted to lay an egg. The first try was a near disaster: the egg broke within her, but she was able to pass it with the help of moisture and heat. She finally laid two whole eggs and incubated them for four weeks while her mate kept busy providing food. Once hatched, the young grew rapidly, appearing to double in size each of the first few weeks. The chicks were brought into the house for hand feeding and fledged at the age of ten weeks.

G. Hosking of England reported on his breeding of Maximilian's Parrot in the April 1983 issue of *The Magazine of the Parrot Society*. His pair were approximately five years old and had been imported four years previously. They were maintained in large flights that were thirteen feet long, six feet wide, and six feet high. In 1980 Mr. Hosking's pair produced three infertile eggs, and in 1981 there were two eggs, one of which was fertile but contained a dead chick. In 1982, a single chick was successfully bred.

SENEGAL PARROTS

When African parrots are mentioned, most people think of the African Grey, Meyer's Parrot, and the lovebirds. There are actually more than a dozen other species of parrot found in Africa; a group that should be better known is the genus *Poicephalus*, which includes the Senegal Parrot, *P. senegalus*.

This Canary-winged Parakeet is a popular member of the genus Brotogeris. Robbie Harris

A White-crowned Pionus. Everett Webb

Senegals are known and loved for their acrobatic ability and comical behavior. Michael DeFreitas

Without a doubt, the most endearing discussion of a Senegal Parrot was provided by Edward J. Boosey, the original proprietor of the famed Keston Bird Farm of England. He describes his bird as being about nine inches long, with a rather simple color arrangement: The body was basically dark green, the wings and tail were even darker, the head was dark gray, the cheeks were silvery, and the beak was black. Its yellowish eyes were set in such dark lores that one might have been tempted to ask, "Who is that masked man?" The abdomen and lower breast were orange-yellow. From Boosey's description, it appears that this Senegal was probably the nominate species, as the two subspecies, *P. s. versteri* and *P. s. mesotypus*, have slightly different markings, the former lacking the orange abdomen and the latter being a lighter green on its upper surfaces.

Boosey obtained his Senegal while still a schoolboy and maintained the bird until it died at the venerable age, for a small parrot, of twenty-one years. He attributes their excellent relationship to hand feeding, although he also credits the ample time he had to devote to this chore, as well as the subsequent weaning from a mash of boiled sweetened corn, a common hand feeding diet of the era, to a regular diet of seeds. Throughout his career Boosey owned hundreds of parrots, but he declares this Senegal "the most charming and delightful pet

of any kind" that he ever owned. She had some verbal skill, and her other achievements included lying in his hand on her back and studiously examining the interior of his mouth when he opened it to yawn. During these observations she would constantly emit clucking sounds as if to indicate that she was viewing an extraordinary sight. This tame and gentle bird lived in a fairly large cage but generally had the freedom of the house, where she would fly down long passages as she followed Boosey from room to room. In all likelihood, this constant exercise contributed to her longevity.

Senegals are widely distributed throughout west central Africa and are native to Gambia, part of Nigeria, and the Ivory Coast, as well as Senegal. The bird was first identified by A. Goffin, for whom Goffin's Cockatoo is named, as early as 1863, and Dr. Greene cites a much earlier but somewhat obscure reference from 1445. At the time of Greene's writing, new imports could be purchased for as little as two dollars.

More current references to this interesting parrot are virtually unanimous in their approval. Pat Sutherland (*The Pet Bird Handbook*, 1981) praises its gentleness and amenability to taming, while Matthew Vriends emphasizes its speech and mimicry abilities and excellent disposition. David

Alderton commends these birds for tameness but suggests choosing only young birds for pets. The highest contemporary recommendations come from well-known aviculturist Cyril H. Rogers (*Parrot Guide*, 1981), who is enthusiastic about their pleasing colors and personality, their willingness to nest in captivity, and their excellent reputation as parents.

Breeding records for these small but engaging parrots go back to 1886, when, according to Prestwich (*Records of Parrots Bred in Captivity*, 1951), four were bred by R. B. Sheridan at Dorchester, England. Boosey himself bred the species in 1957, and there are many later reports from zoos and private breeders throughout the world.

Several years ago on one of my regular visits to the extraordinary aviaries of Alba Ballard, I spent an enjoyable afternoon with Teddy Bird, her Senegal Parrot. He was a confident young male bred and hand fed by Bob Nelson of Coquille, Oregon. Teddy Bird met and exceeded all expectations for the species. Although he did not talk, preferring to make the loud, bussing sound that is typical of the group, he gave kisses and performed acrobatics. He was fearless to the point of recklessness, attempting to boss around some of the cockatoos and other large parrots in the extensive Ballard collection.

A well-bonded Senegal pair. Joan Balzarini

MEYER'S PARROT

This bird is widely distributed throughout central and eastern Africa, and subspecies can be found in Uganda, Tanzania, Kenya, Malawi, Zambia, the Congo, Angola, Lesotho, and South Africa. As is the case with most of the African parrot species, *Poicephalus meyeri* has been familiar to ornithologists since the early nineteenth century. Peters (*Check-List of Birds of the World*, 1937) lists the nominate plus as many as eight subspecies, designating 1827 as the year these parrots were first described and named. A. A. Prestwich (*I Name This Parrot*, 1963) places the discovery a year earlier and praises Dr. Bernhard Meyer, the physician in whose honor this parrot is named, as a man who made an outstanding contribution to the early study of natural history. Meyer, who lived from 1767 to 1836, undertook numerous expeditions for the purpose of studying plants and birds. He visited many European scholars in his travels and they visited him in turn to admire his outstanding bird collection. The famous German poet Goethe was Dr. Meyer's guest on at least two separate occasions.

Forshaw (*Parrots of the World*, 1973) condenses the number of subspecies to six, considering the differences between them generally minor and consisting of variations in intensity of color or areas covered by a particular marking. Geography, of course, is also a factor.

Meyer's Parrot is also appropriately referred to as Meyer's Brown Parrot, Brown Parrot, and Sudan Brown Parrot, due to the grayish brown coloring of the head, the upper parts of the breast, and the back. The rump is a bright turquoise, although this is not normally evident when the wings are folded. There are bright yellow markings at the bend of the wing and on the thighs, the feet and beak are grayish black, and the iris is reddish orange in adults and brown in young birds.

All subspecies with the exception of *P. m. reichenowi* and *P. m. damarensis* have a bright yellow marking on the crown that may account for the nickname "Goldbug" commonly used in Germany. Wolfgang deGrahl (*Color Atlas of the Parrots*, 1973) believes that sex differences between these birds cannot be detected even with a breeding pair. He considers them shy and timid and goes so far as to suggest that during acclimation they be provided with a crate having only one open side to assure maximum privacy.

Rutgers and Norris make reference to the wide distribution and large numbers of these birds in Africa. They add that despite sporadic importation, the species is well known in captivity and was first seen in the London Zoo as early as 1855. W. T.

Greene (*Birds of the British Empire*, 1898) gives a good description of the Meyer's and, unlike many early authors, properly distinguishes it from the Brown-headed Parrot, *Poicephalus cryptoxanthus*.

Sydney Porter wrote with great enthusiasm for his pair of Meyer's Parrots in *Avicultural Magazine*, May 1931. An indefatigable traveler, Porter had seen these birds in the wild in Africa and observed them chattering away furiously as they ate and wasted the fruits of a M'sasa tree. Sometimes the tree seemed to be raining half-eaten fruits, moving Porter to declare that parrots "are surely the most wasteful birds in creation." Whenever a stranger approached the tree, all chatter and other sounds would cease and the grayish-brown birds would become virtually invisible, silently blending with their surroundings. Porter remarks that it is easier to get within reach of an eagle than a "wild Meyer's Parrot and yet no bird makes a tamer or more charming pet." The natives of Porter's time would catch the parrots by locating their roosting spots and placing sticky substances on twigs.

The literature includes a number of reports on the breeding of Meyer's Parrot. Prestwich (*Records of Parrots Bred in Captivity*, 1954) discusses an early achievement by J. B. Rough of South Africa. The birds, which were caught wild on Mr. Rough's farm in the Transvaal, produced a number of young in the spring of 1952.

Another South African success was achieved by J. F. Brauckmann, who described his experience in the March/April 1960 issue of *Foreign Birds*. Mr. Brauckmann had kept Meyer's Parrots for many years but had never bred them. He varied his nest boxes and other conditions and finally placed his birds in a twelve-foot-by-fifteen-foot-by-six-foot aviary with hollow palm tree stumps, a ten-by-twelve-inch-square nest box, and a twelve-inch-square-by-twenty-four-inch-high box.

Three eggs were laid and three chicks hatched, but only one of the young was reared to maturity. In 1959, a new pair of adults produced three more eggs, two of which hatched on the nineteenth and twenty-third day of incubation. The chicks, which resembled baby budgies, were reared, and left the nest after nine weeks. In 1971, Dr. Williams S. Hawkins of Sunland, California, bred a pair of Meyer's Parrots he had purchased in 1969 as immature, newly imported birds. Writing in the

May 1972 issue of *Avicultural Bulletin*, Dr. Hawkins states that the parrots were kept in an indoor flight until spring and then were placed in a four-by-twenty-three-foot outdoor aviary with a ten-inch-square-by-eighteen-inch-deep nest box lined with about four inches of peat. Late in the summer of 1970, the birds began to show an interest in their nest box and three eggs were produced early in September. The hen incubated alone, and although all three eggs were fertile, none hatched. Dr. Hawkins speculated that the record heat in Southern California that summer might have been a factor in this failure. In 1971 the birds again showed interest in the nest box quite early in the spring, and the hen laid three eggs during the first week in February. Despite a severe earthquake that struck the area on February 9, 1971, the hen did not leave the nest. Two eggs hatched on February 21 and the third two days later.

The parents were devoted and attentive, with the male cooperating handsomely. The young appeared similar to baby lovebirds with patches of white down. In October of the same year a second breeding resulted in three fertile eggs that hatched on November 12. The parents again provided good care, but because the weather was turning cold the three downy young were removed for hand rearing. They were fully on their own by the first week in February. Their owner describes them as smaller and duller editions of their parents.

Raymond Franklin of England bred Meyer's Parrots in 1972 and reported on his accomplishment in the November 1972 issue of the *Magazine of the Parrot Society*. He observes that the male had a larger head than the female and more yellow on the crown, features that might, however, have been due to a difference in their subspecies rather than their sex. He furnished his pair with a twelve-by-three-by-six-foot flight that had a small shelter, adding a small hollow log on April 3, 1971. The male fed the female but neither showed interest in the nest until Mr. Franklin filled it with peat, which the hen would throw out as quickly as he replaced it. Mr. Franklin found one egg on May 16 but to his surprise and delight, two chicks were discovered on June 16. They appeared to be about one week old and were covered with down.

One chick began peering out of the nest by July 30 but did not leave until August 10, and a second chick emerged on August 13. Mr. Franklin was further astonished when two more young appeared on August 15, giving him a total of four strong, healthy birds from this first clutch.

The breeding success of H. Mekin in England is recorded in the February 1974 issue of the *Magazine of the Parrot Society*. He had owned two Meyer's Parrots for several years and had always believed them to be a pair. His birds selected a thirty-by-twelve-inch-square nest box from several alternatives he provided. After copulation in April 1974, the hen was not seen again for six weeks. At the end of June, Mr. Mekin decided to risk a peek into the nest and discovered a large chick with patterns of coloring similar to that of his parents. This youngster left the nest after another five weeks.

Alan H. Booton of Riverside, Illinois, has had remarkable success in breeding parrots, although perhaps this success is not so much remarkable as justified given the highly organized way that Mr. Booton has gone about it and the expert help and advice he received early in his career from breeders Ralph and Tina Small of Brookfield, Illinois. As a matter of fact, the breeding pair of Meyer's Parrots he used was loaned by Ralph Small.

As is typical of parrots, the shy parents would retreat into the nest box whenever Mr. Booton entered the room, but their five hand-fed babies would eat from a spoon and were so playful that they would "play dead" in his hand while lying upside down and totally relaxed.

The diet Mr. Booton provided for the parents was three parts sunflower, one part dove mix (without corn), one part safflower, and one-half part parakeet mix. Monkey chow as also included, as well as a variety of fruits and greens. Brewer's yeast was sprinkled on the moist fruits and vegetables just before they were fed and poultry vitamin added to the drinking water on a daily basis. When young were in the nest the amount of safflower and sweet corn and other vegetables was increased.

The flight cage was eight feet long by three feet wide by six feet high. Three such cages were in a special room in Mr. Booton's basement with wooden partitions separating them so that the birds in one flight could not see those in the others. The room was well lit by broad-spectrum fluorescent lamps that were kept on for fifteen hours a day and regulated with an automatic timer and dimmer. Night lights were also provided so that if a parent left the nest it would have no difficulty finding the way back.

Three clutches of three eggs each were produced during the year. In the first clutch one chick hatched, one chick was dead in its shell, and one egg was infertile; in the second, two eggs hatched and one was infertile; and in the third, two eggs hatched and one chick was dead in its shell. Incubation lasted for twenty-four days, and the young were removed for hand feeding when they were three weeks old. The breeding pair used by Mr. Booton were well into their teens, but he estimates that this species can begin breeding at about two years of age.

Mr. Booton reported that the adults and young were all very quiet birds, only issuing an alarm-type call when startled or wanting attention.

CAIQUES

This group includes an excellent selection of small pet parrots. The caiques are small, brightly colored, solid-looking birds with short, square tails. Based on the bone structure of their skulls, some ornithologists see a relationship between this genus and some of the conures. They average ten inches in length, which makes them as large as the smallest of the Amazons. The origin of their name, which rhymes with "dike," may lie in the beak's similarity to the sharply curved canoe used by some South American Indian tribes. Their voices are rather shrill and they have a limited capacity for speech, but watching a pair or trio scramble around a cage is highly entertaining.

The White-breasted and Black-headed Caiques are the most popular members of the genus. They are chronic wood chewers and should be provided with plenty of satisfying and replaceable material or they will probable destroy their perches, which may be at risk in any case.

One of Edward J. Boosey's White-breasted Caiques loved to use the cord from a window shade as if he were a sailor climbing a rope. This bird could jump up a flight of stairs and could also push an imaginary wheelbarrow across the kitchen table.

Many other experts praise their clever and friendly behavior. These amusing little parrots are being bred in the United States and should not be difficult to obtain.

GREY-CHEEKED PARAKEETS

Interest in parrot species frequently follows trends in much the same way that people become engrossed with fashions, music, or automobiles. Of course, economics also plays a role, and just as it is not possible for everyone to own a luxury car, many parrot fanciers must tailor their choices to fit their wallets.

During the 1970s, the Yellow-naped Amazon rose to a peak of popularity that it justifiably retains. It is a handsome parrot that enjoys physical contact with its owners and can virtually be guaranteed to learn to talk. As the demand for these birds grew, prices doubled and eventually trebled. Interest in the Grey-cheeked Parakeet followed a similar pattern in the early 1980s. The Grey-cheek, or *Brotogeris pyrrhopterus*, is also known as the Orange-winged or Orange-flanked Parakeet. It is a close relative of the Canary-winged Parakeet, although the latter never achieved the popularity of the Grey-cheek. Grey-cheeks are compact, stocky birds that are about eight inches long and lime green in color, with a pale blue crown and delicate gray markings on the cheek. The bends of the wings are marked with orange, and there is a slash of yellow under each wing. The sexes do not visibly differ, but young birds can be recognized by their smaller size and muted colors. Although their markings are attractive, the demand for these smaller parrots is based strictly on their personality.

Virtually all Grey-cheeked Parakeets, including those that were imports, are tame and gentle. Many owners consider them among the most docile birds they have ever kept, a quality that is unusual except among the hand-fed, domestically raised specimens of other parrot species. Robbie Harris, in *Grey Cheeked Parrots and Other Brotogeris*, recounts the experiences of a friend who examined a shipment of more than one thousand Grey-cheeks in a quarantine station. As he reached into a flight cage to take out one of the birds his arm was instantly covered with dozens of them. This gentle nature appears to be an inborn trait, similar to speech skills in Yellow-napes and a sense of humor in the white cockatoos, and our generation of parrot fanciers was not the first to discover it. In his 1926

Virtually all Grey-cheeked Parakeets are tame and friendly.
Robbie Harris

book *Parrakeets*, British aviculturist David Seth-Smith, referring to the Grey-cheek, insists that he has "never . . . seen a wild one. They always seem to be perfectly tame when imported and will often allow themselves to be carried about on one's finger from the first."

The range of the Grey-cheek is western Ecuador to southwest Peru. During the period 1982 to 1985, thousands of these parrots were imported and sold. They were priced at about fifty dollars each, while enterprising breeders charged twice that or more for the young they raised. Importation has ceased, of course, but there are many domestic breeding pairs and these delightful birds are readily available.

If you are interested in breeding these birds, obtain a pair that is at least two years old and make sure that they have been sexed either surgically or by the chromosome method. An appropriate breeding flight would be six-by-six-by-twelve feet in size, with a ten-inch-square nest box; Robbie Harris recommends offering at least four different nest boxes

A bluish gray throat and bib provide an attractive contrast to the Grey-cheeked Parakeet's predominantly green plumage (opposite). Dimension Three Photography

and allowing the birds to choose the one they prefer. A normal clutch includes five eggs that are incubated for about thirty days. The chicks should fledge at around five weeks.

If keeping or breeding a small parrot appeals to you, I encourage you to give the Grey-cheek a try.

The White-winged Parakeet is closely related to the Grey-cheek. Robbie Harris

BLUE-NAPED PARROT

Knowledge of this bird dates back to 1766 when, as noted by Peters (*Check-list of Birds of the World,* 1937), a specimen found on Luzon in the Philippines was described and named.

Tanygnathus lucionensis has a great many names for such a small parrot, including Blue-crowned Green Parrot, Luzon Parakeet, Philippine Green Parrot, and Philippine Great-billed Parrot. This last is due to its similarity to a much larger version of *Tanygnathus,* the Great-billed Parrot of Papua and the Moluccas. The Latin name refers to the stretched and extended jaw that is typical of this parrot and the fact that it was discovered on Luzon. It is found on most of the Philippine Islands, as well as islands off northern Borneo and north of the Celebes.

The species is green with a yellowish-green mantle and underparts. The green of the head is quite vivid, contrasts strikingly with the back of the crown, nape, and, occasionally, the lower cheeks, which are blue. The wing coverts are also blue but are bordered with yellow, producing a mottled appearance similar to that noted in the Rosellas. Typically for this genus, the beak is red, becoming

lighter toward the tip. It is relatively large for a small parrot of only eleven or twelve inches in length and gives the Blue-nape a somewhat pugnacious look. Males are larger than females, have bigger beaks, and are more intensely colored.

Forshaw (*Parrots of the World,* 1973) recognizes only three subspecies, having in effect cut the number of subspecies identified by earlier authors from six to three by grouping together those Blue-napes that resemble each other. He notes that they are very common in the Philippines, where they are popular pets. They are also gaining in popularity in the United States as people discover that these clever and friendly little birds have a good potential for speech as well as a pleasant disposition that belies their belligerent countenance.

Mrs. F. Bonestall of California reported in the June 1936 issue of *Avicultural Magazine* on her success in breeding the Blue-nape, which, she was informed by officers of the Fish and Game Commission and Bureau of Science in Manila, was the first record of the Blue-nape having been bred in captivity. She had traveled widely in eastern Asia and the Pacific and brought home many rare birds to populate an outstanding group of aviaries built on extensive grounds on the bank of a narrow, wooded valley in California.

Penny Corbett and her late mother, Jean Corbett of Pittsburgh, shared bird keeping as a hobby. This mother-daughter team successfully bred an imported pair of Blue-naped Parrots in June of 1979. Although the male had at one time been a pet, this did not interfere with his bonding with the hen. A twenty-six-inch-high-by-twenty-inch-square nest box was placed in their cage at the end of January. The female seemed to approve of her nest box and entered it on February 19. Three eggs were laid in the morning between eight and eleven A.M., the first appearing on March 29 and the second and third on March 31 and April 2. Ms. Corbett discovered a broken egg that apparently had been thrown from the nest box on May 2. Its embryo appeared to have been developing normally. Unfortunately, when she candled the other two eggs that were still in the box, she was disappointed to find that their embryos were not alive. She replaced the contents of the nest box with fresh material, but this time added wet peat moss in addition to the wood shavings it had originally contained. The hen dug down into the peat and laid her eggs after hollowing out an appropriate spot in the wet mound. She worked alone, while the male sat on his perch and supervised, even failing to protest when Ms. Corbett entered the room Although he had fed the female before the eggs were laid, he seemed to feel that all of his responsibilities were over once this had occurred.

No obvious signs of courtship were noted except for an unusual cry produced by the hen during copulation. Ms. Corbett reports that it sounded very much like a repetitious, high pitched, "Joey Joey!" On May 17 an egg was dropped from the perch and on May 21 a second egg was finally laid in the nest box. A third egg was also laid in the box on May 23. Once again they were produced between the hours of 8 and 11 A.M. Only the hen incubated and she alone fed the chicks. After the eggs hatched the male began to show some signs of fatherly devotion and he would call out to alert the hen if either of the women entered the room. If a stranger entered he would scream loudly, at which time the hen would join him in screaming and come out of the nest box to participate in an attack on the intruder.

On June 12 the first chick hatched in the late afternoon, emerging completely bald and totally without down. The second egg did not hatch until June 19, a delay Ms. Corbett speculates may have been caused by the hen's frequent departure from the nest to obtain food for the first chick. The chicks did not make any effort to leave the nest box, so Ms. Corbett and her mother took them out for hand feeding when each reached three weeks of age. It was just as well that they did this, as when the younger chick was removed they noticed that his head and the tops of his wings had been plucked by the hen.

These fine specimens were on hard seed and completely independent at the ages of seven and eight weeks. In later reports Ms. Corbett added that both birds appeared to be males and that in contrast to the opinions of other experts, they talk clearly and well.

18

A VARIETY OF UNUSUAL PARROTS

His body was green and the tips of his wings rose-pink; his forehead was blue and his throat golden. Though deaf she can hear the few phrases the bird speaks. Loulou was almost a son . . . to her in her isolated state.

—*Gustave Flaubert,* A Simple Heart

The term *unusual* in this context means "unique," a quality the birds discussed in this chapter have in abundance; not all of them are rare, but they can certainly be considered unusual.

THE VASA PARROT

The genus *Coracopsis* consists solely of the Greater and Lesser Vasa Parrots. Although a considerable body of information is available about these birds, they have always been considered rare, although for several years during the late 1980s they were imported freely and sold in the United States.

I have never found the grayish-black *Coracopsis v. vasa* to be particularly attractive, but those who own them praise their personalities and friendliness.

Specimens average about nineteen or twenty inches in length, consisting of several inches of long tail. The feathers on the lower edge of the wings, flights, and lower back are silver-gray. The eye, surrounded by a ring of ash-gray bare skin, has a very dark brown iris, and the beak varies in color from horn to dull black. According to Rutgers and Norris, the beak is whitish during the breeding season and becomes darker following the molt, but a

group of Vasas recently examined by one of my acquaintances shows approximately equal numbers of dark and light beaks.

Coracopsis n. nigra, or the Lesser Vasa, is sometimes referred to as the Black Parrot. It is, of course, smaller than the Greater, measuring about fifteen inches in length. Its feathering is a dark brownish black and its naked eye ring is a dull rose color. Immediately after the molt the beak is black, but it becomes almost white again following the molting season.

These birds originated in Madagascar, off the eastern coast of southern Africa. Along with the off-shore islands of the Comoros, Reunion, and the Seychelles, it provides a suitable home for a large number of lesser-known parrot genera. Forshaw (*Parrots of the World,* 2d rev. ed., 1978) notes that the Greater Vasa is now found along the entire coast of Madagascar as well as on Reunion Island, where it was introduced, and that the Lesser is found throughout the same coastal region and on some of the islands of the Comoros and the Seychelles.

The duke of Bedford, who wrote extensively about these birds, describes his Greater Vasa Parrot in the August 1914 issue of *Avicultural Magazine* as "an amiable and lively bird which, with little encouragement, becomes very tame and docile." He praises its aptitude for speech and mimicry but considers its natural cries unpleasant grunts and squawks. He sees no visible differences between the sexes and distinguishes the Lesser Vasa from the Greater by its smaller size and the fact that it is less noisy and very affectionate. In the December 1926 issue of the same publication, in an article on African Parrots, the duke reports that Vasas are hardy birds that are only infrequently subject to illness and that, once acclimatized, can even winter in the open. The 1928 edition of his *Parrots and Parrot-Like Birds* makes further reference to the Vasa's lively and intelligent disposition and its capacity for mimicry and affection. He also discusses its unusual habit of extruding internal organs from the vent during the breeding season.

Lex Beatrous, an exotic-bird dealer in Miami, Florida, is very familiar with Vasa Parrots and has examined scores of them. He believes that their beak color may vary according to sex, age, and the time of year. His own Vasas showed a moderate ability for speech but a marked aptitude for mimicking household noises and the sounds of other birds and animals. He insists that even imported adults birds tamed readily and were extremely docile.

JARDINE'S PARROT

Until 1981, these attractive parrots were seldom imported and thus fairly rare in the United States. Then they began to appear on importers' and wholesalers' lists at fairly reasonable prices, and although this little bird has not achieved a great degree of popularity, some of the original imports and a few domestically bred young are available.

Jardine's Parrot, or *Poicephalus gulielmi*, is a member of a large group of stocky birds from central Africa, all species of which bear a strong resemblance to each other and can be easily recognized by their hefty build, formidable beak, squared-off tail, and prominent, naked cere. The Jardine's is named for Sir William Jardine, a well-known nineteenth-century British naturalist who was a contemporary and associate of Lear, Leadbeater, and Swainson, three men who have been immortalized by parrot enthusiasts in the common designations of a spectacular macaw, a beautiful cockatoo, and a lorikeet with exotic coloring.

A Jardine's Parrot pair with the hen shown on the right.
R. J. Richards

The identification and naming of Jardine's Parrot occurred in 1849, and its species name, *gulielmi*, is actually a Latin version of Jardine's first name.

The Jardine's is a twelve-inch-long, green parrot with very dark wing and mantle feathers bordered in a lighter green that gives the bird a scaly appearance. The crown, forehead, and thighs are a reddish-orange color. Forshaw (*Parrots of the World*, 2d rev. ed., 1978) notes three subspecies that differ from the nominate race mainly in the depth of their red-orange coloring, the size of their green feather margins, and geographical origin. They are forest birds, and are not nearly as plentiful as the African Grey, which frequents many of the same locations.

The Jardine's is frequently referred to as the Red-crowned or Red-headed Parrot. A page of photos in Wolfgang deGrahl's *Color Atlas of the Parrots* provides an interesting comparative view of African parrots. Under the picture of a very young Jardine's, which he refers to as a Congo or Red-headed Parrot, he notes that age can be determined by the size of the red-orange forehead marking.

Dr. Greene kept a Jardine's, appropriately named William, that could talk but was, regrettably, a feather plucker. In another early reference in the November 1902 issue of *Avicultural Magazine*, the owner of a Jardine's expresses concern about the way his bird, Jacob, plucks its breast feathers. Jacob was described as an affectionate bird that could dance and do tricks. In a later letter the writer, a Mr. Moerschell, reported that "Jacob" had laid two eggs.

A. J. Stoodley of England recounted his successful breeding of the Jardine's Parrot in the October–December 1978 issue of *Avicultural Magazine*. In 1977, he set up two pairs in a twenty-by-seven-by-six-foot aviary and provided hollow logs as nests. The birds nested and laid eggs, but no chicks hatched. In the spring of 1978, they were moved with their nests to a smaller indoor aviary. Soon after this, eggs were laid, and following an incubation period of approximately twenty-six days, a single chick was hatched. This bird was fully fledged and independent by twelve weeks of age. It was duller in color than the parents and had a smaller red-orange marking.

Lee Buse, a U.S. parrot owner, reports that Belle, her active, tame Jardine's Parrot, enjoys flying around the house. At the time of our first communication, Ms. Buse was under the impression that Belle was a female, but the bird has since been surgically sexed and it turns out that Belle should really be called Bill!

THICK-BILLED PARROT

For what is probably the sake of convenience, the Thick-bill, a native of northern and central Mexico, is usually grouped with the conures. It is, of course, a separate genus, *Rhynchopsitta pachyrhyncha*, the Latin name referring to its heavy beak. The color is a rich, grass green, except for a mass of tightly curled scarlet feathers, similar to those of the Military Macaw, that begin at the base of the upper beak and blend into the crown. This parrot is about fifteen to sixteen inches long, and the male is slightly larger than the female. In many respects I find that they resemble the miniature macaws both in their appearance and their playful manner.

In the 1970 monograph *Mexican Macaws*, Lyndon L. Hargrave indicates that early observers sometimes confused the Thick-bill with the Military Macaw, which shares part of its territory in the pine forests of the Sierra Madre Mountains of Mexico. The Thick-bill feeds voraciously on oil-rich pine nuts, occasionally flying north into Arizona and New Mexico when these nuts are in season.

According to Forshaw (*Parrots of the World*, 2d rev. ed., 1981), Thick-bills originally ranged as far north as northern Arizona, and references to them in that area can be found in reports of a sixteenth-century expedition by Spanish explorers. Archaeological evidence recovered from Indian sites places them in the region even earlier. Thus, they appear to have been natives of what is now the state of Arizona, but are currently only occasional visitors.

Sparks and Soper discuss Thick-bills as "repatriated parrots," referring to the plan to re-establish them in the United States by releasing captive-bred birds in areas where conditions are favorable. There have, however, been critics of the way in which this plan is being implemented, as many of the newly released birds proved to be inept in the wild even after having spent months in flights with wild birds. Although they are sharp-eyed birds, they failed to form groups to protect themselves against various native predators. In addition, they lacked the natural instinct to remove pine cones from trees when searching for food. In California, where human-raised California Condors are being repatriated, great care is taken to avoid allowing the chicks to bond with their keepers. Hand feeding for the condors is done with a mock condor hand puppet. This and other precautions seem to result in a greater degree of success for the condor reintegration group.

The Thick-billed Parrot has an engaging, friendly personality. Karl Plath, in a 1927 article in *Avicultural Magazine*, describes his tame, playful Thick-bill, which had great affection for Plath's young son. Using an odd, shuffling walk, the bird would follow the youngster around while shaking his tail from side to side.

A brief article by R. T. Kyme in the August 1971 issue of the *Magazine of the Parrot Society* discusses breeding efforts at the Jersey Wildlife Preservation Trust in Great Britain, where director Gerald Durell oversaw the production of chicks in 1970. Unfortunately, the young did not survive, as one was accidentally crushed by its parents and the others died a few days later. A commemorative postage stamp issued by the Isle of Jersey postal authorities in 1971 honored the Wildlife Preservation Trust, using the Thick-bill on one of its stamps.

A 1966 article by Kenton Lint in *ZOONOOZ*, the publication of the Zoological Society of San Diego, describes what is probably the first recorded captive breeding of this species. Although the zoo received the female in 1955 and her mate in 1956, it was not until nine years later that success was achieved. During this period the staff patiently varied nest-box size and location, diet, and other factors until a chick was finally born and raised.

FIG PARROTS

The two genera of Fig Parrots are *Psittaculirostris* and *Opopsitta*, the latter including the Double-eyed Fig Parrot, so named because early writers fancied that the blue marking above and in front of the eye resembled a second eye. *Opopsitta* is found mainly in New Guinea and Australia, while *Psittaculirostris*'s native habitat is the Western Papuan Islands and southern New Guinea.

A perfect pair of Salvadori's Fig Parrots. Gunther Enderle, NEKTON PRODUCTS

In general, both species are attractive, compact birds, measuring seven to eight inches in length. *Opopsitta* is somewhat smaller and has a bare cere. Their small size, rapid movement, and ability to blend with their background are probably greater factors in their absence from the pet trade than their lack of availability.

Forshaw (*Australian Parrots*, 2d rev. ed., 1981) notes that the Double-eyed Fig Parrot is not as rare as has been generally claimed and that some subspecies are quite common within their range. He has seen a group of several hundred birds leave a single roosting tree.

Edward's Fig Parrot, or *Psittaculirostris edwardsii*, is a fine example of these small but attractive birds. It is about seven and a half inches long, and has a greenish-yellow crown that blends with a black band stretching from the eyes to the nape. The red and yellow feathers of the face and ear coverts protrude like unruly whiskers and remind one of the Kakapo or Owl Parrot, although these are not related. The throat and breast are red, with a blue band of feathers at the top of the breast, and the tail and upper feathers are green.

Desmarest's Fig Parrot, sometimes called Desmarest's Dwarf Parrot or the Golden-headed Fig Parrot, is a beautifully marked bird with a deep-green body set off by a red forehead that blends with its golden orange crown. A half ring of blue below the eye is matched by a similar blue marking at the top of the breast. Desmarest's is the same size as Edward's and originates in western Papua and southern New Guinea.

Early aviculturists linked these parrots to the lories; Charles Barrett called them "Lorilets." Barrett refers to Coxen's Fig Parrot, *O. d. coxini*, as the Blue-browed Lorilet and adds that it was named by Gould in 1867 for a Mr. Coxen of Brisbane. Barrett confirms the species' ability to blend with the background foliage and escape detection as it feeds in tall jungle fig trees.

Bates and Busenbark (*Parrots and Related Birds*, 1978 ed.) consider the Fig Parrots to be "extremely fascinating birds . . . with the size and shape of lovebirds and the personalities of Lories."

Discussing their diet, Rutgers and Norris note that, since it is so heavy in fruits, the droppings of the Fig Parrots, like those of the lories, have a large liquid component. This should not deter the bird enthusiast, however, as cages can be designed for easy cleaning and diets can be modified to alleviate the problem.

HAWK-HEADED PARROT

It is the striking appearance and colorful erectile ruff of the Hawk-head that most people consider so impressive. Although the Vinaceous and Double Yellow-head Amazons can also raise the feathers of their nape and crown, their display is not nearly as startling as the large fan-shaped ruff of the Hawk-head. The deep red feathers of the head are edged in light blue, and, when erected, resemble bunting for a patriotic occasion.

The nominate species, *Deroptyus accipitrinus*, which is generally the one seen in the United States, originates in Venezuela, Surinam, and Guyana. This parrot has a light or buff-colored crown and forehead and is often referred to as the Buff-crowned Hawk-head.

The rare subspecies found farther south in Brazil is *D. a. fuscifrons*, which has a brown crown and a forehead with occasional streaks of buff or cream. The Brazilian specimens have never been plentiful, and current restrictions make it almost impossible to obtain them. People who are fortunate enough to own Buff-crowned Hawk-heads are usually searching for males, as most of those imported into the United States have turned out to be females and hybridizing these parrots with the subspecies is universally frowned upon.

Ramon Noegel, who consistently breeds many rare parrots, reported on his Hawk-heads in the September 1980 issue of the *Avicultural Bulletin*. He has what may be the only breeding pair of Brazilian Hawk-heads in the United States. In his article, Noegel describes the three-by-four-by-nine-foot suspended aviary in which he placed his pair in the summer of 1975. A fertile egg was produced in the spring of 1976, from which a chick hatched after twenty-eight days. Unfortunately, this bird did not survive because the parents covered it with nesting material and by the time it was discovered it was not possible to save it. The male was eight years old at this time and the female was partly responsible for this tragedy. In February 1976, three fertile eggs were laid at three- to four-day intervals. One of these eggs was pulled for incubation and hand raising, while the other two were hatched by the hen. The prolific pair produced three additional clutches of two eggs each, for a total of nine chicks in one year.

Noegel suggests that only one pair be kept at a time, as these parrots are extremely territorial and will react adversely to another pair within seeing or even screaming distance.

KEA

If you were asked to guess the identity of the most clever, talented, and ingenious member of the parrot family it is doubtful that you would choose the Kea. It is a large, rather dumpy-looking olive-green bird whose general mode of transportation consists of moving along the ground in an undignified waddle with an occasional little hop to avoid obstacles. But do not be deceived by first impressions. This intelligent bird is blessed with such a keen sense of curiosity that it frequently comes into close contact with humans and the structures they build. Unlike other parrots, which generally avoid unfamiliar objects for several days to be sure that they pose no threat, within hours of a camper's arrival in a Kea's natural territory the Kea will enter the tent, examine the contents of a backpack, or play with the windshield wipers of the car.

Nestor notabilis is eighteen to nineteen inches long and is unique to the South Island mountain region of New Zealand. It should not be confused with its relative the Kaka, *Nestor meridionalis*, which can be found on both the North and South islands of New Zealand.

The olive-green colors of the Kea are mottled with delicate traces of blue and yellow relieved by orange-red bars under the wings and a dull red rump. It has a long, slender upper beak that is thought to be more sharply arched in males, but there has been no verification of this. The call of the Kea, which is usually heard when the bird is in full flight, is a high-pitched scream that sounds like "Kee-ah," obviously the source of the parrot's name.

Barry Preston (*Birds of Paradox*, 1967) encountered the Kea during a camping trip to the mountains of New Zealand. His first-hand descriptions of his experiences with these birds include a scene in which he awoke to find one perched on his chest and peering at his nose. Preston notes that they live in groups of twenty or more and breed in secluded locations high among the rocks. Wolfgang DeGrahl

(*Color Atlas of the Parrots*, 1978) confirms their amusing personalities but notes that they are generally sleepy during the day while becoming quite lively at night—a reversal of normal parrot behavior. DeGrahl also discusses several successful breedings of this bird in the Zurich Zoo.

Dr. Greene describes the Kea as a sprightly and active parrot that in a flight or cage will spring from perch to perch "with the agility of a sparrow." He quotes his colleague, Reverend Dutton, on the Keas' ability to escape from their cages at the London Zoo; ultimately these enclosures had to be padlocked, as the Keas were able to open virtually any ordinary fastenings.

An informative article on the Kea appeared in the March–April 1947 issue of *Avicultural Magazine*. Dr. J. M. Derscheid confirms the night behavior of the Kea, describing it as one of the large-eyed semi-nocturnal birds. He also observes that its diet is not that of the typical parrot, as it uses its sharp beak to dig up roots and insect grubs as well as to strip bark from the trees to obtain additional insects. He was once sent a pair of these birds by friends in New Zealand. Although they arrived in excellent condition, he was surprised at the box in which they had traveled, which was covered in sheet metal and padlocked. The reason for these precautions soon became apparent, however, as within a week the new arrivals had done more damage to wooden cages and opened more clasps and bolts than all the other residents of the aviary had done in the previous year. Remarkably, their efforts did not involve brute force, but were instead a group endeavor to seek out weak spots, which they then successfully exploited.

Dr. Derscheid draws some interesting conclusions regarding the sexing of these birds. His pair had identical plumage but a great deal of variation in body conformation.

The larger of the two, believed to be the male, was heavier and bulkier, with a massive head. The bird with the slighter build and the more reclusive personality was considered the female.

An article in the June 1987 issue of *American Cage-Bird Magazine* describes Michael Levine's visit to New Zealand and his affectionate confrontation with a band of Keas that attacked his clothesline, pulled out his tent pegs, and begged for food by tapping on the sliding glass door of the ranger's quarters at Mt. Cook National Park, where Mr. Levine spent the night.

His research into the charge that Keas are sheep killers resulted in the observation that although these animals might scavenge the carcass of a dead bird and rogue Keas might attack a sick or injured sheep, all other claims of Keas turning into sheep-killing carnivores are distasteful exaggerations.

part III

SPECIAL DELIGHTS

19 PARROT POTPOURRI

ver the last few years, many "tidbits" about parrots have come our way. Some are clever and useful, while others are simply appealing if you love parrots.

James K. Page, Jr., has a parrot that says "hello" when he comes home and "bye" when he leaves. Writing in a recent issue of *Smithsonian*, Mr. Page told the story of two white pigeons that could do even more. These birds had been taught by the famous psychologist B. F. Skinner to communicate using symbols. Jack and Jill, as they were named, operated a keyboard with which they could answer questions and say "thank you" when they received a snack reward. Intelligence or simple conditioning?

Even a simple change in the way you perform a routine task such as placing paper in your cages can save you work and time. If you use four sheets of newspaper, which is suitable for most cages, put the two front sheets on top of the back sheets in such a way that the front sheets, which generally get most of the droppings and seed husks, can be lifted off and replaced without disturbing the back papers.

Tutu, my Greater Sulphur-crested Cockatoo, always sits on an outside perch when I am cleaning and feeding. She demands and receives lots of attention, including neck scratching and kisses. If she fails to get a kiss she clicks her upper and lower beaks together rapidly in a loud, clattering imitation of a kissing sound. I think Tutu probably also belongs to a special subspecies of Cockatoos known as the Fat and Silly Greater.

The *Australian Stamp Bulletin*, published monthly, points out that almost twenty percent of their collectors specialize in a common theme or subject, one of the most popular of which is birds. One issue featured an attractive full-color photo of the rare Golden-shouldered Parakeet that also appears on one of Australia's ten-cent stamps.

A gentleman in Kingsport, Tennessee, has devised a method of encouraging his parrots to ingest more of the cuttlebone and vitamins that he provides. Since they all love peanut butter, he now mixes the vitamins and ground cuttlebone with a peanut butter treat. They devour every bit of this nutritious mess, which pleases him greatly.

A pair of Hyacinth Macaws in breeding condition. Michael DeFreitas

"The Drowning Pool," an old movie that still makes the rounds of late-night TV, is a sequel to the detective movie "Hooper." In the second film, Hooper, played by Paul Newman, visits the estate of a rich client whose large outdoor aviary features Double Yellow-heads and Blue and Gold Macaws. In one scene, she paid more attention to the parrots than to the detective.

Advertisers constantly find parrots an ideal eye-catching device. One ad for Sheraton Hotels in Latin America was dominated by a beautiful photo of a large Scarlet Macaw. The cover of an Avianca South American Tour Guide was also graced with a Scarlet Macaw, while an inside picture of another Scarlet is captioned, "Come and see me in the Amazon." Fortunoff's, a New York department store, featured a Blue and Gold Macaw, a Yellow-naped Amazon, and, although it really doesn't belong in the picture, an Umbrella Cockatoo on both the front and back covers of a "jungle" ad for summer furniture and similar products.

Bloomingdale's, the upscale New York department store, ran a cosmetic ad in which the model had a Moluccan Cockatoo on her shoulder. A few weeks later, T-shirts decorated with very colorful Macaws were selling at various Greenwich Village boutiques for anywhere from $20 to $120. When asked why he was featuring a parrot T-shirt, the owner of one store replied, "Who knows? But the shirts are flying out of the store."

Bloomingdale's buyers must love parrots! In a spring fashion mailing a women modeling a bathing suit had a beautiful Moluccan seated right on top of her head. Not to be outdone, one manufacturer of TV projection devices advertised the product with a picture of a large Scarlet Macaw that appears to jump from the screen towards a man and his cat who are watching from an armchair. Parrots are constantly used in fashion and other types of ads.

Does your parrot become nervous when you attach the hose to your vacuum cleaner? It is possible that the hose reminds him of a snake. Parrots

As with most parrots, the Yellow-headed Amazon occurs in a number of subspecies. Shown here is an example of the oratrix *and* tresmariae *subspecies.* Mike Gluss

are terrified of snakes, their natural enemies in the wild, and perhaps the sight of the curved, thick hose awakens a buried atavistic memory of a deadly adversary.

Feather plucking is a serious problem for many parrot owners. A rather extreme approach, when all else fails, is to have your veterinarian notch the plucking parrot's lower beak. After this is done the upper and lower beak no longer can finely articulate and although the parrot can still crack seeds and engage in other normal activities, feathers will slip through. The treatment must be repeated when the notch grows in, and your vet should be very careful not to split the beak.

Parrot owners quickly discover that their birds resent and resist change. Frodo, one of my Scarlet Macaws, had a large swing in his cage, which was destroyed by several days of vigorous chewing at both ends. I made an easy repair by

shortening the swing, but when I replaced it in his cage, Frodo acted as if he had never seen it before, backed away screaming, and refused to mount it. Eventually, he sat on a nearby perch and tore the swing to pieces as if enraged by its very presence.

If you watch reruns of the TV show "Alice," keep your eyes open for the episode in which one of the waitresses in Mel's Diner loses her parrot when Mel frightens it to death. He replaces the bird with a Mealy Amazon named Irving, the largest Mealy I have ever seen.

In the first "Rocky" sequel, Rocky's wife plays a scene with a Greater Sulphur-crested Cockatoo. The timid woman screams in fright when surprised by the parrot, and the crest of the equally frightened Cockatoo pops up instantly in response.

"The Lady Killer," a movie staring Alec Guiness, contains scenes with a plump and charming Greater Sulphur-crested Cockatoo. The parrot plays no real role in the movie; he just sits on his perch looking smug as the action goes on around him.

Parrots are not really as critical or disapproving as they sometimes look. With its eyes widely spaced on either side on the skull and having relatively little muscular control over eye movement, a parrot must move its head to change the field of vision. This cocking of the head to look at an object contributes to their comical and slightly disapproving appearance.

Herman, an Amazon that was something of a fixture at a waterfront motel bar in Miami, was shot and killed by a tipsy patron who was unhappy about being evicted from the bar. Herman had been entertaining customers with a running stream of chatter for over twenty years, and was buried on the beach by the mourning bartender, who said, "He will be missed." The gunman was charged with assault, shooting in an occupied dwelling, and cruelty to animals.

If the feeding cup setup in your parrot's cage is arranged with one cup closer to you than the other, assign the closest spot to the water cup. If one of your birds is in a biting frame of mind or if you have someone doing the feeding for you, the easily spilled water cup will be less difficult to replace. You can also tell substitute parrot feeders that a quick spray from a plant mister will cause most threatening birds to back away from the cup openings long enough to allow them to slip the dishes in.

Stevie Wonder, the pianist, held a party to celebrate a new album. Part of the entertainment included some macaws and cockatoos. One of the birds, a Scarlet Macaw, bit anyone who got near him. Frodo, my Scarlet Macaw, would have approved of this.

Recently I clipped the nails of Jaco, one of my African Greys, both for her comfort and for the benefit of a visitor who wished to learn the technique. I noticed that Jaco watched the operation even more closely than the visitor to make sure that I did not cut carelessly.

To assist you in the training of a newly arrived parrot, wire a short length of perch inside the cage door the day before training begins. (Doing it the day before gives the parrot a chance to get used to it.) This simple device will encourage the parrot to climb to the top of his cage, where it will be a lot easier to work with him.

Bob Hope and Hedy LaMarr starred in an oldie called "My Favorite Spy." In one scene the villain's house burns down but fortunately his bird collection is rescued. If you watch carefully you can spot a Lesser Sulphur-crested Cockatoo as well as a very calm Scarlet Macaw that casually moves his head out of the way each time a fire hose or other piece of fire-fighting equipment comes too close.

A good container for toys can be purchased in any restaurant supply house. It consists of a stainless-steel wire basket that can be attached to the side of the cage. Bits of food and other material will drop through, but the toys will be kept clean and available in the basket.

Parrots scold loudly when angry, frightened, or distressed. My wife calls our birds "watch-parrots," as they also make a lot of noise when they hear a stranger. If I come into the bird room late at night after lights are out, the birds grumble and mumble and I imagine they are saying, "What does he want at this late hour?"

Jan Breughel's seventeenth-century masterpiece "Hearing," which hangs in the Prado Museum in Madrid, includes two Blue and Gold Macaws, a Lesser Sulphur-crested Cockatoo, several Amazons, and an Indian Ringneck.

Fiorello, one of my Scarlets, and Tutu, my Greater, used to take turns each evening on a large trapeze perch. As I would take Tutu off with one hand and install Fiorello with the other, Fiorello would engage in a game of gently pulling Tutu's tail. Tutu simply pretended to ignore him.

A British study showed that elderly people who lived alone and who were given a budgie to keep and care for experienced a vast improvement in general attitude and self-image. A control group that was given flowers to care for instead of budgies did not do nearly as well.

Parrots and artists seem to go together. Adolf Sehring of Culpeper, Virginia, is a well-known and talented painter whose work hangs in many collections and museums. Mr. Sehring is the owner of two handsome Blue and Gold Macaws that he has bred several times. The late Alfonso Ossario of East Hampton, New York, a well-known sculptor and painter, owned an African Grey whose attractive cage was truly a work of art. Ray Ellis, acclaimed for his paintings, sketches, and watercolors of the Savannah, Georgia, area, frequently paints with his Yellow-nape, Rama, sitting on his shoulder. Rama is known in the community for the time he escaped to the top of a tree in a park and was finally found when he started to scream, "Where's Ray! Where's Ray!"

If you are planning vacation travel with your parrot, have your veterinarian carefully examine your pet a week or two before your departure to be sure that he is fit to travel. Ask the vet about safe medications or natural foods that might be helpful in calming the bird so that he will adjust quickly to new surroundings. If you are flying, get to the airport early and do not let the reservations clerk put your parrot's cage on the baggage conveyor belt. Instead, carry it to the boarding area, where you can ask an airline employee to make sure personally it gets on the aircraft. Reverse this procedure at the other end. A tip to the employee might be appropriate. If you can avoid traveling during peak periods your chances of special care are greater.

Moving a bird in or out of the country is quite a chore. There is a lot of red tape and paper work, but if you do some research and planning you can make things go a little more smoothly. Write to the Chief Staff Veterinarian, Import Birds and Poultry Veterinary Services, Department of Agriculture, Federal Building, Hyattsville, Maryland 20782, for their latest checklist and forms for birds entering or re-entering the country. Another useful publication is issued by the Department of Health, Education and Welfare, Public Health Service Center for Disease Control, Atlanta, Georgia 30333, and is titled *How To Import Pets But Not Disease.*

One episode from the television series "Love Boat" featured a Scarlet Macaw, which several of the characters on the show had taught to say, "Captain Stubing is a jerk!" He learned it faster than any parrot I have ever known.

An eerie Australian motion picture, "Picnic at Hanging Rock," is set in Australia at the turn of the

Gentle handling, nutritious food, and generous love can win the confidence of any parrot, even one that may have been abused. Robert Czarnomski

century. The scenery is beautiful and one particularly vivid bit of photography shows a Blue and Orange Lory flying from branch to branch.

Our local newspaper carried an article about a report of psittacosis afflicting the owner of a cockatiel that had died. The victim went into the hospital emergency room with a temperature of 105 degrees. When the doctor asked if anyone in the household had been sick and the wife replied, "Our bird died this morning," the doctor's eyes widened. An autopsy on the bird confirmed the psittacosis. No other members of the family, human or avian, came down with the disease.

Parrot owners often wonder why on some occasions their birds bite while at other times they are sweet and gentle. Many parrots have strongly developed personalities and also seem to know their rights; they will play when in the mood but become ill-tempered if disturbed when they do not wish to be handled. Using discretion may spare you a lot of nips.

An interesting story in the *St. Petersburg Times* dealt with Cortez, a very old Purple-capped Lory that was one of the items contested in a local divorce case. Judge Robert Beach concluded that the Lory should spend six months with each owner but that neither was to influence him against the other. (In other words, the husband was not to teach the parrot to say things like "Mommy serves wilted vegetables!")

The smallest member of the Los Angeles Police Department is eighteen inches tall and weighs three pounds. Officer Byrd is a Blue and Gold Macaw that gives safety shows for children, demonstrating safe methods of using bikes, skateboards, and roller skates. Although he uses bird-sized equipment, the children get the message and enjoy it.

With parrots you really have to keep in mind the saying that actions speak louder than words. At least two of my parrots scream "no bite!" just before they nip.

Tom Wilson, who writes and draws the cartoon *Ziggy*, often uses a parrot in the cartoon. Tom doesn't keep a parrot, but his son does, and that bird is the inspiration for the clever things the cartoon version often says or does.

Rosie, my Moluccan, isn't much of a talker but she is skilled at making whooping sounds that are very much like those heard in movies just before a submarine dives. This is typical of Moluccan Cockatoo vocalization, although I have heard other owners of these delightful parrots describe the noise as sounding like an unconventional train whistle.

If you let your larger parrots occasionally fly free in your bird room, be careful not to startle them by sudden noises or movements. While the long-tailed macaws are well equipped for short stops, lowering their tail feathers to lose lift, a bird such as a cockatoo or Amazon will generally hit a wall or some other object if it engages in vigorous indoor flight.

The Australia Bulletin reports that the rare Night Parrot, *Geopsittacus ocidentalis*, has been rediscovered in the far north of South Australia. This bird, which was thought to be extinct, is one of Australia's unusual Ground Parrots and no prior authenticated sightings had been made in the last sixty years.

Shapes are important to parrots. If you have been feeding carrots and find that your birds ignore a portion served in the unusual cylindrical fashion, try making carrot sticks or using a french fry cutter to achieve other interesting shapes. You may be surprised at your bird's reaction to a mere cosmetic change of contour.

A well-known watch company used a television ad in which a large Scarlet Macaw dropped an inexpensive watch from a great height and, after retrieving it, squawked that the watch still worked. The bird was a beauty, but, of necessity, the voice was dubbed.

There were once three beautiful Macaws in the Pan American Union Building in Washington. They lived in a lush, beautiful garden provided by the Organization of American States. They would scream at employees during working hours and drop an occasional feather into cocktails during diplomatic receptions. The trio consisted of a pair of Scarlet Macaws named Paz and Chapina, plus a Blue and Gold female named Pancho Villa. There have been Macaws in the building on and off since 1948. The first two birds, which were provided by the American Naval Attaché from Brazil, died in the mid 1950s and were replaced by the president of Guatemala, who offered to fill the vacancies while he was visiting President Eisenhower. It was President Eisenhower's niece who named the birds. The young Caroline Kennedy would frequently visit the birds after hours when the employees had gone home. In 1985, these colorful creatures that had been admired by the first family as well as by many heads of state were moved to a basement cage in the National Zoo. Telephone calls from people who missed the parrots elicited the news that the decision to move them was for their own good, as they seemed to be getting nervous and aggressive. The source of this information suggested that their move should be considered retirement rather than banishment.

In a way, their story typifies life in Washington. One day you are being visited by heads of state or the president's daughter, and the next day you are in the basement of the National Zoo.

Firms that sell factory equipment offer wire-mesh partitions in various panel sizes. These are quite sturdy, as they are made of number-ten-gauge wire in a half-inch diamond pattern. All types of doors, windows, and accessories are available, and it is obvious when you look at a catalog that this material, which is generally used to set up secure tool or equipment rooms, would be ideal for the construction of an aviary.

In the sequel, "Butch Cassidy and the Sundance Kid—The Early Days," Butch and the Kid visit a place of entertainment decorated with a Blue-fronted Amazon that is an expert at twisting his head in all directions. He reminded me very much of Fogel, my own Blue-front, who was also very good at manipulating his head.

Several years ago Johnny Carson had a baby Scarlet Macaw on his late-night talk show. The young woman who was handling the bird demonstrated hand feeding and the macaw obliged by eating the food and then, in a typical baby fashion, jerking its head back and trying to take the spoon with it. When Johnny attempted to wipe the baby's chin, the ungrateful macaw squawked loudly, flapped its wings, and frightened him off.

During another program Johnny featured a Greater Sulphur-crested Cockatoo, a Mealy Amazon, and a young Double Yellow-head that were touted as outstanding talkers and performers. The birds didn't do very well, so Johnny produced a film clip from an earlier show in which the most talented parrot I've ever heard sings, "I Left My Heart in San Francisco" and "Springtime in the Rockies." All of this was done on command and in a very clear voice.

A friend in Colombia advised me that the most popular name for parrots in Cartagena is "Pepe," and that they are not taught to say "Polly want a cracker!" Instead they say, *"Lorito, Lorito Real,*

The temptation to give a parrot pet outdoor time is great. Done carelessly, though, it can result in the escape and permanent loss of the bird. Properly handled, it can benefit the bird and increase the owner's pleasure in its company. George Allen, III

visto de verde y soy Liberal!" This is considered very humorous, as it roughly translates to "Royal parrot, dressed in green and I am liberal," and the official color of the liberal party in Cartagena is red. There appears to be a conspiracy on the part of all maids and children to teach this statement to parrots.

People who are not familiar with parrots may not believe that they are capable of facial expressions, which are produced largely with the eyes, beak, and facial feathers. Birl, my Mealy Amazon, generally maintained a smiling and contented look if things were going well for him. If things went wrong, however, he would immediately develop a pop-eyed look of terror. This could result from something as minor as my accidentally brushing against the table under his cage.

Birl was surprisingly nimble for a rather fat parrot. He would climb from his cage when I opened the door and have a grand old time chewing up the cardboard boxes stored behind his cage. On one occasion, when I wanted to cut some wooden blocks for the birds, I discovered that Birl had also been chewing the power cord on my electric saw.

Not surprisingly, Birl appeared to prefer and show affection for people who are somewhat boisterous or noisy. Perhaps he cherished those who, like himself, spent their lives making loud noises.

The *New York Times* reported on several U.S. families living in New Guinea and working for one of the large number of construction companies that are changing the face of the land. One woman was shown holding a large Triton Cockatoo. She indicated that the bird visited her on a daily basis and that she fed him cookies and sweet tea, which were his favorites. The cockatoo looked docile but rather plump in the photograph—perhaps too many cookies and too much sweet tea?

The San Diego Wild Animal Park had a demonstration of a Scarlet Macaw that was trained as a seeing-eye bird. A friend who attended reports that it was not a successful demonstration; the macaw appeared to be distracted by the audience, keeping him from paying attention to where he was going. Even more interesting was the African Goose that kept dive bombing the audience in the middle section of the amphitheater in repeated attempts to get to his usual roosting place.

If your parrot opens nuts and bolts on or in his cage, you can stop this by slightly deforming the ends of the threaded portion of the nuts. You will still be able to remove the nut but the parrot will not have the strength to do so.

Police officer Wayne Frampton from Suffolk County, Long Island, is a bird lover. When a group of cockatiels, parrots, canaries, lovebirds, and one cockatoo were seized from a pet shop by the ASPCA, Office Frampton volunteered to care for the 175-bird collection. When a New York State Supreme Court judge ordered the birds returned to their owner, Frampton, commenting on the birds' breeding activities, noted that more birds were going back than had been confiscated.

Many people would like to give their parrots a taste of the outdoors but hesitate to do so because of the risk of escape. During warm weather, try bringing the parrot's cage out onto your lawn and placing it on an area that is clean and has not been fertilized or otherwise sprayed with chemicals. Slide out the bottom tray and the sheet metal safety shield and allow your parrot the thrill of being able to walk, play, and dig in the clean, moist grass of your lawn or garden. Take care when replacing the tray and metal retainer to be sure that they are properly inserted so that they do not fall away when you lift the cage to return your parrot to the house.

Always caution visitors, particularly those with children, to use discretion when admiring your parrots. You might remind them that a parrot's beak can close with force of 350 pounds per square inch, so putting your finger through the bars of a parrot cage is not a wise move.

A friend who lives in Mexico reports that the prices of parrots in his country are still quite low. He notes, however, that the price can change radically if the *pajarero* (bird seller) sees that you are not a local or that you do not know anything about birds. One American visitor paid about $400 for a baby Mexican Red-head, probably because he asked, "How much are the little macaws?" My correspondent, however, paid as little as four dollars each for the same birds.

A movie from Holland, "Soldiers of Orange," deals with the Dutch resistance during World War II. In one garden scene, an attractive Moluccan Cockatoo is seated on a hoop stand watching some young people play tennis. A stray tennis ball hits the hoop and the agile Cockatoo simply slides to the bottom of the hoop while loosely holding on with her claws and beak. Because they originate in Indonesia, a former Dutch possession, these cockatoos have always been popular in Holland.

Here's a great rarity: a Spix's Macaw baby at age two months (opposite). Paolo Tiengo

Several years ago NBC aired a program on the unhappy childhood of wealthy heiress Gloria Vanderbilt. During the program, her aunt, Gertrude Whitney, was shown with her attractive Greater Sulphur-crested Cockatoo named Cecil. He was in a large wrought-iron cage and appeared to be a rather quiet bird. Little Gloria was permitted to feed him a carrot in one scene, a treat for both Cecil and little Gloria.

In the James Bond film "For Your Eyes Only," the mystery of the missing secret equipment was solved when a Blue and Gold Macaw spilled the beans about its location.

A delightful movie called "Rich Kids" included a Lesser Sulphur-crested Cockatoo, along with some budgies and finches. The Lesser is a bit ragged and tends to hiss at people he doesn't like.

Police inspector Enio Aravjo knew something was up in the Brazilian town of Canoas when he heard Blondi the parrot screaming, "baboa!" "baboa!" (Big Baby! Big Baby!). Big Baby is the nickname of a local eighteen-year-old with a record of bird snatching. The thief claimed he had received the bird as a present, but when the bird's owner appeared, Blondi immediately recognized him and fluttered to his arm. Big Baby was then arrested.

The *Los Angeles Times* described an influx of what appear to be Yellow-fronted or Orange-winged Amazons in Arcadia, California. The flock of parrots, appearing to number almost a hundred, was disturbing residents with noise, damage to plant life, and general nuisance behavior. Speculation on the origin is that some escaped from private homes, while others were freed by parrot smugglers who were about to be caught and simply decided to release the evidence.

The 1934 version of the old Robert Louis Stevenson classic "Treasure Island" is still making the rounds on TV, starring Wallace Beery, Jackie Cooper, and a scowling Yellow-naped Amazon. Mr. Beery is gone and Jackie Cooper has changed a lot, but the Yellow-nape may still be around screaming, "Pieces of eight!"

A friend who is something of a philosopher recently noted that a parrot is the only creature gifted with the power of speech that is content to repeat just what it hears without trying to make a good story out of if.

Fiorello, one of my younger Scarlet Macaws, could be very affectionate and playful at times, while at other times he was capable of such mean actions as nipping my wrist as I changed his newspapers or attempting to crush a finger if he was offered a tasty treat. You might wish to consider my approach with your own birds if you have the same problem: When he was in a good frame of mind I would play with him and enjoy his company, while also taking the opportunity to do his major cage cleaning and straightening. When his attitude was unfriendly, I would back off and avoid contact, since one can hardly force oneself on an unfriendly macaw.

I once read that the owner of a bird store filed a two-million-dollar lawsuit against the company that air conditioned his building, claiming that the faulty equipment had caused the death of Coconut, a Hyacinth Macaw. Why two million dollars? The owner indicated that Coconut was not only an invaluable business asset but also a dear friend.

Parrot behavior patterns vary widely. One aspect of their behavior that is common, however, is the use of a portion of their cage as a toy when permitted. Jaco and Duda, my African Greys, enjoyed lifting the handle that held their food and water dishes in place. Naturally, the dishes would fall out, making a mess and depriving the birds of their contents. I solved the problem by crimping the loops that ride on the upright bars. Although this made it more difficult for me to insert and remove the food dishes, it was impossible for the birds to drop them out of the cage.

Do you have a bird that ignores the wooden blocks or twigs you offer him? If so, drill a series of holes through the wood, even to the point of creating several splits in it. Many of my parrots ignored wooden chewing blocks unless I provided several starter holes. Once they had a few holes drilled through them, the parrots would reduce them to splinters in short order.

Technological Horizons in Education, a journal devoted to the use of computer equipment in schools, featured a brilliantly colored Scarlet Macaw in one of their issues. The macaw is sitting on top of a piece of exotic equipment, which is quite appropriate—one exotic helping to advertise another.

A while back, the *New York Times* reported on *The Macquarie Dictionary*, a 2,062-page volume of Australian usage produced after eleven years of work. A great deal of Australian slang as well as many aboriginal terms have been incorporated into the English spoken in Australia, and this dictionary is an excellent source of clarification. The *Times* article was illustrated with a small section of the page beginning with Galah, which is described as a common small cockatoo. A line drawing of a Galah, or Rose-breasted Cockatoo, is also shown, and following the English word itself is the slang expression "Galah session," meaning, "A time set aside for the women of isolated outback areas to converse with one another by radio."

I have always provided small blocks of wood for my birds to chew and play with. If the wood is dropped to the bottom of the cage, it tends to become soiled, so I prefer to hang it from large-link metal chains attached to threaded rods with an eye on one end. For a large parrot, such as a cockatoo or macaw, use a two-inch eye bolt and, to fit on the bolt, get a good-sized piece of wood that will last for several days. I used to have a problem with the nut, which could fall off the threaded rod and be lost in the debris at the bottom of the cage, and if I failed to notice this it would be thrown out with the trash. However, my local hardware store recently provided me with a plastic insert. With a brisk twist, the nut is now virtually locked in place, and is easy to remove with a small wrench.

People who have had experience with parrots often make generalizations about their behavior. For example, I have always believed that most parrots show a preference for individuals of one sex or the other, and I have also maintained that only

birds that have been hand-fed are quick to transfer affection from one individual to another. Polly, a Yellow-fronted Amazon I owned for several years, followed the first rule to the letter. Her original owner's husband had declared, "Either the bird goes or I do!" because the parrot attacked him without provocation whenever she was out of the cage. I assumed that with patience and love I would be able to establish some sort of relationship with Polly, but we never became good friends. I was fascinated when a young woman visitor was able to scratch her, touch her feet, and feed her seeds all within the space of half an hour. My two years of devoted feeding, cleaning, and supplying of treats and toys counted for nothing; Polly simply preferred females. On the other hand, Otto, my Lilac-crowned Amazon, was an imported bird that had passed from shop to owner to owner. He is at ease with everyone and permits anybody who wishes to do so to handle and scratch him. We just have to accept the fact that there are exceptions to every rule.

An issue of *The Instructor*, a magazine for teachers, features a full-page advertisement for a manufacturer of spelling books. A photo of a large Scarlet Macaw, looking very much as though he can spell and add, dominates the page.

Telecom-Australia is having a problem with cockatoos that are playing with and destroying the feed windows of long-distance telecommunication antennas. Apparently, the cockatoos are attracted to the windows and have made a game of picking at and damaging them.

There have been many discussions regarding the use and misuse of the terms *lutino* and *albino*. Lutinos are not pure white; they show color and markings on some parts of their bodies. Albinism is a gene defect resulting in a lack of the enzyme that produces color pigment. Although it is not as rare as generally supposed, albino birds seldom survive in the wild for any length of time, as they are easily spotted by enemies and even darkness does not offer them safety. Due to the lack of pigment formation, the feathers of such birds are white, while their irises show the pink color of blood in the capillaries.

A Knoxville, Illinois, couple were awakened one morning at about 2 A.M. when their Green-winged Macaw hopped from his perch onto their bed and began to make a fuss. They were shocked to discover that their apartment was filling with smoke from a fire on the floor below. The trio successfully escaped the smoke-filled apartment, and Carlos, the big hero, is now referred to as a green-feathered smoke detector.

PARROT Q&A

E ducators have long been aware that one of the first steps in learning is knowing how to ask a good question. The following are some very useful questions, which (along with the answers, of course) should be helpful to all parrot fanciers.

Q: I recently purchased a Yellow-fronted Amazon. Are the sexes distinguishable? If I decide to buy another parrot, is either sex considered superior as far as speaking ability is concerned?

A: There is no accurate visual method of distinguishing between male and female Yellow-fronts or most other Amazons. Some people claim there is a size difference, but I do not recommend setting up pairs on that basis.

Neither sex has the advantage over the other in speech capability.

Q: How long does it take before a baby parrot begins to talk? I have a four-month-old African Grey, and all he does is make funny sounds.

An Umbrella Cockatoo adding to the beauty of its surroundings. D. Shaugnessy

A: The "funny sounds" are very likely the beginning of speech and might be compared with human baby talk. An African Grey, if it is going to learn to talk, will generally begin mimicking speech at four or five months. Some start earlier and, of course, some later. Encourage your budding conversationalist with enthusiastic responses such as laughing, bringing in other members of the family to hear him, or best of all, offering a small treat.

Q: My female parrot is constantly laying eggs. Should I be concerned about this?

A: You are right to be concerned, as excessive egg laying can be debilitating and can also deplete the bird's calcium level, causing her bones to weaken. Ask your vet about Synthroid or other hormones that, properly administered in her drinking water, should put a stop to the egg laying.

Q: My African Grey weighs about eleven ounces. My Blue-fronted Amazon is harder to weigh but he appears to be about one pound. Are these normal weights for the species?

A: Your African Grey is on the slim side, while the Blue-fronted Amazon could be considered hefty. Both birds, however, are within normal weight ranges.

Q: Is it dangerous to let my bird chew at the metal clapper of his bell? Sometimes he can actually remove it and then I have to wire it back in.

A: The clappers in many bells are often made of lead or lead compounds. I would remove this bell and replace it with another toy, as lead poisoning is a serious threat to birds. If you want to keep the bell, replace the clapper with a heavy steel nut that should be firmly attached to the bell. You won't get quite the same melodious sound, but your bird will be safer.

Q: What are the symptoms of psittacosis in humans?

A: It resembles a serious case of the flu or the early stages of pneumonia: Symptoms include a high temperature, headache, and chills. Any bird owner who has a severe respiratory infection or lives with a relative in this condition should immediately inform the family doctor of the bird's existence. Prompt treatment with tetracycline will usually cure psittacosis in humans. A doctor who diagnoses this ailment may order a lab test for the psittacosis organism.

Q: I own a Lesser Sulphur-crested Cockatoo that is a dream bird. She can talk, do tricks, and is tame and loving. However, I am concerned about her health because she does not gain any weight. I can even feel her breastbone with my fingers. Is there something wrong with my cockatoo?

A: After a reasonable time a healthy bird should gain sufficient weight that the breastbone is covered and does not stick out like a sharp keel. Locate a veterinarian who knows birds and insist on a complete workup, including an examination of the waste products for parasites. There are also certain diets that help birds to gain weight, but I suggest you first determine the cause of this problem before using any of them.

Q: Can anything be done about smoking in pet shops and, even worse, at bird shows? I personally don't care for the smoke, but I am even more concerned about the captive birds that are forced to inhale these fumes.

A: Enough complaints to the owner of a pet shop should help bring about a change in the shop rules. Why not start a campaign? As far as smoking at shows, there is already a movement to bar smoking. Many clubs now ban smoking in show halls where birds are benched and judged.

Q: I hate the job of cutting by parrot's nails since he really balks when I attempt to do so. As a result, his nails are quite long, and I recently noticed that several are growing in a misshapen fashion. Are they damaged permanently?

A: Overly long nails may assume odd shapes. If a long nail was injured or twisted by catching on a bar or in a cage opening, the root may be damaged and the twisted growth permanent. If not, you can improve the situation by trimming off small pieces of the nails once or twice a week until you get them down to a manageable size. The bird may balk (and squawk) but he will move around more easily and not be in danger of getting hung up when you trim the nails regularly and properly.

Q: My gray cockatiel has normal droppings for one or two days. Then, for about six hours, he will have almost clear and watery droppings. This happens on and off at irregular intervals. His appetite is good, and, in addition to seeds, he eats celery, apples, and a few other fruits and greens. Do you think he might have worms?

A: It is possible that he is reacting to the volume of water in the celery. The cycle you are describing sounds very much as if the loose stools are a response to food or some other material he is ingesting. Try removing suspect items one by one until you note a change in the pattern. You might also hold off on all fruits and vegetables for a few days, and if the droppings stabilize, observe what happens when you feed the first green. This should help you to determine which food is responsible for the problem.

Q: My young Orange-wing Amazon occasionally sits with his feathers fluffed up. I am always concerned when he does this, as I have read that this is a sign of illness. He appears to be perfectly healthy and eats quite well. Do you think he has a problem?

A: Any bird, including one that is in perfect health, can and will on occasion fluff or ruffle up his feathers producing pockets of air that conserve heat and keep him warm, similarly to the way you might wear several layers of clothing on a cold day. Very young birds tend to tire more quickly and frequently during the day than mature birds. Thus, it is not unusual for a young bird to sit dozing occasionally with his feathers fluffed if the room is cool.

Of course, if the room is not cool, repeated fluffing of feathers can definitely be a sign that the bird is ill. If this is the case, you might want to check for other symptoms, such as loose stools or a decrease in appetite, to determine the significance of your observations.

Q: I would like to try my hand at breeding parrots. Can you suggest a good species with which to begin?

A: Good birds for beginning breeders include lovebirds, cockatiels, and Quaker Parakeets. All are free breeders and in the case of cockatiels, it is easy to distinguish males and females at a fairly early stage.

Q: About six months ago, I bought a young bird that was sold to me as a Blue-crowned Amazon. He is now almost a year old and does not have any noticeable blue on the crown. The people I bought him from say that he will develop the blue crown when he gets older. Does this sound accurate to you?

A: Blue-crowned Amazons belong to the Mealy Amazon group, within which there are several subspecies differing in size, dullness of body feathers, and blue markings on the head. *A. f. guatemalae* has the most obvious blue crown marking and is thus named the Blue-crowned Amazon. The blue crown, or some degree of it, should be visible at the age of one year, with some blue eventually extending to the nape and shoulders. If your pet shop made an error in identification it is an innocent one, as all members of the Mealy group are of equal talent and value.

Q: I am confused about a parrot that has been offered to me as a Blue-crowned Amazon. It is a good-sized bird that looks very much like a Mealy Amazon but has a deep blue crown.

A: See the previous question and answer. The Blue-crowned Amazon, also known as the Guatemalan Amazon, is a subspecies of the Mealy Amazon, only differing from the Mealy in being a bit larger and more colorful. The Mealy Amazon tends to be underrated, as many are talented talkers that can also become very affectionate pets.

Q: Our Umbrella Cockatoo is extremely affectionate to my husband and me but appears to be terrified of anyone else who comes into our home. Do you have any suggestions that would help us to get her to adjust to strangers?

A: Most Cockatoos engage in exaggerated forms of behavior and it is possible that a lot of your Cockatoo's hissing and puffing up, which you interpret as fear, is just for show; she may not be as frightened of strangers as you think. Try taking her out of the cage before the visitors enter the room, but make sure she has a clear flight path back to her cage in case she decides to flee.

Q: I have frequently seen the term "stick training" used in books and articles about training a new parrot. What does it refer to?

A: A bird that either avoids or bites your finger may be difficult to get out of his cage. Since getting the bird out of the cage is crucial to his training, you can try substituting a short perch for your finger. You may be pleasantly surprised to watch a parrot that has refused any contact with your hand climb amicably upon the stick, which to him represents a familiar object, similar to his own perch.

Q: My young Scarlet Macaw recently hit the floor rather hard even though he can fly. To my horror, I noticed large drops of blood forming when I put him back in his cage. I used peroxide, which has been recommended for bleeding injuries, and while it seemed to help for a moment or two, every time Red moved, he would start to bleed again. I spent a very uneasy night, and when I checked him in the morning, the bleeding finally stopped, although it was obvious that he had lost blood during the night. The bleeding seemed to come from his feathers. Why does this happen? I have read that you can cut flight feathers without any risk of injury.

A: When the shaft of a functioning feather is broken too close to the skin, it can cause the type of hemorrhaging you describe. This is comparable to your injuring a fingernail deeply and close to the cuticle. If peroxide does not stop bleeding, silver nitrate will, but since this potent chemical compound actually cauterizes the wound it should be used by a veterinarian. Vets generally have silver nitrate available on cotton swabs and after dipping the swab into sterile water, they can stop even severe bleeding almost immediately. You might also remove the stump of the broken feather a few days after the bleeding has stopped, as this will encourage new feather growth and remove a possible source of irritation.

Q: Despite the care with which I cut my cockatoo's nails, there is always some bleeding, so I put this job off until I cannot hold her because of her painfully sharp claws. Why is it that her nails always bleed when I cut them no matter how careful I am?

A: The blood vessels in the nails recede if the nails are regularly trimmed. Because you have been avoiding the job, the vessels have extended almost to the tip of the nails. If you cut only the sharp tips, gradually the blood vessels will recede so that you can cut slightly more each time. Bleeding can be stopped with peroxide or styptic powder.

Q: I have just purchased a very active Severe Macaw. Having always visualized parrots on stands, I also purchased a T-stand for him. A friend now advises me that a cage is best for any parrot. Is this correct?

A: A T-stand gives the illusion of freedom, but since you will not permit the parrot to climb down from the stand and walk about the floor at will, the only space he has to move about on is the length of the stand. A cage has six surfaces, allowing a healthy parrot to move up, down, and across. I prefer a cage or, as a compromise, a cage with a playpen on top of it.

Q: As an officer of a humane organization, I need to know the standard cage sizes for exotic birds in pet shops. Can you help?

A: I share your concern about the humane handling of animals in pet shops. Fortunately, most shop owners are equally concerned. The minimum cage size for an Amazon would be about twenty-four by twenty-four by thirty inches. For the smaller conures, cockatiels, and budgies, cages measuring eighteen by eighteen by twenty-four inches are adequate. Larger macaws and cockatoos should be in cages that are at least three to four feet square.

Q: Is there a risk in buying a baby parrot that still requires hand feeding?

A: If you have never fed a baby bird before, there is some risk, as it is vital that the baby be fed regularly and that the food enter its food tube and not its windpipe. Eye droppers with their tips cut off or similar devices can be used for this feeding. The food must also be warmed to the proper temperature and ideally should be the same mix that the baby was getting from its breeder. I would recommend having an expert demonstrate the technique for you at least once or twice before you do it yourself for the first time.

Q: My parrots make so much noise that they are disturbing my neighbors. Cuca, a Red-fronted

Conure, and Pecato, my Scarlet Macaw, are the worst offenders. Can you suggest any method to make them less noisy?

A: Noise and parrots generally go together, to the pleasure of some people and the resentment of others. Suggestions that may help include playing a radio or tape-recorder during the day when you are not at home. If the parrots also scream when you are around, it is possible you are not spending enough time with them. The old technique of covering the cage and putting out the lights also helps with some birds. A word to your neighbors explaining that you are working on the problem might also be in order.

Feeding baby birds is a useful skill, but it takes preparation and observation before attempting it for the first time. Linda Greeson

Q: Can the offspring of hybrid parrots reproduce young of their own?

A: If a hybrid is to be able to reproduce, it has to come from parents that were similar enough that their chromosomes match. If the parents were not related closely enough, either no offspring will result from a mating or the offspring that do result will themselves be infertile. Such animals are referred to as mules. Hybridization of the larger parrots is not considered an acceptable avicultural practice.

Q: Sometimes my Yellow-fronted Amazon loves to chew his wooden toys while at other times the blocks of wood are just tossed to the bottom of the cage. Are there particular types of wood that parrots prefer?

A: Pine scraps that can be obtained either free or for a nominal price at any lumber yard are an excellent choice of wood to offer parrots. The piece of wood should not be so large that he cannot manipulate it, and several holes should be drilled in it to make it more interesting for him; even a piece that has been previously rejected will prove enticing once several holes just the right size and shape for inserting a beak are provided. Be sure to remove any nails that may be in the wood. You will also find that knotholes are impossible for a parrot to chew.

Q: I recently purchased a wooden ladder for use in my African Grey's cage, but he seems to avoid it. Is this the right toy for this type of parrot?

A: Virtually any new object placed in a cage will be avoided by a typical parrot. This is a healthy expression of caution and, of course, it is a trait that helps animals to survive in the wild. After a day or so his fear should diminish. However, he will not really benefit very much from this type of toy if it is used in the usual way, as he can already climb up and down the bars of his cage with great ease. Try mounting the ladder horizontally across the back of the cage as an extra perch or platform. You may find that this gives him a comfortable and pleasurable place to roost.

Q: While stationed overseas I owned a parrot. The odor from his cage was so unpleasant that now that we are back in the States my wife does not want to get another parrot. Do all parrots pose this problem?

A: If you have a healthy bird and maintain normal sanitary conditions, there is no reason for unpleasant odors. Although most parrots have a characteristic odor that is not at all disagreeable, I would suspect that your original bird might have had a problem with his digestive tract. The odor could also have been linked to the particular diet you fed the bird.

Q: Why are Goffin's Cockatoos sold at such comparatively low prices?

A: The law of supply and demand also works with parrots. Goffin's, which come only from the island of Tanimbar, were imported in very large numbers as the extensive cutting of forests on the island made it easier for locals to collect these parrots. Many of the original imports are now breeding and producing a steady supply of young, hand-fed domestic Goffin's. Closely related to the Bare-eyed Cockatoo, this parrot is among the most clever of the cockatoos and makes an excellent pet as well as a fine potential breeder.

Q: About how many years can a pair of Triton Cockatoos continue to breed?

A: Prolific breeding of the larger white cockatoos can go on during their prime years, from age seven to about age twenty-five. There have been some notable exceptions that continued to breed well into their thirties.

Q: Why do so many authorities recommend the addition of vitamins and minerals to a parrot's diet. I provide Poco, my Blue-front, with a high-quality parrot mix. Isn't this adequate?

A: Although high in phosphorous, even a good seed mixture can be low in calcium, so ground oyster shell or cuttlebone should be provided. Since most pet parrots do not get much sunlight, a vitamin preparation containing Vitamin D is also important. If a concentrated vitamin is added to the water or sprinkled on the parrot's food, you are guaranteeing that he will get the vitamins and additives he needs. You might also consider adding a high-quality pellet ration to his diet.

A Blue-fronted Amazon in excellent condition, a tribute to its good care. Linda Greeson

Q: I cannot decide whether to use vitamins in liquid or powder form. Any suggestions?

A: Assuming that the vitamins are equal in quality, the main consideration should be to choose the vitamin your parrot will ingest most readily and in the necessary quantity. Water-soluble liquid vitamins generally have a pleasant smell and taste and can be completely dissolved in the parrot's water dish. The difficulty here is that many parrots drink only a limited amount of water. If powdered vitamins are sprinkled on top of the seed dish, much of them will be shaken down to the bottom. A good alternative is to use a powdered vitamin on your parrot's fruit and greens, which will be moist after having been washed. You might even consider providing a separate dish for these items. Also, be sure to choose a vitamin designed for birds rather than one simply adapted from a cat or dog formula.

Q: Is it safe to use liquid vitamins in my parrot's water dish in warm weather?

A: I share your concern, since bacteria can multiply rapidly in a nutrient solution such as a mixture of vitamins and water. In warm weather, either change the water several times a day or switch to powdered vitamins added to the seed dish or sprinkled on fruits or greens for the summer months.

Q: My bird room is overrun with mice. Their droppings appeared right after the first cold spell this fall. We keep all food in covered containers, and while the traps I have set are working, it is obvious that the mice are still around. A friend suggested a poison that would be brought back to the rodent's nest to end the problem. Is poison safe to use?

A: Sweep and vacuum two or three times a day, or more if necessary. Set out more traps and change their location regularly if they do not work. Do not place traps where family members, birds, or other pets can get at them. Check possible points of entry such as the boundaries between the outside walls and floors and fill any openings with a mixture of steel wool and cement. The best time to check for such openings is on a sunny day; if you search for potential entry areas while in a darkened room, the openings will be visible to you because of the sunlight behind them.

Poison should not be used under any circumstances, as the poisoned bait, which is usually in the form of seeds, could be tracked to where your birds might get at it, with deadly results. You might want to try one of the sonic devices that manufactures claim will drive away rodents without bothering you, your birds, or other family pets.

Q: My recent purchase (and my pride and joy), a baby African Grey, does not drink much water. I have a Double Yellow-head that practically empties his water cup, while the Grey hardly touches his. Is this something to be concerned about?

A: Parrots vary greatly in the amount of water they drink. This variation can be due to species differentiation or just differences between individuals. Be sure that the water is palatable and without unpleasant additives or a high concentration of chlorine from your town water purification system. Also, don't forget that he gets a certain amount of liquid from the fruits and greens you provide.

Q: I have noticed that some people are able to make the bars of the parrot's cage practically disappear when they take pictures of their birds. How is this done?

A: You need a camera with a variable F-stop setting. If there are bars obstructing the view of the parrot (and you can't get him out of the cage, which is really the best way to photograph him), then set the F-stop, which is an indication of the size of the lens opening, to the smallest number (or largest opening) compatible with the amount of available light. Then focus on the parrot. Since a wide lens opening provides a very limited depth of the field, only the parrot will be clearly visible in the resulting photograph.

Q: Every time I try to take closeups of my Sulphur-crested Cockatoo, her features are washed out. Is there some method of photographing birds that can help me resolve this problem?

A: This is a dilemma peculiar to white birds or birds that have a large area of white on the face or body. I presume you are using a strobe or other type of flash device and that the white feathers are reflecting too much light. Try aiming your strobe at the ceiling, which will give you some very nice lighting effects, or, if your camera permits, closing down the lens by one F-stop. You could also, of course, eliminate the problem by taking your photos in existing light or, if weather permits, taking the photos out of doors.

Q: I am rather new to the hobby of parrot keeping. Could you explain how and why one clips a parrot's wings?

A: Wings are clipped to discourage rapid or distant flight. This is to prevent a bird from flying within your home and hurting himself, as well as to keep a bird from flying away if you permit him outdoor freedom, which is not recommended.

The most common and probably the safest method is to clip all the primary feathers down to the primary coverts. If this is only done in one wing, the bird will not be able to fly in a straight line, but will still be able to break his fall if he loses his balance. Some people leave the outer two or three primaries uncut for the sake of appearance and symmetry, but I consider this risky, as a bird clipped in this fashion may unexpectedly be able to fly.

This Hyacinth Macaw is the "official greeter" in a well-managed pet store. Note that several of its flight feathers have been trimmed short to prevent flight and possible escape. James Robinson

Q: Our Yellow-nape has a deformed feather that we would like to remove because he seems sensitive in that area. Is there a painless and safe way to do this?

A: Mist the feather and the surrounding area with lukewarm water for about a week. Then grasp the feather and rotate it gently several times. It should come out without bleeding or difficulty.

The area of yellow feathers will grow larger as this young Yellow-nape matures. Sharon and Ray Bailey

Q: Is there some sort of "tonic" I can give my Double Yellow-head to perk him up?

A: An interesting tonic recipe used at Chicago's Lincoln Park Zoo seems to touch all the bases as far as nutritional supplements are concerned. It is fed once a week.

4 tablespoons Gevral
2 tablespoons calcium lactate
1 teaspoon Vionate
4 cups guava juice
12 ounces carrot juice
2 cups canned milk

Add sufficient water to make a gallon and refrigerate. Do not keep for more than a week.

Q: My Yellow-fronted Amazon began to sneeze and scratch her nostrils shortly after we switched parrot mixtures. Is it possible that she is allergic to something in the new diet?

A: Practically all seed mixtures contain a certain amount of dust and other debris. The very best are screened several times in an effort to remove this material. Try some additional screening, as I suspect your parrot is reacting to the dust particles and is not actually allergic to a particular seed.

Q: I would like to add some variety to the diet of Blu, my very stubborn Blue and Gold Macaw. Sunflower and peanuts is about all he will eat. Are there any other seeds you can suggest that might tempt him?

A: Although your pet can survive on the seeds you mention, a greater variety will add to his potential for a longer and healthier life. Try offering seeds such as canary; millet; millet spray, which may appeal to him because of the activity involved in removing the seeds from the spray; rape, a rather small seed, although its strong flavor may attract him; hemp, which is expensive but attractive to many parrots because of its size, ease of opening, and pungent odor; and safflower, a valuable seed that is often overlooked. You should also try offering him high-quality pellets. If he accepts these your troubles will be over.

Q: I would like to increase the amount of protein in my cockatoo's diet. Could you recommend some protein-rich foods that are safe for parrots?

A: Cooked chicken, ground beef, hard-boiled eggs, and cheese are all rich sources of protein that many parrots enjoy. American cheese is a particular favorite in my bird room. As usual, you will have to experiment to see who likes what and, of course, be particularly careful not to let these perishable foods lie around for very long. All the pellet diets available contain protein. When choosing a pellet, be sure to note the difference between those for active breeding birds and those for sedentary birds. You do not want to feed the high-protein version for very active parrots to a pet leading a relatively quiet life.

Q: Can you suggest an appropriate diet for my mixed collection of Amazons, African Greys, cockatoos, and macaws?

A young Tres Marias Amazon showing heavy yellow markings. Mike Gluss

A: The basic seed ration should consist of sunflower, large canary, safflower, millet, hemp, thistle, oats (or groats), and buckwheat. At least two-thirds of the above mixture should be made up of the sunflower, canary, and safflower seeds. A peanut or two in the shell may also be provided. Some people also supplement seeds with rich protein sources such as chopped meat or cooked egg, which should not be left available for too many hours, as they can spoil. Fruits and greens are also important components of the diet for the larger birds. Choose fruits from among apples, grapes, cherries, plums, bananas, and pears, and if you have other fruits readily available, give them a try. Fresh corn on the cob, beet tops, carrot

tops (including the leaves and stems), carrots, dandelions, string beans, green beans, and virtually any other common vegetables my be tried. Avoid those with a huge water content, such as lettuce. Walnuts and other large nuts are also a welcome treat, but will probably need to be started with a slight crack for most birds. Remember that rich nut treats will cause your parrot to eat a smaller amount of his regular seeds.

Remember that all fruits and greens must be washed thoroughly, and never feed any fruit or vegetable that is wilted or appears spoiled.

Q: I have often seen references to a food called "monkey chow" in articles on parrot feeding. What is this and where can I purchase it?

A: Monkey chow is one of a series of animal diets produced by a large feed manufacturer whose products include diets for rodents, chicks, rabbits, and other animals. It comes in the form of a small biscuit and contains many nutrients and vitamins, along with trace elements. Some experts feel that its high protein content makes it unacceptable for birds. Consider pellets made for birds instead.

Q: How often may I spray my Blue and Gold Macaw with water? Is it okay to spray a cockatoo?

A: During warm weather you can spray your birds every day; they will particularly welcome spraying on hot, humid days. Try to spray early enough in the day that the bird will be completely dry before it goes to sleep. You can spray all year round, but I recommend spraying less in cold weather and not at all when it is bitterly cold.

These guidelines apply to cockatoos as well. You will find that the feather quality and the appearance of all your birds will be remarkably improved by regular spraying.

ANNOTATED BIBLIOGRAPHY

Note: Although many of the books listed are out of print, for the most part they do exist in public and university libraries. Many libraries will perform a search for you if you provide sufficient information, thus giving you access to libraries outside your own area. The Library of Congress in Washington, D.C., can also be helpful, and readers with access to the now famous "information superhighway" can make use of their computers to search further afield, even in different countries.

BOOKS

Adventures with Talking Birds. Catherine Hurlbutt. Neptune, N.J.: TFH Publications, 1981.

Most people assume that parrots and mynah birds are the only avian species that learn to mimic speech or sounds. The author provides a wealth of information on other talented talkers, including crows, ravens, magpies, jays, and other species that either are taught to speak or pick up the sounds of speech by themselves. Some of the examples of speech by talented birds almost defy credibility. A chapter on teaching birds to speak has many suggestions that will be useful to parrot owners. Two additional chapters on bird breeding and bird care also contain valuable hints. The photos all appear to be new and many are quite charming.

The African Grey Parrot. Eve Wicks. Bedford, England: Parrot Society, c. 1970.

If you want to breed African Greys this booklet will help to ensure success. The author's personal observations, listed in diary form, take you through the successful breeding of a pair of Greys. Some very interesting photos and drawings are included.

The Age of Birds. Alan Feduccia. Cambridge, Mass.: Harvard University Press, 1980.

This study of the evolution of birds will appeal to a wide spectrum of readers. Many of Feduccia's ideas are new, and all of them are presented in a manner that led one reviewer to describe this book as "bird watching on a cosmic scale."

All About the Parrots. Arthur Freud. New York: Howell Book House, 1980.

An Orange-winged Amazon. Michael DeFreitas

This is an interesting mixture of facts and anecdotes on the most commonly kept parrots. It includes numerous quotations and attributions to other writers, particularly from earlier eras, and very good photos.

Atlas of Conures. Thomas Arndt, Neptune, N.J.: TFH Publications, 1993.

This is a greatly expanded and vastly superior version of an earlier work that appeared in 1982. Conures are rapidly becoming more important to the parrot fancy and this book will prove very useful to those who wish to expand their knowledge. The arrangement of the book has obviously been modeled after Forshaw's *Parrots of the World,* even to the layout of the photos and water colors that are of the highest quality.

Australian Aviculture. Graeme Hyde, ed. Melbourne: Avicultural Soc. of Australia, 1987.

This book offers a selection of outstanding articles culled from the last forty-two years of the magazine of the Australian Aviculture Society. Topics covered include housing, feeding, management, behavior, health, plantings, and much more.

Australian Cockatoos. Stan Sindel and Robert Lynn. New South Wales, Australia: Singil Press, 1989.

This is a balanced combination of information from both field and aviary studies. Having forty years of experience with parrots behind them, the authors are eminently qualified to produce such a book. Their approach is fairly standard, with early chapters on housing, diet, care, and health, followed by chapters on the different cockatoo genera. The photographs are unique in their variety. When discussing the Galah, for example, the authors provide not one photo, but fifteen, in order to indicate clearly the differences between the nominate race and the subspecies, as well as mutations and stages of development. In an interesting bit of irony, the photos of nestling Palm Cockatoos were supplied by the late Richard Schubot of the Avicultural Breeding and Research Center in Florida rather than from an Australian source.

Australian Lorikeets. Stan Sindel. New South Wales, Australia: Singil Press, 1987.

It is always a pleasure to read information provided by an author who has actually kept or bred the species about which he is writing. Sindel knows his lories and lorikeets well and writes about them in an enthusiastic and informative manner.

Australian Parakeets. 5th ed., H. G. Groen. Groningen, Holland: Dijkstra Niemeyer Press, c. 1960.

Dr. Groen deals with the larger, long-tailed parakeets, including the Grass Parakeets. For many years this was the only book on the topic of these birds. Although others now exist, Groen's book is well worth including in your reading.

Australian Parrots. 2d rev. ed. J. M. Forshaw, with illustrations by William T. Cooper. Lansdowne Editions. New York: Mereweather Press, 1981.

This second edition substitutes lithographs for hand-tipped photos, which, although preferable, are no longer really feasible because of labor costs. The text's layout is an improvement over the first edition and includes a considerable amount of new information on breeding.

Australian Parrots. Neville W. Cayley. Sydney, Australia: Angus and Robertson, 1938.

Cayley was a vice-president of the Royal Zoological Society of New South Wales, as well as an officer of several ornithologists' organizations, who was interested in all Australian birds. The artwork for the book was done by Cayley, who was an accomplished artist as well as an ornithologist—two careers that have flourished together on more than one occasion.

Australian Parrots, A Field and Aviary Study. B. R. Hutchins and R. H. Lovel. Melbourne: Avicultural Society of Australia, 1985.

This is a completely revised version of the original work published in 1973–1974. It emphasizes the smaller Australian parrots such as the lories and lorikeets, King Parrots, swifts, rosellas, and others. Since most books about Australian parrots dwell on the cockatoos, this book fills a void. Unfortunately, other than range maps, it lacks illustrations, but the text is excellent.

Australian Parrots in Bush and Aviary. Ian Harman. North Pomfret, VT: David and Charles, 1981.

Ian Harman spent many years in Australia. His interest in birds developed early in life and the part of his childhood spent in Tasmania was a fortunate opportunity to become familiar with many Australian birds. The language in this book is consistently clear and well chosen, and the author covers all significant areas. It is obvious that he has kept birds, as his information and comments are eminently practical.

In an interesting bit of history, he challenges the derivation of the name "rosella," which many of us had long believed came from Rose Hill, the town where this parakeet was first observed. Harman suggests that the birds were actually named rosetta parrots in honor of Rosetta Angas, the wife of an early Australian pioneer, and that through a slip of the pen European collectors of these birds recorded their name as rosellas. The photos accompanying each chapter are noteworthy and you will enjoy going over the details in some of them, such as the Golden-shouldered Parrot with its wings and tail spread or the Red-collared Lorikeets, whose colors and charm make them look like a pair of characters from "The Muppet Show."

Aviary Birds in Color. Dennis Avon, Tony Tilford, and Frank Woolham. Dorset, U.K.: Blandford Press, 1974.

Why is it that only a few photographers produce color prints that are sharp, clear, and faithful to the living bird? The answer, of course, lies with the choice of equipment and the use of techniques that make the most of lighting and the rare opportunities that most bird models grudgingly provide. The authors of this book have gone a step further, and have skillfully elicited poses that invariably reveal the definitive characteristic of their subject.

Aviculture in Australia. Mark Shephard, Australia: Reed Books, 1989.

This large volume is extremely comprehensive in its information on birdkeeping. All the Australian parrots are covered, along with many other species. Many color photos and line drawings, as well as charts and tables, help to make this book useful as a research tool.

Behavioral Enrichment in the Zoo. Hal Markowitz. N.Y.: Van Nostrand Reinhold Company, 1982.

Although this book does not really deal with pet birds, the ideas and suggestions for enriching the lives of caged animals are valuable to individual bird owners. In the past, the average zoo was a barred enclosure that bore an unfortunate resemblance to a prison cell. Indeed, the beasts behind the bars would frequently pace back and forth like human prisoners. Mr. Markowitz points out that in recent years there has been a revolution in the development of zoo exhibits, with constant striving toward the goal of naturalism, so that the animals are presented in settings very similar to the wild. Unfortunately, while these developments may enhance the appearance of the animals and provide a learning experience for their viewers, they do not necessarily result in behavioral enrichment for the zoo animal, which should be the primary focus of attention. Its health and comfort are an everyday concern, whereas the average visitor only attends the zoo once or twice a year at most.

Bird-Keeping in Australia. Ian Harman. London: Angus and Robertson, 1980.

Although this book devotes some space to finches, canaries, and doves, the bulk of the text deals with parrots. Harman lived in Australia for many years, and his information comes from first-hand observations of the aviaries he visited in this extremely bird-oriented country. The photos are helpful, but unfortunately all are black-and-white.

A Birdkeeper's Guide to Long Tailed Parrots. David Alderton. Morris Plains, N.J.: Tetra Press, 1989.

A Birdkeeper's Guide to Parrots and Macaws. David Alderton. Morris Plains, N.J.: Tetra Press, 1989.

These are two of a series of small books by Alderton that cover all parrots. These books are concise and informative and include many fine photographs by well-known British photographer Cyril Laubscher. The second portion of each book, which deals with individual birds, provides only basic information, but this, along with the well-written picture captions, is a very useful vehicle for parrot identification.

Birdland. Len Hill and Emma Wood. New York: Taplinger Publishing Co., 1976.

Photos and drawings help make this book outstanding. One photograph of Leah and Mac, the Hyacinth Macaws that became Birdland's trademark, is so charming that it probably caused an increase in the price of Hyacinths. Another impressive photo of a Yellow-backed Lory is sharp enough that one can see the individual feather barbs.

Birds of the British Empire. W. T. Greene. London: The Imperial Press, 1898.

This is a small volume from the prolific Dr. Greene. I found it particularly interesting in that it was written several years after his masterpiece, *Parrots in Captivity,* and some opinions and descriptions had changed slightly. Keep in mind that this book was written when the British Empire included many of the parrot-producing areas of the world, such as Australia, India, parts of Central America, and South Africa.

Birds of Paradox, Birdlife in Australia and New Zealand. Jack Pollard, Melbourne, Australia: Lansdowne, 1967 ed.

This unusual book includes essays, poetry, news articles, and other material on the vast birdlife of Australia and New Zealand. Although the parrot family birds are the ones that may interest you the most, you will not be able to resist reading the other chapters.

Breeding Cockatoos. Ann Nothaft. Neptune, N.J.: TFH Publications, 1979.

I feel a close link to the author of this book, from whom I purchased Tutu, my Greater Sulphur-crested Cockatoo, in 1974. Mrs. Nothaft and her husband wisely obtained pairs of many cockatoos species in the mid-1960s and went on to build a set of ideal aviaries in the backyard of their (then) rural location in southeastern Suffolk County, New York. This small book recounts their breeding experiences and is filled with tips that would be valuable to anyone hoping to breed cockatoos.

Breeding Conures. Robbie Harris. Neptune, N.J.: TFH Publications, 1983.

This was one of the first books on conures and its strength lies in the author's successful background in breeding many of these smaller parrots. In addition to chapters on housing, feeding, breeding, and rearing, there are two lengthy breeding case histories and the information provided here can be extrapolated to other breeding situations. Conures are rapidly gaining in prominence and this useful book can help breeders as well as fanciers.

The Budgerigar Book. Ernest Howson. Surrey, U.K.: Saiga Publishing, 1981.

A comprehensive guide to budgie care and breeding that covers five major areas, including maintenance, feeding and nutrition, showing budgies, genetics, and disease. Many black-and-white photos and drawings add to the usefulness of this book. In addition, there are two full-page color plated drawings of twelve of the most popular budgie forms, clearly delineating markings that are not always easy to spot on a photo of the live bird.

A Tres Marias chick (opposite). Walter Hansen

Cages and Aviaries. Curt Af Enehjelm. Neptune, N.J.: TFH Publications, 1982.

Information on cages for breeding softbills, parrots, budgies, and canaries, and information on hospital cages are all included in this book. In addition, material is provided on indoor aviaries, bird rooms, outdoor aviaries, nest boxes, and food and water containers. An extensive variety of clear and meaningful photos adds interest and, as has often been said, a picture can be worth a thousand words.

Did you ever think of stretching a large chain across a parrot cage to provide a combined perch and activity device for your bird? The photo of a male Eclectus on such a chain perch may inspire you, as it did me, to adopt the arrangement immediately.

Checklist of Birds of the World. J. L. Peters. Cambridge, Mass.: Harvard University Press, 1937.

This book contains the definitive list of birds and bird names. It's old but still quite useful.

Clovis. Michael Fessier. New York: Turtle Point Press, 1993.

This fictional account of Clovis, the African Grey, will make you laugh if you like or keep Greys. It depicts the hilarious adventures of a highly opinionated and strong-willed parrot. Many of the episodes are obviously based on the author's experiences with his own Grey Parrot.

Cockatoos, A Complete Pet Owner's Manual. W. and S. Lantermann. New York: Barron's, 1989.

All books in this series follow a similar useful pattern. Advice regarding purchase, housing, equipment, acclimation, feeding, health care, and breeding information and color photos of individual species make the book a winner in its price range. Be sure to look at the photo of a Rose-breasted Cockatoo skimming the surface of an Australian lake to get a drink while still in flight.

Cockatoos and Parrots. J. T. Walton and C. Smith. Bedford, England: Parrot Society, 1969.

One of a series of excellent booklets produced by this active group of parrot fanciers, it offers a guide to the aviary care and breeding of several cockatoos, African Greys, and Jardine's Parrots. The useful, practical information includes advice on nest boxes, hand feeding, incubation periods, and more.

Color Atlas of the Parrots. Wolfgang deGrahl. Walsrode, Germany: Horst Mueller Verlag, 1973.

Although written in German, you can still identify all the parrots in this beautifully illustrated book as the scientific names are familiar. The photos are outstanding and the commentary on each parrot is useful and well written. If you have a smattering of German, it will increase your pleasure in this book immensely.

The Complete Bird Owner's Handbook. Gary A. Gallerstein, D.V.M. New York: Howell Book House, 1994.

This is a completely revised and expanded second edition of Gallerstein's earlier book, which has been so helpful to thousands of bird owners. This is truly a user-friendly medical guide that will help the average bird owner deal with signs of illness as well as those sudden problems that always seem to come up late at night or on a weekend. The unique index of signs can help the bird owner locate the possible answers to emergency questions in a matter of seconds. Buy a copy of the book for yourself and another copy as a gift for your avian vet.

A Complete Guide to Eclectus Parrots. K. Wayne Arthur, Fred Bauer, and Laurella Desborough. San Francisco: Parrot Publishing Co., 1987.

A major strength of this book is the clear way in which it helps readers to distinguish between the subspecies of Eclectus. It is supplemented by an excellent series of photographs, including closeups of tail and wing feathers that in many cases are the only way to tell one group from the other. Unfortunately, a later paperback edition omits all these photos, so be sure to get the original hardcover version.

Dear Parrot. John Phillips. New York: Clarkson N. Potter, 1979.

This is a clever bit of whimsy by an author who lives with and loves parrots. Although obviously written with tongue in beak, it will be appreciated by all who love animals and enjoy seeing them exhibit a sense of dignity and independence. The carefully executed line drawings by William Bramhall reflect an excellent understanding of parrot anatomy and disposition, adding greatly to the pleasure of reading this mini-text.

Diseases of Parrots. E. W. Burr, D.V.M. Neptune, N.J.: TFH Publications, 1982.

A ragged and plucked Citron-crested Cockatoo stares plaintively from the cover of this book and seems almost to be asking for help. Dr. Burr has bred the parrot and was also involved in parrot disease control in Southeast Asia. *Diseases of Parrots* differs from other medical books in that it deals only with parrots and has been designed to present the current picture of the state of their care, management, diagnosis, and treatment. An entire chapter is devoted to respiratory diseases, a common affliction of many parrots. Other chapters deal with the digestive system, parasites, feather and skin disorders, and problems encountered in breeding and rearing young. Although some of the reading is pretty heavy, a series of appendices will help to clarify the material. These include charts on diet, common infections, and antibiotics, along with appropriate dosages. An extensive glossary will also prove useful to the lay reader.

Even though much of the book may be too technical for the nonprofessional, it will help you to describe problems and symptoms clearly to your veterinarian.

Encyclopaedia of Aviculture. A. Rutgers and K. A. Norris. London: Blanford Press, 1972.

This oversized, three-volume set is highly inclusive and has always been a valuable source for me to fall back on for information that cannot be found elsewhere. Forshaw was a major contributor to the section on the Australian species and this work preceded the publication of his own books on parrots. In many respects I prefer this book to Forshaw's work, as there is a much larger amount of anecdotal material that makes for enjoyable reading as one searches for information. The color plates are merely adequate, but this is made up for by 250 excellent line drawings.

Encyclopedia of Amazon Parrots. Klaus Bosch and Ursula Wedde. Neptune, N.J.: TFH Publications, 1984.

A good translation from the German as well as an excellent assortment of photos makes this a truly useful book for the Amazon fancier. Virtually all the Amazons are included, and the material about their habits in the wild may assist you in maintaining and breeding them in your own aviary.

Encyclopedia of Conures. Thomas Arndt. Neptune, N.J.: TFH Publications, 1982.

This is an interesting and useful book, but it is not nearly as good as Arndt's 1993 work, *Atlas of Conures*, which covers most of the same topics in much greater detail and with many more illustrations.

Encyclopedia of Parakeets. Kurt Kolar and Karl Spitzer. Neptune, N.J.: TFH Publications, 1990.

This well-illustrated book includes some of the parakeets we know as Budgies, but it devotes the bulk of its contents to the larger, long-tailed Rosellas, Grass Parakeets, Ringnecks, and such non-Australian parakeets as the Brotogeris, Quakers, Nandays, and other conures. The illustrations and text are well done.

Endangered Parrots. Rosemary Low. Dorset, England: Blandford, 1984.

The author provides a wealth of information on the reasons why so many parrot species are endangered. She accurately notes that it is deforestation rather then bird exportation that is mainly at fault. Photos of slash-and-burn forest and jungle areas make it obvious why birds cannot survive in such locations. Blandford published a revised, paperback version of this book in 1994.

Feeding Cage Birds, A Manual of Diets for Aviculture. Kenton Lint and Alice Lint. London, U.K.: Blandford, 1988.

The title of this book provides an apt description of its contents, written by a curator of birds at the San Diego Zoo, which Kenton Lint was for many years. If you need advice on diets for a finicky parrot of any type, you'll find it in this book.

Foreign Bird Keeping. Edward J. Boosey. London, U.K.: Dorset House, 1949.

The author's love of his birds comes through in everything he writes. He takes the same affectionate approach in his later book, *Parrots Cockatoos and Macaws*.

Grey-Cheeked Parakeets and Other Brotogeris. Robbie Harris. Neptune, N.J.: TFH Publications, 1985.

Robbie Harris's book appeared at the time the Grey-cheek was rising to heights of popularity because of its remarkable good nature. These birds have been bred in large numbers, and thus Harris's book has been helpful to an entire generation of parrot fanciers who chose (and still choose) this inexpensive and delightful pet.

The Grey Parrot. Wolfgang deGrahl. Neptune, N.J.: TFH Publications, 1987.

This is a fine book on one of the most popular parrots. DeGrahl keeps Greys and apparently thinks highly of them, as reflected in his comments.

Guide to Cage Birds. David Alderton. Surrey, England: Saiga Publishing, 1980.

Although this book deals with a number of different types of pet birds, the parrots are well represented. The prolific Alderton offers descriptions of the birds as well as advice on their suitability as pets, breeders, or outdoor aviary creatures. He also includes material on health and care. The book provides black-and-white photos and drawings along with a few full-page color plates.

A Guide to Diagnosis, Treatment and Husbandry of Caged Birds. Jim Stunkard, DVM. Edwardsville, Kan.: Veterinary Medicine Publishing Company, 1982.

The appendices in this book are worth their weight in gold. Appendix V on drugs and dosages provides a formula for calculating the amount of medications to be added to a bird's drinking water based on the volume of the container and the weight of the patient. More than a dozen pages of medications follow, with specific information on when their use is called for and what dosage to give. Appendices VII through X are in chart form and provide specific information on diseases caused by bacteria, viruses, fungi, and parasites. Critical signs, diagnosis, and treatment are all indicated. The treatments in this appendix are keyed to the list of drugs and dosages in Appendix V. A phenomenal amount of work appears to have gone into the collection and collation of the data in this book.

A Guide to the Names of the Parrot. A. A. Prestwich. Hertford, U.K.: Stephen Austin & Sons, 1969.

The Guatemalan subspecies of the Mealy Amazon group shows a distinctly blue forehead and crown. Paolo Tiengo

This is basically an appendix listing the scientific names, species, derivation, and English names of many parrots. It is very useful in determining the particular parrot to which an author or speaker is referring if proper nomenclature is not being used. The derivations are fascinating; for example, Prestwich points out that *Amazon barbadensis*, the Yellow-shouldered Amazon, does not come from Barbados, but is actually a native of Venezuela.

A Guide to Neophema and Psephotus Grass Parakeets. Toby Martin. Queensland: Australian Birdkeeper, 1989.

This slim book is heavily illustrated with excellent photos of the Grass Parakeets. The attention paid to pointing out male and female characteristics in the birds pictured is especially welcome.

Guide to a Well-Behaved Parrot. Mattie Sue Athan. New York: Barron's, 1993.

A fine guide to working with your parrot by taking stock of body language, activity patterns, territoriality, and other aspects of parrot behavior. This new approach can help to solve many problems if readers are willing to follow through with the author's suggestions.

Halfmoon and Dwarf Parrots. William Allen. Neptune, N.J.: TFH Publications, 1967.

Combining the Halfmoon, or Petz's Conure, with some of the other birds discussed in this book such as Bee Bees, Caiques, Cockatiels, lovebirds, and others makes little taxonomic sense. However, the material on the Halfmoon is good, so if you are a fan of these conures, look for this small volume.

Handbook of Aviculture. Frank Woolham. Dorset, U.K.: Blandford, 1987.

This comprehensive text by a well-known author and breeder deals with many types of exotic birds. His notes on parrots are accurate and informative.

The Handbook of Cage and Aviary Birds. David Alderton. London: Blandford Press, 1993.

This book contains 366 pages of information and photos on 450 different species, with 230 color illustrations. Details are provided on all aspects of bird-keeping, with emphasis on flight building, feeding, and breeding.

Handbook of Lovebirds. Horst Bielfeld. *Diseases of Parrots*. Manfred Heidenreich. Neptune, N.J.: TFH Publications, 1982.

Two books in one deserve two titles and two authors. This volume offers an inclusive treatise on lovebirds and a long, useful section on parrot diseases. The photos are outstanding and a look at the photographer credits tell you why. The sequence in which the author presents the birds is intriguing: He groups them based on relationships among their characteristics. Each section begins with a clear range map and a photo of the bird under discussion.

Hookbills I Have Known. Marie Olssen. New York: Audubon Publishing, 1975.

Marie Olssen is an historical figure in the field of exotic aviculture. She was one of the first individuals to raise cockatiels, and her work with Australian Parakeets brought her into contact with the duke of Bedford, who was also enthusiastic about the group. They engaged in a mutually helpful correspondence for many years. This hand-illustrated book stresses the Ringnecks and their relatives and provides insights based on Olssen's firsthand experiences with these parrots.

How To Hand Raise Baby Birds. Joe Goldsmith. Wisconsin: Avian Publications, 1983.

This is a booklet consisting of twenty-four pages of useful material prepared in a highly readable and easily understandable form. For example, Joe Goldsmith, whose degrees are in biology, begins his first chapter on the physiology of birds with two drawings of a chick that show the intimate relationship of the tongue, trachea (windpipe), and esophagus (food tube), thereby providing an instant lesson in the safe feeding of baby birds.

The topics of other chapters include sour crop, materials needed for hand feeding, hand feeding procedures, weaning, helpful hints, and formula recipes. The author answers just about every question that might occur to a first-time hand feeder.

The Human Nature of Birds. T. X. Barber. New York: St. Martin's Press, 1993.

This unusual book delves into bird behavior with a very open mind. The author is willing to accept bird intelligence of the highest order and he writes with a warmth that shows he has a fondness for his subject. Of course, he mentions the famous African Grey, Alex, but he also describes a number of other standouts, such as

Lorenzo, a male jay who understood games and would seek to lure his keepers into playing hide and seek with him. Delightful!

Importance of the 13 Essential Vitamins for Pet and Aviary Birds. J. Lafeber, D.V.M. Niles, Ill.: Dorothy Products, 1980.

This interesting little book on nutrition is unique in that it was written with birds in mind; virtually all other material on this topic is written for animals in general and has to be adapted to the special needs of birds.

I Name This Parrot. A. A. Prestwich. Hertford, England: Stephen Austin and Sons, 1963.

The author provides an odd arrangement for this book, which is filled with brief biographies of individuals in whose honor various parrot species and subspecies were named. It is alphabetical by the scientific name of the species or subspecies, and thus you have to know that name to look up the honoree. In spite of this, it is very useful if you wish to delve deeply into early work on the discovery, classification, and identification of parrots.

The Jungle Crusade of Holly Parrot. David R. Zimmerman. *New York Times Magazine*, New York, August 6, 1978.

Keeping and Breeding Parrots. Karl Aschenborn. Neptune, N.J.: TFH Publications, 1990.

The original version of this book first appeared in German in 1971. It has, however, been updated, and additional material has been added. Discussions of housing, nutrition, breeding, and general maintenance are followed by descriptions and photos of the individual species that strengthen the text.

King Solomon's Ring. Konrad Lorenz. New York: Harper and Row, 1952.

Lorenz, a behavioral psychologist, was well known for his work in measuring the intelligence of animals. His anecdotes about clever ducks, loving cockatoos, and brilliant African Greys provide charming and informative reading. Lorenz was the individual who is remembered by college psychology students as the man who was followed by ducklings whom he imprinted to regard him as their parent.

Lovebirds. Matthew M. Vriends. New York: Barrons, 1986.

This is part of the publisher's Complete Pet Owner's Manual series, and it is a fine book with valuable information, interesting drawings, and excellent photos. The information on interpreting lovebird behavior by body and head movements is unique and helpful.

Lovebirds and Related Parrots. George A. Smith. Neptune, N.J.: TFH Publications, 1979.

The material on lovebirds is top-notch and includes housing, care, breeding, genetics, and more. There is also a fascinating discussion of the production of color in parrots based on an understanding of feather structure. The color illustrations are also quite good. What I find confusing, however, is the addition of material on Ringnecks, Great-billed, Eclectus, and Hanging Parrots. I see no linkage of these groups to the lovebirds and their inclusion serves no purpose other than to make this a larger book.

Lovebirds and Their Colour Mutations. Jim Hayward. Dorset, U.K.: Blandford Press, 1979.

This is a brief book but very much to the point; I don't believe there is a wasted line or phrase. The author's information and opinions on housing, feeding, breeding, and dealing with health problems are very well presented. The color plates are among the best I have seen and readers will appreciate their labeling, which identifies the sexes and draws attention to the characteristics of immature birds.

Lovebirds . . . Care and Breeding. Jo Hall, Austin, Texas: Sweet Publishing Company, 1979.

These twenty-six chapters of useful information, written in Jo Hall's usual engaging style, offer highly detailed information from an individual who kept and raised birds and who experienced and solved the problems she wrote about.

Lovebirds, Cockatiels, Budgerigars: Behavior and Evolution. R. Kavanaugh. Los Angeles, California: Science Software Systems, Inc., 1987.

The Manual of Color Breeding. Jim Hayward. Oxford, U.K.: Aviculturist Publications, 1992.

The topic of color breeding is normally of great interest to breeders of canaries, finches, budgies and cockatiels. Hayward's book can be used with these groups but it is primarily aimed at parrots. The charts and other information are clear and useful. This book is truly one of a kind.

A Monograph of Endangered Parrots. Tony Silva. Pickering, Ontario: Silvio Mattacchione and Co., 1989.

This large book is fantastically illustrated with prints that were especially commissioned for the text. If you obtain this book, spend the first evening looking at and enjoying the illustrations, and then read the text. The artwork is so powerful that you probably will not be able to do it any other way.

Mexican Macaws. Lyndon Hargrave. Tucson: University of Arizona Press, 1970.

Macaws lived in Mexico thousands of years ago, and Hargrave's monograph provides interesting proof in the form of photos and drawings of their skeletal remains.

My Parrot, My Friend: An Owner's Guide to Parrot Behavior. Bonnie Munro Doane and Thomas Qualkinbush. New York: Howell Book House, 1994.

This is the first book on normal and problem parrot behavior, as well as parrot behavioral modification, written specifically for the ordinary bird owner. The book shows how and why psittacines respond to specific stimuli, and it shows how to handle unacceptable conduct in these birds. With this helpful reference, bird owners can avoid the onset of bad habits such as biting, screaming, or feather picking, and they can correct those that do exist.

Natural History of Birds. Buffon, c. 1779.

Buffon was a French naturalist who studied and wrote about the exotic birds being imported into Europe from Asia and Africa long before most people even knew what most of these birds looked like. He was honored by having a subspecies of macaw (a large version of the Military Macaw) named for him.

The New Parrot Handbook. Werner Lantermann. New York: Barron's, 1986.

This book is part of a series by Barron's that is similar to their Complete Pet Owner's Manual series. Lantermann is well known in the field of aviculture, and his information on housing, nutrition, health, training, and the nature of individual species will be appreciated as it is firsthand rather than derivative. The photo choices are made with an eye to providing pairs where possible and also to show typical behavior, as in the four-photo layout of an African Grey assiduously preening.

Parrakeets. David Seth-Smith. London, 1926.

Smith was the expert in his day on many exotic bird types. The "parrakeets" referred to in the title are the long-tailed, large bird variety that he bred and studied.

The Parrot Family. Wolfgang deGrahl. New York: Arco, 1984.

Although he does not cover all the common parrots, the author does provide worthwhile information on keeping and enjoying the birds he discusses. His detailed chapter on housing is particularly useful, as it includes methods of adapting existing rooms for birds. The color and black-and-white photos are quite good.

Parrot Family Birds. Julian L. Bronson. Fond du Lac, Wisc.: All-Pets, 1955.

The Bronson name is still associated with the sales of exotic birds and animals. This book discusses many parrots, but has particularly interesting material on magpies, mynahs, crows, and other non-parrot species that are included only for their ability to speak.

Parrot Guide. Cyril H. Rogers. New York: Pet Library, 1981.

For a number of years this was the book people carried to pet stores when they needed a method of identifying confusing Amazons and other look-alike species. It has now been surpassed by many other volumes, but it's still worth a look.

The Parrot in Health and Illness. Bonnie Munro Doane. New York: Howell Book House, 1991.

This book has been very popular from the first day it appeared, because the author approaches the important problem of dealing with health questions at a higher level than many elementary books on bird health and yet keeps the material readable and understandable. This is a book to give as a gift to your avian vet so that you and he or she can compare notes when you think your bird is ill.

Parrots. David Alderton. Morris Plains, N.J.: Tetra Press, 1992.

This oversized publication would be worth reading for the incomparably brilliant photos by British photographer Cyril Laubscher. Alderton, however, provides even more with his coverage of all the common parrot groups. The section on housing could be a book in itself, as it deals with every form of parrot habitation from cages to outdoor flights with exploded views that provide valuable construction hints.

Parrots. David Alderton. London: Whittet Books, 1992.

This fine little book is not nearly as large or heavily illustrated as some of the others produced by this prolific author, but it is excellent reading. The line drawings by John Cox catch the spirit and humor of parrots, making it a pleasure to leaf through in search of topics of particular interest.

Parrots. A. Scott. New York: Congdon and Weed, 1982.

This enjoyable little book consists of illustrations accompanied by poems or quotations dealing with parrots such as this rather mean one from George Bernard Shaw: "Parrots are amusing and never die. You wish they did."

Parrots: A Natural History. John Sparks and Tony Soper. New York: Facts on File, 1990.

Unique and sometimes obscure details, both historical and biological, make this a fascinating source of information or, in some cases, speculation. For example, according to the authors, a parrot belonging to King Henry VIII fell into the Thames River and was saved when it screamed for a "boat!" More believable is the information that breeding in the wild is frequently geared to rainfall, which brings an abundance of food. Great photos accompany such gems and make this a book you will want to read for pure pleasure as well as for research purposes.

Parrots: Their Care and Breeding. Rosemary Low. Dorset, U.K.: Blandford Press, 1992, 3d rev. ed.

This is an attractive compilation of photos and information about many parrots. It includes a good bibliography that may lead you to other sources.

Parrots and Other Talking Birds. Charles N. Page. Des Moines, Iowa: 1906.

This self-published little volume gives a good look at bird keeping at the turn of the century. It is amazing how so many of the author's observations on particular species are still made by writers today.

Parrots and Parrot-like Birds in Aviculture. Marquis of Tavistock. London: F. V. White and Co., 1930.

This is the original version of a book that provided many parrot fanciers with their first detailed information on the hobby. The author, later the duke of Bedford, kept a fantastic collection on his estate at Worburn Abbey. He and his staff are credited with many first-time or early breeding successes of parrots. Modified editions of the book were subsequently published.

Parrots and Related Birds. Henry J. Bares and Robert L. Busenbark. Neptune, N.J.: TFH Publications, 1978.

This book and the duke of Bedford's *Parrots and Parrot-like Birds in Aviculture* were pretty much all many of us had to work with when we got started with parrots in the 1970s. The book is enhanced with black-and-white photos and a large section of color photos that add to its charm and informative nature. These are generally useful for identification purposes. The text covers feeding, housing, taming, health, and more. The descriptions of behavior and habits are largely based on the authors' experiences at their Palos Verdes Bird Farm breeding facilities.

Parrots, Cockatoos and Macaws. Edward J. Boosey. Silver Spring, MD: Denlingers, 1956.

The author was the proprietor of the famous Keston Foreign Bird Farm in England, one of the earliest establishments to devote itself to breeding and so well known that a casual reference to "Keston" was always understood. Boosey was a prominent figure in the golden age of British parrot keeping, and this book includes comments from some of the best known aviculturists of the period.

Parrots Exclusively. Karl Plath and Malcolm Davis. Fond du Lac, Wisc.: 1957.

Plath was curator of birds at the Chicago Zoo at the time that this book appeared, while Davis filled the same position at the Smithsonian's National Zoo in Washington, D.C. This was one of the first parrot books to become popular and it still makes interesting reading. Malcolm Davis went on to star in a long-running television program called "Wild Kingdom," where his enthusiasm inspired watchers to keep tuning in.

Parrots for Pleasure and Profit. C. P. Arthur. London: F. Carl, c. 1900.

This book is an historical oddity, as well as an interesting look at attitudes and ideas about psittacines at the turn of the century. The line drawings are fascinating and in many cases intentionally humorous.

Parrots in Captivity. 3 vol. W. T. Greene. London: George Bell & Sons, 1884.

A difficult book to find but well worth the effort. Try a university library if your local library can't help you. Greene's descriptions of parrots and their behavior and qualities are for the most part just as accurate today as they were more than a century ago. His droll wit is also something to appreciate and the color lithographs are magnificent.

Parrots, Lories and Cockatoos. David Alderton, Surrey, U.K.: Saiga Publishing, 1982.

This title is not as revealing as it might be since the book really covers many more groups, including parrotlets, lovebirds, hanging parrots, lorikeets, caiques, and macaws. The distribution maps cover vast territories and are useful in showing the range of many parrots, but they would have been more valuable if the author had added familiar landmarks to orient the reader. Color plates by Michael Stringer are outstanding and represent their bird models with complete accuracy and clarity. A large selection of black-and-white photos and drawings adds information and interest to the various chapters.

Parrots, Macaws and Cockatoos. Elizabeth Butterworth. New York: Harry N. Abrams, 1988.

This folio-sized book has only a small amount of text. However, the illustrations are remarkable and in a number of cases offer a valuable comparative study. This is particularly true in the case of the Lears and Glaucous Macaw paintings, which are extremely useful in clarifying the differences between these closely related parrots.

Parrots of Australasia. Charles Barrett. Melbourne: N.H. Seward Pty. Ltd., 1949.

Although old, this book is fascinating, as it gives information on the haunts, habits, and, where possible, the histories of many of the Australian psittacines. Rare photos of parrots in their nests in the wild, nesting sites, young birds, and typical scenes of the parrot habitat are material seldom found in other books.

Parrots of the World. Joseph M. Forshaw. New York: Doubleday & Co., 1973.

This was the first of a series of editions and revisions of a great attempt to describe and illustrate the entire range of parrots. The first edition is rare and has since become a collector's item, selling for approximately ten times the original price. It is a large, imposing book that provides detailed material on species, subspecies, ranges, background, breeding successes, and other vital data. It also offers excellent range maps and a unique method of illustration: The birds shown in the color plates by William T. Cooper are keyed numerically to small black-and-white versions that identify them, allowing males and females as well as nominate and subspecies to be compared in the same plate. Cooper should be given great credit, as it is his work that makes the book as impressive as it is. Some of the later editions and reprints do not always do the book justice, containing poor reproductions that in at least one case are badly placed, preventing readers from comparing the text with the illustrations. Choose carefully when looking for this book. You are not likely to find the original version, but the 1983 reprint of the third revised edition is the next best thing.

The Pet Bird Handbook. Patricia Sutherland. New York: Arco, 1981.

The book follows a logical progression and moves from choosing the right bird through behavior, feeding, hygiene, housing, and training. It includes a unique chapter, "Miscellaneous Information," that deals with questions often asked but seldom answered. High-quality photographs are another plus.

The Politics of Extinction. Louis Regenstein. New York: Macmillan Publishing Company, 1975.

In addition to informing us about animals that are endangered, this book indicates why, and in some cases who, is causing the loss of life. It names the state and federal agencies responsible for protecting wildlife, information that could be helpful if you become aware of actions endangering wildlife in your own community.

Popular Parakeets. Dulce Cooke and Freddie Cooke. London: Blandford Press, 1989.

The authors deal with the larger, long-tailed parakeets in a competent and helpful manner. Although this edition is out of print, a paperback version with the same text and photos became available in 1993.

Popular Parrots. Matthew Vriends. N.Y.: Howell Book House, 1983.

The author is probably the most prolific of the bird writers and this comprehensive book provides detailed coverage on a wide range of topics. Vriends is at his best when he describes personal experiences in the field and he quotes widely from notes made during his travel in Australia. The book includes excellent color and black-and-white photos.

Popular Parrot Species. Werner Lanterman. New York: Arco, 1986.

This book contains fine photos and a good translation from the German.

Portraits of Mexican Birds. George M. Sutton. Norman: Oklahoma University Press, 1972.

Sutton lived and painted in Mexico for many years. His watercolors are very attractive, showing many parrots and other birds in flight, at nesting trees, and living in the wild. His descriptions are also quite apt.

The Proper Care of Parrots. Martin Skinner. Neptune, N.J.: TFH Publications, 1992.

Skinner offers basic information on a large variety of parrots and includes many photos.

Records of Parrots Bred In Captivity. A. A. Prestwich. Hertford, U.K.: Stephen Austin and Sons, 1949–1954.

Prestwich was an early member and officer of the British Avicultural Society and as such had direct access to and input from many of the greatest names in aviculture. He made the most of these contacts, and his information is invaluable for research as well as good reading if you enjoy the trivia and minutiae of parrot lore. This series of slim volumes is available for research at the library of the Museum of Natural History in New York City.

The Royal Natural History, vol. IV, Birds. Richard Lydekker. London: Frederick Warne and Co., 1895.

The remarkable color and black-and-white illustrations of parrots and other birds in this volume are impressive. The text is even more fascinating as we read highly accurate descriptions of Keas, Kakas, Black Palm Cockatoos, and other unusual parrots. Some names have, of course, been modified in the last hundred years, but the basic facts have not changed and Lydekker presents them in an appealing and interesting manner.

Sexing All Fowl, Baby Chicks, Game Birds and Cage Birds. Loyl Stromberg. Pine River, Minn.: Stromberg Publishing Company, 1977.

A soft-covered compilation of more than fifty articles dealing with sexing. Just about all types of birds are covered and there is generally more than one technique suggested for each species.

The Speaking Parrots. Karl Russ. London: Upcott Gill, 1884.

Russ was a contemporary of the celebrated parrot enthusiast Dr. W. T. Greene, who often quoted him. This very rare English version of the original German manuscript has many pleasing anecdotes along with a considerable amount of factual material. With the exception of the beautiful representation of an Alexandrine Parakeet that opens the book, illustrations are in black-and-white, but they are still quite useful.

The Talking Parrot and its Care. Armisted Carter. Chicago: Audubon Publishing Co., 1952.

A slim booklet that is valuable for its historic aspects as well as for the information it offers. The material on parrot medical care and nutrition has some valuable tips but it is even more interesting to see how far the fancy has progressed since the 1950s.

To Save A Bird In Peril. David R. Zimmerman. N.Y.: Coward, McCann, Inc., 1975.

The author advocates interceding in a bird's life cycle or environment when the species population has fallen below fifty. Such birds are so close to being lost that more than the standard conservation techniques of legal protection and habitat preservation are needed. He also gives an excellent description of the Patuxent Project at Laurel, Maryland.

Training Your Parrot. Kevin Murphy. Neptune, N.J.: TFH Publications, 1983.

The author addresses the first thing that most new parrot owners must consider: taming and training their new pets. He does a fairly good job of answering questions and bases many of his responses on his own work with Sigfried, a good-looking Double Yellow-head.

Tropical Birds. S. Sitwell, from Plates by John Gould. London: Batsford Ltd., 1948.

This small volume has remarkable color plates that represent a portion of Gould's *Birds of New Guinea and the Adjacent Papuan Islands*. You will want to take the book apart and frame these brilliantly tinted representations of birds, but do resist the temptation. Sitwell's comments show an unusual depth of knowledge as well as a true understanding of the parrot personality.

Understanding Your Parrot. Irene Christie. London: H.F.& G. Witherby Co., 1990.

The author discusses choosing and keeping an appropriate bird and offers realistic advice on diet, care, health, feather problems, clipping wings and nails, and just about all the problems that parrot owners must eventually face. Her discussion of body language is both novel and useful and provides suggestions for understanding and working with neglected parrots. Excellent photos by Cyril Laubscher accompany the text and heighten one's pleasure in reading this book.

Vanishing Birds. Tim Halliday. N.Y.: Holt, Rinehart, and Winston, 1978.

The author's views on conservation, captive breeding, and reintroduction to the original habitat may not agree with yours, but books that alert us to the dangers of extinction serve a vital purpose. Sixteen color plates, including a very lively picture of the Carolina Conure, are an attractive bonus.

What Bird Is That? A Guide to the Birds of Australia. Neville W. Cayley. Sydney, Australia: Angus and Robertson, 1948.

Caley's specialty was the habitat of birds, and in this book he indicates how they could thrive in the proper habitat. Although many groups of birds are covered, he does full justice to the parrots. Excellent photos of the regions in which they live, as well as full-page color plates, add to the pleasure of using this book.

The World of Cockatoos. Karl Diefenbach. Neptune, N.J.: TFH Publications, 1985.

This book follows the tried and true pattern of starting with general information on behavior, nutrition, housing, and general care. A second section describes the habits of the individual cockatoos. The photos are helpful and, where possible, identify specimens by both sexes and maturity.

The World of Macaws. Dieter Hoppe, translated by Arthur Freud and Raul Ugarte. Neptune, N.J.: TFH Publications, 1985.

Because it is a large-format book, it offers opportunities for excellent full-page photos and photo spreads that add to the beauty and usefulness of the book. Its use of geographical distribution maps, together with the text's information on the characteristics, range, and way of life of Macaws is similar to Forshaw's *Parrots of the World* but is much more readable.

Yellow-Fronted Amazon Parrots. Edward J. Mulawka. Neptune, N.J.: TFH Publications, 1982.

We live in an age of specialization, and this book is no exception; *Amazona ochrocephala* and its species are the only parrots covered. Of course, this group includes some of the most popular pets kept in the United States, such as the Double Yellow-head, the Tres Marias, the Yellow-naped Amazon, the Panama Amazon, and the Yellow-fronted Amazon. A few lesser-known groups are also described. The format is logical, beginning with some general characteristics of *A. ochrocephala* along with a description of its behavior and distribution in the wild, followed by a chapter on breeding, and finally, detailed descriptions of the individual members of the family. The information provided in the descriptions includes size, markings, appearance of immature birds, range, and behavior as a pet.

SPECIAL MAGAZINES (ANNUAL INDEXES ARE AVAILABLE FOR MOST OF THE MAGAZINES LISTED BELOW)

American Cage-Bird Magazine was published monthly from 1928 until February 1994, when it was sold to Fancy Publications and acquired a new name, *Bird Breeder*. This was the premier publication among U.S. bird magazines, with a serious approach to the care and breeding of exotic birds. Many libraries have complete collections. Full indexes are available from 1985 through 1993.

Australian Aviculture. Published monthly by the Avicultural Society of Australia, 52 Harris Rd., Elliminyt, Victoria, 3249, Australia.

This publication offers high-quality articles and notes on many Australian birds. Its greatest emphasis is on finches and parrot family birds.

It provides excellent photos and many useful tips and hints for bird keepers.

Avicultural Magazine. Founded in 1894 and now published quarterly by The Avicultural Society, c/o Bristol, Zoological Gardens, Clifton, Bristol, BS8 3HS, England.

This is probably the finest of the bird publications, as nothing quite compares to the variety of articles and their level of quality. Unfortunately, over a period of years, publication frequency has dropped from monthly to quarterly. One cannot fault the magazine for this as publication is strictly a labor of love by volunteers and unpaid authors.

The authors are from all over the world, and this is a truly international publication. It dates back more than a hundred years, and many back issues from its earliest days are still available. These can be ordered at reasonable prices, and if you also obtain an index you can select those issues with topics of interest to you. The Library of the American Museum of Natural History in New York has a complete run of the publication, and you can check the indexes there.

Magazine of the Parrot Society. Published by the Parrot Society, 108b Fenlake Rd., Bedford, MK42 OEU, England.

Each issue contains noteworthy articles on parrots and related topics with a great emphasis on breeding. Excellent photos began to appear several years ago and are now a monthly staple. Many helpful bits of advice and tips on new trends appear in each issue. Some back issues are available.

ZOONOOZ is published by the Zoological Society of San Diego (which most people call the San Diego Zoo). Complete collections are available in some libraries.

INDEX